The Correspondent Breeze

ESSAYS ON ENGLISH ROMANTICISM

The Correspondent Breeze

ESSAYS ON ENGLISH ROMANTICISM

M. H. ABRAMS

With a Foreword by Jack Stillinger

 W·W·Norton & Company

NEW YORK   LONDON

Published simultaneously in Canada by Stoddart, a subsidiary of General Publishing
Co. Ltd., Don Mills, Ontario.
Printed in the United States of America.

The text of this book is composed in Baskerville, with display type set in Deepdene
Italic. Composition and manufacturing by The Maple-Vail Book Manufacturing
Group.

Library of Congress Cataloging in Publication Data

Abrams, M. H. (Meyer Howard), 1912–
    The correspondent breeze: Essays on English Romanticism.

    Includes bibliographical references and index.
    Contents: Wordsworth and Coleridge on diction and
figures—The correspondent breeze—English Romanticism
—[etc.]
    1. English literature—History and criticism—Addresses,
essays, lectures.   2. Romanticism—England—Addresses,
essays, lectures.   3. Wordsworth, William, 1770–1850—
Criticism and interpretation—Addresses, essays, lectures.
4. Coleridge, Samuel Taylor, 1772–1834—Criticism
and interpretation—Addresses, essays, lectures.
I. Title.
PR457.A2   1984   820'.9'145   83-19359

ISBN 0-393-01837-7

W. W. Norton & Company, Inc., 500 Fifth Avenue, New York, N.Y. 10110
W. W. Norton & Company Ltd., 37 Great Russell Street, London WC1B 3NU

1 2 3 4 5 6 7 8 9 0

Contents

Foreword

M. H. Abrams, Class of 1916 Professor of English at Cornell and author of *The Mirror and the Lamp* (1953), *Natural Supernaturalism* (1971), and a sizable list of shorter works, is our preeminent historian and interpreter of English Romanticism. He is also a very modest man, and it took some fancy rhetoric on the part of his friends and the publisher to persuade him to approve and lend a hand in this collection of essays—journal articles, occasional lectures, symposium contributions, book chapters, and an introduction—on his principal lifelong topic of research and contemplation. These essays originally appeared in three countries, and in several kinds of publication: scholarly book, commercial book, learned journal, Festschrift collection, and so on. Most of them are already well known and widely cited by scholars who have traveled a good deal in the library stacks to seek them out. The present volume, bringing them together within a single set of covers, now makes them available to a more general readership.

Written over a period of three decades, the nine essays bear somewhat the same figurative relationship to *The Mirror and the Lamp* and *Natural Supernaturalism* as Wordsworth's "minor Pieces" (in the analogy of Wordsworth's Preface to *The Excursion*) bear to the poet's larger works then published and in progress: they are "the little cells, oratories, and sepulchral recesses" surrounding the main edifice of a (in this instance two-towered) cathedral; less metaphorically, they are prefigurings, epitomes, examples, and amplifications. They examine Wordsworth's and Coleridge's innovations in their theories about the language of poetry; the prevalence, sources, and significance of a key Romantic image, the "correspondent breeze"; the pervasive revolutionary "spirit" of Romanticism; the defining characteristics and chief exemplars of the most distinctive poetic genre of the age, the "greater Romantic lyric"; the relation of Coleridge and Wordsworth to modernist poetics and literature; the philosophic and scientific backgrounds of Coleridge's thinking; the numerous manifestations of apocalypticism in the Romantic period, characterized in the final essay as "the most apocalyptic cultural era since the century and a half in Hebrew civilization which preceded and followed the birth of Christ." But there is no need to expound their contents here: the essays have beginnings, middles, and ends; they announce what they are about and stick to the subject; they are examples of an increasingly rare type of academic writing about literature—critical explanation that ordinary readers can actually understand. Consider the following, from the second paragraph of "Structure and Style in the Greater Romantic Lyric":

> They [a group of ten poems that Abrams is describing as a class] present a determinate speaker in a particularized, and usually a localized, outdoor setting, whom we overhear as he carries on, in a fluent vernacular which rises easily to a more formal speech, a sustained colloquy, sometimes with himself or with the outer scene, but more frequently with a silent human auditor, present or absent. The speaker begins with a description of the landscape; an aspect or change of aspect in the landscape evokes a varied but integral process of memory, thought, anticipation, and feeling which remains closely intervolved with the outer scene. In the course of this meditation the lyric speaker achieves an insight, faces up to a tragic loss, comes to a moral decision, or resolves an emotional problem. Often the poem rounds upon itself to end where it began, at the outer scene, but with an altered mood and deepened understanding which is the result of the intervening meditation.

These four sentences together have more substance than some other critics' entire books.

In method the essays represent a combination of historical and biographical interpretation, explication of specific texts, and the study of sources, genre, and style; less formally, they represent the application of knowledge and intuition based on several decades of reading, thinking, and life experience. They employ, that is, the customary tools of what is sometimes nowadays referred to as "traditional humanism"; as Lawrence Lipking says in an introductory note to a recent volume of essays honoring him (*High Romantic Argument*, 1981), Abrams "believes in history, evidence, reason, meaning, authors, texts, himself." The most fashionable present-day critical theorists (those, for example, who find nourishment in viewing "an event in a text . . . [as] the shifting of a persona across the borders of a semantic field") now and then write as if such beliefs, and the various approaches to literature based on them, were quaintly naive—vestigial lingerings of a time gone by. But fashions have a way of succeeding one another rather quickly. In the long history of literary criticism, the steadiest recurrent phenomenon, constituting the foundation from which virtually all theoretical innovations take off, peak, and thence subside, is precisely the set of interests and values (literary history, biography, textual investigation, "philology") that we have at hand. Abrams' work locates itself at the center of this stable, fundamental standard of critical endeavor and serves as a model of useful practice. His position also allows him a dispassionate view of some higher-reaching, less satisfying schemes. Here, from the final section of "The Correspondent Breeze," is part of his description of Maud Bodkin's well-known discoveries of archetypal patterns:

> These are astonishing equations, but the logical procedure by which they were achieved is simple enough. It consists in treating loose analogy as though it were identity. This strategy, to be sure, has a singular virtue; it cannot fail. Only leave out enough of the qualities that make a poem, or any complex

experience, distinctive, and it can be reduced to an abstract
pattern—almost any abstract pattern. . . . A procedure which
ingeniously contrives to reduce all—or at least a great many—
serious poems to variations upon a timeless theme is not much
to the purpose of the literary critic, whose chief concern is with
the particularity of a work. . . .

Though first published in 1957, these sentences could be
applied tellingly to a great deal of structuralist and poststruc-
turalist critical activity in the quarter-century that has followed. Not surprisingly, Abrams in recent years, in a series
of trenchant essays with titles like "What's the Use of Theorizing about the Arts," "The Deconstructive Angel," and "How
to Do Things with Texts" (theoretical essays soon to be collected in a companion volume), has expanded his range to
become one of our most clear-sighted commentators on current theorizing about literature.

The main topic of the present collection, "Romanticism,"
is, as Wordsworth said of poetry, "a word of very disputed
meaning." Abrams' position in the matter is, in brief, that
this is as it should be—the more the disputes, the better the
understanding that results. "Romanticism," he comments near
the beginning of the essay "English Romanticism: The Spirit
of the Age," first published two decades ago, "is no one thing.
It is many very individual poets, who wrote poems manifesting a greater diversity of qualities . . . than those of any preceding age. But some prominent qualities a number of these
poems share, and certain of these shared qualities form a
distinctive complex which may, with a high degree of prob-
ability, be related to the events and ideas of the cataclysmic
coming-into-being of the world to which we are by now
becoming fairly accustomed." In spite of the careful wording
of this statement, and of several others like it in his writings
elsewhere—wording that points to "*some* prominent qualities
. . . *a* distinctive complex" without denying the existence of
other qualities and complexes that may be equally prominent
and distinctive—reviewers and critics have sometimes
attributed to Abrams an "essentialist" view of Romanticism;
they have in effect constructed a self-limiting definition of

the period on the basis of his multiplicity of instances and then argued against the definition, as if Abrams had in fact proposed it. This is a harmless activity, and on the positive side it has produced, in the evidences marshaled against a supposed "essence," further testimony to the richness, vitality, and complexity of the period. But it is not exactly fair to Abrams, who knew what he was doing all along.

His own best defense of his writings (though none was needed) is the essay entitled "Rationality and Imagination in Cultural History" (*Critical Inquiry*, 1976), in which he plainly declares his pluralist and "nominalist" (as opposed to essentialist) position—"I don't believe that there exists an abstract entity, named 'Romanticism,' whose essential features are definable; or . . . that we can set the necessary and sufficient conditions for the correct use of the term"—and even, in response to a challenge, outlines an alternative history of Romanticism based largely on authors, works, themes, and events that he has *omitted* from his own writings on the subject. His modest statement there concerning *Natural Supernaturalism* applies generally to the essays in the present volume as well:

> I claim no more than that the interrelated topics which I have elected to treat, and the writings in which these topics are instantiated, were very important in their own time and continue to be of great interest to us today; that to tell this chosen story with any adequacy is quite enough for one book to try to do; and that if I have done my job properly, both the historical importance and continuing human interest of these selected topics are confirmed and expanded in the course of their historical exposition.

The real test of Abrams' historical explanations is of course whether or not they "work"—whether, when we apply the criteria of correspondence and coherence (just as in interpreting a poem), they "make sense" out of the particulars at hand and produce useful generalizations even in the face of competing historical interpretations. Abrams' work continues to hold up. There seems no doubt that (to paraphrase another sentence in the same essay), while he may be telling only a *part* of the truth, it is, after all, a part of the *truth*.

Details of original publication are given at the beginning of each series of notes at the back of the book. The texts have in every case been slightly revised, mainly in the documentation (to make the older consistent with the more recent). Author and publisher alike wish me to express their gratitude to the copyright holders for generous permission to make use of the pieces here.

Jack Stillinger

The Correspondent Breeze

ESSAYS ON ENGLISH
ROMANTICISM

ONE

Wordsworth and Coleridge on Diction and Figures

THE TYPICAL NEOCLASSIC THEORY of poetry was a rhetorical theory, in the basic sense that it conceived poetry, like rhetoric, to be an art of achieving effects on an audience, and looked upon the various elements of a poem chiefly as so many means toward that end. Accordingly neoclassic critics usually treated diction as a topic common both to rhetoric and to poetry and differentiated the treatment in the two provinces largely in terms of whether the primary effect in view was to persuade or to please (and sometimes to instruct) the auditor.

We can think of Wordsworth's Preface to *Lyrical Ballads* as related to this antecedent theory in two important ways. The root principle of the Preface was the statement, twice uttered, that poetry is the overflow of powerful feelings; and feelings, of course, are most readily conceived to flow over into words. But Wordsworth also said that "poetry is the *spontaneous* overflow of powerful feelings"; and this spontaneity, although it may follow upon prior thought and practice, and may be an attribute of "emotion recollected in tranquillity," is not compatible with the artful manipulation of words to the deliberate end of affecting the reader. From our present point of view, therefore, Wordsworth's Preface is notable first, because it made the topic of diction, rather than plot, character, or design, the central and engrossing subject of critical inquiry, and second, because it sheared away the rhetorical frame in which this topic had been traditionally treated. Commentators have always remarked that Wordsworth, in his Preface, attacked the neoclassic use of diction in poetry. It is worth making the point that Wordsworth also attacked the poetic theory on which this use of diction was commonly justified, and that he did so by the drastic expedient of subverting its premises.

For a statement of the kind of theory about poetry and poetic diction against which Wordsworth rebelled, we may turn to James Beattie's *On Poetry and Music As They Affect the Mind,* published in 1776, which provides a convenient summary of conservative opinion in the generation before Wordsworth. Beattie echoes Aristotle—poetry, he says, "is an imitation of human action"—but like almost all critics of the eighteenth century, Beattie assimilates the mimetic concept of Aristotle's *Poetics* to the pragmatic framework of Aristotle's *Rhetoric.* "Every art or contrivance," he says, "which has a meaning must have an end"; and "the end of poetry is, TO PLEASE."[1] Poetry's prime reason for being is to give pleasure; the achievement of pleasure is what distinguishes it as an aesthetic from a persuasive or purely didactic form of discourse; and the aim of pleasure compels, in the diction which is the medium of poetry, a figurative departure from literal and unadorned imitation. As Beattie presents this thesis, syllogistically:

> If it appear, that, by means of Figures, Language may be made more *pleasing,* and more *natural,* than it would be without them; it will follow, that to Poetic Language, whose end is to *please* by imitating *nature,* Figures must be not only ornamental, but necessary.[2]

The characteristic pattern of neoclassic reasoning about diction, therefore, was dichotomous, in accordance with an underlying conception of poetry which looked both toward the nature it must reflect and toward the reader it must affect. "The end of Poetry," Beattie said repeatedly, "is to please by imitating nature"; or as Dr. Johnson put it, "poetry is the art of uniting pleasure with truth."[3] This dual obligation was often reflected in a systematic and progressive distinction of the verbal medium of a poem into the two components of matter (satisfying the claims of truth to nature) and ornament (satisfying the claims of aesthetic pleasure). On the one level, for example, as Johnson expressed the commonplace, language as a whole "is the dress of thought." The language in turn can be divided into plain sense and ornamental figures of speech; figures, said Hugh Blair, "properly employed, have a similar effect on Language, with what is produced by the rich and splendid dress of a person of rank." Ultimately even a single figure of speech can be analyzed as though itself a poem in little, possessing the double aspect of sense and ornament. Thus, Lord Kames said that all figures have a double signification, presenting both a "principal object" and an "accessory" object: "the principal makes a part of the thought; the accessory is merely ornamental." Or in a more famed passage from Johnson: "A simile, to be perfect, must both illustrate and ennoble the subject" and "is required to exhibit, independently of its references, a pleasing image."[4]

Present-day commentators are often moved to contempt, if not indignation, at this stubbornly laminating tendency of the typical eighteenth-century theory of poetic language and at the associated application to stylistic matters of the metaphor of a body and its covering garment, or of a garment and its ornamental jewels, or of other equally venerable devices for making graphic the distinction between literal speech and the heightened language of poetry. But in that theory, the successive distinctions between matter and ornament were kept from hardening into isolated and independent divisions by that basic neoclassic unifying principle, the concept of the decorum, or decency, or appropriateness of the component parts. Pope's extended discussion of the subject in *An Essay on Criticism* plays the changes on the varied terms and images of his day for establishing on the one hand the distinguishability, but on the other hand the unity-by-congruity, of matter and style when properly employed. Incompetent critics are

> Pleased with a work where nothing's just or fit,

and skill-less poets

> With gold and jewels cover every part,
> And hide with ornaments their want of art.

But

> True wit is Nature to advantage dressed,

and true expression

> gilds all objects, but it alters none.
> Expression is the dress of thought, and still
> Appears more decent, as more suitable.

This linguistic decorum, furthermore, was a complex principle, and one which was capable, at the hands of critics like Dryden or Johnson, of a flexible and subtle application. For example, it held (we find all these concepts in Beattie's essay) that in each instance the expression must be intricately adjusted to the poetic kind (high or low, tragic, epic, or lyric), to the matter signified, and to the exact pleasurably emotional effect intended, as well as to the permanent character, incidental situation, and momentary mental state of the speaker who gives it utterance.

The last requirement—that language be appropriate to the state of mind of the speaker "imitated" in a poem—directed attention to the relation between figurative language and passion. Tropes and figures, as Beattie declares, "are often more *natural*, and more *imitative*, than proper words," for "it would be impossible to imitate the language of passion without them." His reasoning is that since poetry imitates nature, "the *language of Poetry* must be an imitation of the *language of*

Nature," and by *"Natural Language,"* he says, he means speech "which is suitable to the speaker and to the occasion," including the passions which move the speaker at the moment of utterance.[5]

These passages from Beattie include terms and criteria which became the sacred words in Wordsworth's Preface. A brief comparison of the way the terms function in the two critics, however, will indicate how radically different are the underlying theoretical schemes.

1. Reference to the passion of the speaker, which in Beattie had been one of the numerous factors determining the propriety of diction in a given instance, becomes in Wordsworth almost the single source and sanction for the language of poetry—indeed, the defining quality for poetry in general. "Words, a Poet's words more particularly," Wordsworth wrote in 1800, "ought to be weighed in the balance of feeling. . . . For the Reader cannot be too often reminded that Poetry is passion."[6] In the last analysis, moreover, this passion is the poet's own, not merely that of the character imitated. It is the poet's overflowing feelings which, recollected in tranquillity, make the matter of a poem, even when by a kind of proxy, as Wordsworth twice expressed it, "the Poet speaks through the mouths of his characters."[7]

2. "The language of nature," "natural language," remained Wordsworth's criterion, as it had been Beattie's. But by Wordsworth "natural," instead of being construed as an imitation of speech "suitable to the speaker and to the occasion," is given a genetic and psychological significance, and either parallels or coincides with his other prime criteria, "spontaneous," "genuine" (as in his phrase "the genuine language of passion"), and (somewhat later) "sincere."[8] The equivalence between the "natural" language of the poet and the prose language "really spoken by men" is a genetic equivalence, in that both originate instinctively, under the impulse of actual feeling. The standards of valid poetry were set by "the earliest poets," who, Wordsworth said, "generally wrote from passion excited by real events; they wrote naturally, and as men: feeling powerfully as they did, their language was daring, and figurative." The divers ills of modern poetry began

when poets, "without being animated by the same passion," mechanically applied these figures of speech "to feelings and thoughts with which they had no natural connection whatsoever," and eventually produced a language "differing materially from the real language of men in *any situation*."[9]

3. To Wordsworth, as a consequence, the only valid figures of speech are the natural and integral embodiment of feelings. The poet's subject, as he says, "will naturally, and upon fit occasion, lead him to passions the language of which . . . must necessarily be dignified and variegated, and alive with metaphors and figures." Provided a selection has been made to eliminate "the vulgarity and meanness of ordinary life," the pleasure of the reader will follow inevitably from such language, so that there is no need to deviate from natural expression "either for elevation of style, or any of its supposed ornaments."[10] Any additions originating in motives outside the spontaneous urgency of the poet's feelings are invalid, so that "ornament" in Wordsworth's criticism becomes an entirely pejorative term. All such supplements to diction are "arbitrary and capricious," "false refinement or arbitrary innovation," "transitory and accidental ornaments," and "corruptions." In thus eliminating the dual reference to the subject imitated and the effect upon the reader as determinants of style, Wordsworth also cancels the correlated distinction between matter and ornament, by substituting an integral for the old differential analogues of style. "The artifices which have overrun our writings in metre since the days of Dryden and Pope," he wrote in 1810, involve abandonment of

> those feelings which are the pure emanations of nature . . . and those expressions which are not what the garb is to the body but what the body is to the soul. . . . If words be not (recurring to a metaphor before used) an incarnation of the thought but only a clothing for it, then surely will they prove an ill gift.[11]

This point is worth dwelling on for a moment, because it illustrates Wordsworth's characteristic procedure of making a part of earlier theory into the whole. The history of the concept of an intimate and vital union between word and thought goes back, ultimately, to the Aristotelian theory of the relation between matter and form, the Neoplatonic notion of the irradiation of a body by the beauty and goodness of the indwelling soul, and even (as Wordsworth's term "incarnation" suggests) the Christian logos-doctrine of the Word made flesh. In Renaissance and later rhetoric the image of body-and-soul was occasionally used to illustrate or supplement an ornament-and-decorum theory of style and figurative language.[12] With the emergence of the concept of poetry as natural rather than artful expression, however, the analogue of body-and-soul was put in explicit opposition to the hitherto coordinate analogue of body-and-garment and converted into the single criterion of valid poetic language. Herder, for example, wrote in 1767 that in the modern as in the primitive poets "the thought must be related to the expression . . . as the soul is to the body in which it dwells. . . . [The poet] must express feelings." All the life died out of poetry in those cultivated times "when expression became nothing more than art, and was separated from that which it was to express. . . . Thought and expression! And these related as a garment to its body? . . . Thought and word, feeling and expression are related to one another as Plato's soul to the body."[13]

Later Flaubert and the critics of *l'art pour l'art* in France and England adopted this or similar analogues to characterize the inseparability, or even identity, of form and content, and to denounce what A. C. Bradley called "the heresy of the separable substance."[14] One needn't plead, in these days of its triumph, the virtues of the integrative concept of diction; though it is well to remember that this, as well as the more traditional concept, has the defect of its virtues. If the difficulty in the neoclassic view is how to get the elements of a poem tightly enough together, it is no less difficult in the post-Romantic view to separate them for the indispensable purposes of analysis and discussion.

The difference in theory of diction between Beattie and Wordsworth is reflected in their applied criticism of texts; to demonstrate the difference, I purposely choose an instance in which the two critics seem most nearly in agreement. To illustrate a "natural" use of language in poetry, Beattie cites Desdemona's premonitory speech to Emilia:

> My mother had a maid called Barbara;
> She was in love, and he she loved proved mad,
> And did forsake her. She had a song of willow;
> An old thing it was, but it expressed her fortune,
> And she died singing it. That song to-night
> Will not go from my mind. . . .

This is a language, Beattie comments, "so beautifully simple, and so perfectly natural, that one knows not what to say in commendation of it." The passage, however, if "translated into the *finical style,* which, whatever be the subject or speaker, must always be descriptive, enigmatical, and full of figures, would perhaps run thus." Beattie then presents this *ad hoc* example of Shakespeare in red heels and periwig:

> Even now, sad Memory to my thought recals
> The nymph Dione, who, with pious care,
> My much-loved mother, in my vernal years,
> Attended: blooming was the maiden's form,
> And on her brow Discretion sat, and on
> Her rosy cheek a thousand Graces play'd. . . .

And so through the melancholy tale, to the sad conclusion:

> She sat; the weeping willow was her theme,
> And well the theme accorded with her woe;
> Till fate suppress'd at length th' unfinish'd lay.
> Thus on Meander's flowery mantled side
> The dying cygnet sings, and singing dies.

"I hope," Beattie adds, "my young readers are all wiser; but I believe there was a time, when I should have been tempted to prefer this flashy tinsel to Shakespeare's fine gold."[15]

At first sight, Beattie's engaging commentary seems almost the precise equivalent of Wordsworth's attack against "poetic diction"—against what Wordsworth calls the "false refinement," the "family language," and the "motley masquerade of tricks . . . and enigmas" characterizing most eighteenth-century verse. The full context of Beattie's discussion, however, shows that he appealed to quite different grounds for his judgment. "Natural language," he said, must be "improved in poetry by the use of poetical words" and by means of "ornamental" tropes and figures; and he cited approvingly Gray's statement that "the language of the age is never the language of poetry." This was the very statement for which Wordsworth was to indict Gray, as being "at the head of those who, by their reasonings, have attempted to widen the space of separation betwixt Prose and Metrical composition."[16] It turns out that Beattie used the passage from Shakespeare to illustrate the critical thesis, common in his day, that only the more violent passions "are apt to vent themselves in tropes and figures" and that to copy a depressed state of mind, such as Desdemona's, requires "for the most part a plain diction without any ornament." Concerning his own substituted passage, Beattie makes haste to point out that "I do not say, that in themselves these lines are all bad," and "in some sorts of composition the greater part might perhaps be pardonable; but I say, that, considered in relation to the character and circumstances of Desdemona, they are all unnatural, and therefore not poetical."[17]

In short, Beattie decries his modernized version of Shakespeare as "unnatural," not because it is ornamented, but because its ornaments are in their place inappropriate. For him the essential failure is a breach of decorum. When Wordsworth attacks an abuse of diction, it is for a different reason. He cites, for example, Cowper's lines:

> But the sound of the church-going bell
> These valleys and rocks never heard,
> Ne'er sighed at the sound of a knell,
> Or smiled when a sabbath appeared.

He says that the two lines beginning "Ne'er sighed" are "an instance of the language of passion wrested from its proper use . . . and I should condemn the passage . . . as vicious poetic diction."[18] Wordsworth is outraged because Cowper, in attributing feelings and physiognomy to valleys and rocks, has used personification without warrant in genuine passion. To the neoclassic critic nature, as Dr. Johnson had put it, "cannot be properly opposed to *art;* nature being . . . only the best effect of *art.*" But to Wordsworth, at least in his earlier years, all art—in the basic neoclassic sense of the proportioning of diction and ornament to sentiment, and of these, ultimately, to the response anticipated from the reader—was in his phrase "the adversary of nature."[19] And in rejecting this art for a reliance in composing on the natural, or spontaneous, flow of feeling into words, Wordsworth rejected the long-enduring rhetorical understructure of poetic theory.

In the *Biographia Literaria* Coleridge tells us that he agrees with Wordsworth's attack against the "falsity" in the modern poetic style, attributable to the use of figures and metaphors which have been "stripped of their justifying reasons" and "converted into mere artifices of connection or ornament." He disagrees, however, with certain parts of the reasoning on which Wordsworth based his attack, and in particular with Wordsworth's thesis that the proper model for the diction of poetry is the language (in Coleridge's words) "which actually constitutes the natural conversation of men under the influence of natural feelings."[20] The dialectical machinery by which Coleridge attempted to come to terms with Wordsworth on this fundamental issue is too elaborate to reconstruct here in detail, but for our purpose two aspects of Coleridge's argument need to be emphasized.

1. The most revealing clues to Coleridge's standpoint and intention in his debate with Wordsworth are to be found in a sequence of letters written in 1802, in which he voiced his growing doubts about Wordsworth's recently published theories, doubts which had not been allayed by their subsequent discussions of the subject. Although Wordsworth's Preface was "half a child of my own Brain," he told Southey,

> I rather suspect that some where or other there is a radical Difference in our theoretical opinions respecting Poetry— /

this I shall endeavor to go to the Bottom of—and acting the arbitrator between the old School & the New School hope to lay down some plain, & perspicuous, tho' not superficial, Canons of Criticism respecting Poetry.[21]

In this passage Coleridge announced his awareness that Wordsworth's Preface was no less a revolution against the older poetic theory than against the older poetic practice. He announced also—and this, I think, has been overlooked at the expense of misinterpreting Coleridge's own theory—his own intention to act "the *arbitrator* between the old School & the New School." The "Canons of Criticism" which Coleridge promised to lay down, it seems plain, were conceived in accordance with his ruling principle of method, that truth lies in the reconciliation of opposing doctrinal systems,[22] and were intended to save the valid elements in both the traditional and the innovative theories of poetry and poetic diction.

When Coleridge made good his promise some fifteen years later in the *Biographia,* he demonstrated his belief that Wordsworth, in the zeal of his opposition, had thrown out the baby with the bath, by setting out to rescue the elements of earlier theory which he thought indispensable for a criticism adequate to its tasks. This part of Coleridge's enterprise centered on his treatment of what he called a "poem," in distinction from what he called "poetry." You will notice that his definition of a poem is quite in accord with the old rhetorical pattern, making it out to be the disposition of various means, including diction, to the end of effecting pleasure in the reader:

> A poem is that species of composition, which is opposed to works of science, by proposing for its *immediate* object pleasure, not truth; and from all other species . . . it is discriminated by proposing to itself such delight from the *whole,* as is compatible with a distinct gratification from each component *part.*

With this concept Coleridge incorporated a number of traditional terms and distinctions which Wordsworth had either minimized or renounced. For example, he differentiated the subject matter from the form of a poem; he distinguished between thoughts and feelings, and between these mental elements and the diction in which they are conveyed; he even discriminated various conventional levels of diction and style. In this context of discussion unity is conceived according to the old principle of decorum, or what Coleridge calls "appropriateness" among the poetic parts, while failures of unity are denoted by such terms as "incongruity" or "disproportion."[23] By this mode of reasoning Coleridge retained the seemingly indispensable conception, of which there is almost no hint in Wordsworth's Preface, that while we can make predications about poetry in general, we must also recognize that there are diverse kinds of poems, each a unity of its relevant subjects, thoughts, feelings, words, and imagery, and each achieving its own effect and a discriminable kind of aesthetic pleasure.

Most persistently Coleridge set himself to prove that Wordsworth's opposition of nature and spontaneity to art was untenable because at odds with many observable facts of a poem and of poetic composition. Poetry, he says, as "Mr. Wordsworth truly affirms, does always imply PASSION," and all figures of speech (including, as Coleridge says elsewhere, even puns and conceits) must indeed be grounded in a state of emotion.[24] Coleridge's point, however, is that the feelingful language and figures of a poet must differ from the spontaneous and feelingful language spoken sometimes by men in real life, in that the poet, after all, sets himself to the artificial act of composing a *poem*, which is a conventional, metrical medium for producing foreseen effects. The "natural language of excitement," Coleridge says, is therefore altered by the fact that the elements of a poem are "formed into metre *artificially*, by a *voluntary* act, with the design and for the purpose of blending *delight* with emotion."

> There must be . . . an interpenetration of passion and of will, of *spontaneous* impulse and of *voluntary* purpose. Again, this union can be manifested only in a frequency of forms and figures of speech (originally the offspring of passion, but now the adopted children of power) greater than would be desired or endured, where the emotion is not voluntarily encouraged and kept up for the sake of that pleasure.[25]

2. So much for Coleridge's retention of certain neoclassic concepts of poetry and diction. But it is obvious that Coleridge also moves on a quite different level of theory and that this additional element is what marks the *Biographia Literaria* as a great innovative document in the history of English criticism. On the very first page Coleridge announced as one principal object of the book "a settlement of the long continued controversy concerning the true nature of poetic diction." This enterprise, then, helped set off that philosophical chain reaction which led Coleridge through a critical review of the entire history of philosophy, from Aristotle through Hartley to Kant and Schelling. The terminus of this review (which Coleridge eventually reached, but only with the help of a pseudonymous letter to himself advising him to postpone the philosophical details for treatment elsewhere) is to be "the deduction of the Imagination, and with it the principles of production and of genial criticism in the fine arts." His view of the imagination Coleridge summarized in a triple parallel intended to be exhaustive of all forms of creation— cosmic, epistemological, and poetic. In each instance creation is conceived as a productive conflict or tension of opposites, resulting in a synthesis in which the opposing parts are reconciled in a new whole. At the top of this parallel is the divine archetype—"the eternal act of creation in the infinite I AM." This act is repeated in the "primary imagination," or creative process which constitutes all human perception of the sensible universe; and it is repeated once more—through the dissolution of the images of this perception and their fusion or reconciliation into a new unity with diverse aspects of human thought and feeling—in the act of recreation by the "secondary imagination" of the poet of genius. In the fourteenth chapter of the *Biographia* Coleridge finally brings this cumulative concept to bear on his original problem, the nature of poetic diction, by his definition of "poetry" as distinguished from a "poem." For in Coleridge's description the essential factor in producing poetry—regarded as the product of "the whole soul of man" in activity—is explicitly the operation of the secondary imagination, which fuses or reconciles "opposite or discordant qualities" (the hallmark of any kind of creation) into an organized whole.[26]

What Coleridge has done by this long train of reasoning is to supplement the rhetorical view of poetry as an art of adapting diverse means to given aesthetic ends by a profoundly different mode of dealing with the subject—one which calls into play a total philosophy of the universe and of mind. The supreme imaginative passages—the poetry of a poem— are no longer regarded as the disposition and adjustment of words, nor, in Wordsworth's fashion, as the simply "natural" correlates of passion. They are regarded as acts of the mind in which the universe of sense is created anew and made into a whole compounded of subject and object ("the idea, with the image"), by a process blending both "the natural and the artificial." And the unity which in the rhetorical discussion of a "poem" had been an appropriateness or just matching of discernible parts becomes in "poetry" a unity by organic synthesis, in which the parts lose their identity by the nature of their relation to the other parts and to the whole—becomes, in a phrase Coleridge uses elsewhere, a "higher third," in which the parts are *alter et idem,* different though the same.

In this new region of discourse Coleridge is able to reconsider the question of figures of speech, whether valid or invalid, from the standpoint of the operation of the powers and elements of mind on the objects and images of sense. For example, the typical "rhetorical caprices" of eighteenth-century poetic diction he now describes as "the native produce neither of the fancy nor of the imagination," but "the juxtaposition and *apparent* reconciliation of widely different or incompatible things," and therefore "a species of *wit,* a pure work of the *will.*" And all of Coleridge's specific examples of fancy and imagination, it should be noted, are what in the rhetorical mode are classified as figures of speech. Thus, Shakespeare's metaphors in the lines

> Full gently now she takes him by the hand,
> A lily prison'd in a gaol of snow,
> Or ivory in an alabaster band,

are a product of fancy, in that the images—although in contrast to the ornaments of bad poetic diction they have one or

more entirely relevant points "of likeness distinguished"—
remain discernibly the "fixities and definites" of perceptual
memory. Shakespeare's simile, however,

> Look! how a bright star shooteth from the sky,
> So glides he in the night from Venus' eye

is a proof of imagination in that one image or feeling is made
"by a sort of *fusion to force many into one*," so that the component parts are lost in the new whole. And at its supreme level
in Shakespeare the imagination demonstrates itself in the
passage of sustained prosopopoeia uttered by King Lear on
the heath, "where the deep anguish of a father spreads the
feeling of ingratitude and cruelty over the very elements of
heaven."[27]

It has seemed to various commentators remarkable, perhaps a sign of Coleridge's veiled animosity to Wordsworth,
that while approving Wordsworth's objective in reforming
the diction of contemporary poetry, he should have drawn
up such heavy philosophical artillery against the arguments
by which Wordsworth had tried to achieve the objective. But
to Coleridge it helped very little to be right in intention if
one was wrong in principle. To him more than to almost any
critic principles were important, and not only in judging but
also in writing poetry, for as he said, "in energetic minds,
truth soon changes by domestication into power; and from
directing in the discrimination and appraisal of the product,
becomes influencive in the production." In Wordsworth's
writings Coleridge thought he detected proofs that inadequate theory was producing bad poetry by a first-rate poet.
This was to him a matter of supreme concern, because he
believed that Wordsworth was the one man capable of producing the "FIRST GENUINE PHILOSOPHIC POEM," and still more
because Wordsworth's early poetry, by its special excellence,
had been the instance on which Coleridge had shaped the
keystone of his own system of poetic criticism.[28]

In recounting the development of his theory of poetry and
poetic diction in the early chapters of the *Biographia Literaria*,
Coleridge cites three milestones in his progress. The first of

these was the instruction of the Reverend James Bowyer, a hardheaded, heavy-handed, and on the whole quite eighteenth-century rationalist, not unlike Dr. Johnson. Bowyer taught Coleridge to judge poetic thoughts and diction by the criteria of "truth," "plain sense," and "universal logic"; to recognize that the "fitness" of the words in a poem is subject to a causal logic "as severe as that of science"; and on grounds of "sound sense" not to say "lyre" when he meant pen and ink, or "Muse" when he meant the nurse's daughter, or "Pierian spring" when he meant the cloister pump. The second important stage, which occurred in 1789, was Coleridge's discovery of the newly published sonnets of William Lisle Bowles, which, departing from the fashion represented by Erasmus Darwin, demonstrated in practice the very combination of "natural thoughts with natural diction" for which the Reverend Mr. Bowyer had prepared him in theory. Coleridge's utter intoxication with Bowles's poems, which seem to us so undistinguished, is a commonplace of literary history. In the course of the following decade, however, Coleridge's enthusiasm waned, and the reasons for his disenchantment are pertinent to our topic.

Speaking summarily, one may characterize Bowles's poems as a transfer to the sonnet form of a major neoclassic invention, the topographical, or meditative-descriptive, poem. Dr. Johnson defined the type as the poetical description of a particular landscape, "with the addition of such embellishments as may be supplied by historical retrospection or incidental meditation."[29] The essential rhetorical tactic of such a poem was to ornament or, in Johnson's terms, to "embellish" an element in the external scene with a relevant thought or reminiscence suggested to the observer; one of its most characteristic figures, accordingly, was the presentation of a parallel, explicit or implied, between ethos and perceptual object. John Denham's *Cooper's Hill,* the prototype of the genre, also presented an instance of its central trope, which, in its perfect poise between natural phenomenon and moral analogue, bewitched the sensibilities of eighteenth-century readers and worked its way into the substance and cadence of thousands of later couplets:

O could I flow like thee, and make thy stream
My great example, as it is my theme!
Though deep, yet clear; though gentle, yet not dull;
Strong without rage, without o'erflowing full.

A century and a half later Bowles's many rivers—the Itchin, the Cherwell, the Wainsbeck, the Tweed—still flow recognizably in the rhetorical manner of Denham's Thames. The "incidental meditation" in Bowles has become almost invariably pensive and self-pitying, and is managed without allegiance to the fashion of wit-writing which had showed itself in the ingenious particularity of Denham's match between river-vehicle and moral-tenor. We still detect, however, as the element on which the poem usually turns, the meditative-descriptive parallel. A sonnet begins,

> Evening! as slow thy placid shades descend,
> Veiling with gentlest hush the landscape still,

and ends,

> Alas for man! that Hope's fair views the while
> Should smile like you, and perish as they smile.

Coleridge spelled out the reasons for his dissatisfaction with Bowles's poetry in a letter written in 1802, not many weeks after he had expressed his dissatisfaction with Wordsworth's theory of diction. He objected to Bowles's "perpetual trick of *moralizing* every thing" by connecting natural appearances "by dim analogies with the moral world." Nature, Coleridge insisted, "has her proper interest"; and

a Poet's *Heart & Intellect* should be *combined, intimately* combined & *unified,* with the great appearances in Nature—& not merely held in solution & loose mixture with them, in the shape of formal Similes. . . . The truth is—Bowles has indeed the *sensibility* of a poet; but he has not the *Passion* of a great Poet.

From this perception Coleridge went on, after referring to the difference between Greek and Hebrew religious poetry, to make his first formal distinction between fancy and imagination; a distinction which was still free from the immense conceptual elaboration he was later to derive from German metaphysics, yet contained in germ the substance of what he was to say:

> At best, it is but Fancy, or the aggregating Faculty of the mind—not *Imagination,* or the *modifying,* and *co-adunating* Faculty. This the Hebrew Poets appear to me to have possessed beyond all others—& next to them the English. In the Hebrew Poets each Thing has a Life of it's own, & yet they are all one Life.[30]

The grounds of Coleridge's objection to Bowles's procedure are clarified if we recall that this was the very time Coleridge was turning away from Hartley's associationism to a philosophy positing a more intimate relation between subject and object, mind and nature. Rhetorically speaking, Bowles's characteristic yoking of subject and object in parallel is a kind of simile, or "loose mixture," which Coleridge says is well enough in its way: "I do not mean to exclude these formal similes; there are moods of mind in which they are natural . . . but they are not [the poet's] highest and most appropriate moods." The device, as he might have put it later, is proper to a poem, but it is not poetry. In terms of mental powers and operations, Bowles's links between external scene and moral reflection are analyzable as associations by contiguity in past experience (as W. K. Wimsatt has pointed out in his illuminating essay on "The Structure of Romantic Nature Imagery"),[31] or as associations by similarity in form, function, or feeling. Accordingly, Coleridge attributes this poetic mode to the "fancy," or purely associative process of poetic invention: "the faculty of bringing together images dissimilar in the main by some one point or more of likeness distinguished."[32] What Bowles lacks is the higher power of imagination, which acts not by yoking, but by "co-adunating" passion, intellect, and the images of nature—or man's life and the life in nature—into a new whole.

What had given Coleridge this new perspective point, which served to reduce Bowles's poetic stature so drastically, was his exposure to Wordsworth's poetry; and this experience, as Coleridge describes it in the *Biographia,* marked the third and final stage in the development of his theory of poetry. In 1796 he heard Wordsworth recite a manuscript poem (part of which was later published as *The Female Vagrant*), and he says, "I shall hardly forget the sudden effect produced on my mind." Coleridge sets out to define the special qualities of this poem, and his procedure is revealing. His initial description is entirely in rhetorical terms, and by this description Coleridge merely demonstrates that Wordsworth's poem exhibits the same naturalness and mutual appropriateness of the component parts—thoughts, diction, and images, elements of mind and of nature—that he had found earlier in Bowles. "There was here," he tells us, "no mark of strained thought, or forced diction, no crowd or turbulence of imagery," while "manly reflection, and human associations had given both variety, and an additional interest to natural objects." The "style" of Wordsworth's poem had no peculiarity except such "as was not separable from the thought and manner," and even Wordsworth's use of phrases taken from ordinary speech was authorized by suitability to the Spenserian stanza, "which always, more or less, recalls to the reader's mind Spenser's own style."

But when everything which can be said in this rhetorical mode has been said, something remains unaccounted for; and this is the element, Coleridge says, that "made so unusual an impression on my feelings immediately, and subsequently on my judgement." For Wordsworth's poem is not only a poem, but also poetry; and to explain this aspect Coleridge moves into a different province of terms and concepts, based on the modifying activity of mind which reconciles the opposites and disparates of all experience, mental and material.

It was the union of deep feeling with profound thought; the fine balance of truth in observing, with the imaginative faculty in modifying the objects observed. . . . To find no contradiction in the union of old and new; to contemplate the ANCIENT of days and all his works with feelings as fresh, as if all had then sprang forth at the first creative fiat . . . to combine the

child's sense of wonder and novelty with the appearances, which
every day for perhaps forty years had rendered familiar . . .
this is the character and privilege of genius, and one of the
marks which distinguish genius from talents.

This excellence, Coleridge tells us, "which constitutes the
character of [Wordsworth's] mind, I no sooner felt, than I
sought to understand." And the end of his seeking, he goes
on to say, was the discovery "that fancy and imagination were
two distinct and widely different faculties," as different as
Otway's "lutes, lobsters, seas of milk, and ships of amber" is
from King Lear's "apostrophe to the elements."[33]

Coleridge, then, the greatest of the Romantic critics, owes
his eminence in no small degree to the fact that he was a
deliberate moderator between the old and the new and that
he retained control of the analytic tools of earlier criticism at
the same time that he assimilated the innovations of German
aesthetic philosophy. The powers of this double critical vision,
by which poetic passages can be regarded both as rhetorical
structures and as products of the soul of man, are demonstrated in the two chapters of the *Biographia* (the twentieth
and twenty-second) which Coleridge devotes to a detailed
critique of Wordsworth's poetry. Here Coleridge, having
shown what, using the antique distinction, he calls the characteristic "defects" and "beauties" of Wordsworth's poetry,
climaxes his *examen* with the proof that in power of imagination Wordsworth "stands nearest of all modern writers to
Shakespeare and Milton; and yet in a kind perfectly unbor-
rowed and his own."

The passages from Wordsworth which Coleridge selects
for special attention and praise are all densely figurative. It
is noteworthy that the figure most conspicuously represented
is that of personification, which assimilates man to nature in
a peculiarly intimate way, and of which the abuse by eighteenth-century poets, in the absence of justifying reasons, had
moved both Wordsworth and Coleridge to the highest indignation. Coleridge even cites one example of the personification of abstractions in Wordsworth's poem the *Yew Trees,*

> beneath whose sable roof
> . . . ghostly shapes
> May meet at noontide—FEAR and trembling HOPE,
> SILENCE and FORESIGHT—DEATH, the skeleton,
> And TIME, the shadow. . . .

He gives several examples of Wordsworth's personification of inanimate objects, such as that in *The Blind Highland Boy*, where, as Coleridge observes, Wordsworth brings all the "circumstances of a sea-loch before the mind, as the actions of a living and acting power." Finally, Coleridge instances Wordsworth's most characteristic and unexampled kind of personification—it is no less a depersonification—in which, before the poet's fixed and visionary stare, single and solitary human figures transform themselves into something which is both less and more than human. In the passage Coleridge quotes, Wordsworth's old leech gatherer, after a sequence of prior metamorphoses, is modified into an archetypal figure haunting the imagination of the race:

> While he was talking thus, the lonely place,
> The old man's shape, and speech, all troubled me:
> In my mind's eye I seemed to see him pace
> About the weary moors continually,
> Wandering about alone and silently.[34]

According to the rationale underlying the *Biographia Literaria,* such achievements occur in the form of a poem, which is an artful, verbal medium adapted to the achievement of certain ends. They can therefore be analyzed, in a way for which Wordsworth's own theory made no allowance, as modes of diction, partly literal and partly metaphorical, appropriate to the subject, thought, and feeling expressed, to the diction of the rest of the poem, and to the aesthetic effects intended. But these achievements are also, to Coleridge's way of thinking, instances of the poetry in a poem; so that a merely rhetorical analysis, while pertinent, must be supplemented by reference to the powers of the human mind, at once spontaneous and controlled, ordered and self-ordering, to remake and humanize the world of sense. What to the traditional view had been a matter of the kinds and sanctions of figures of speech are now viewed also as the works of the esemplastic imagination of man; and for these Coleridge makes the towering claim that they are the nearest analogue in the finite world to "the eternal act of creation in the infinite I AM."

TWO

The Correspondent Breeze:
A Romantic Metaphor

I

Writing in 1834, Henry Taylor noted that
Wordsworth's attacks on eighteenth-century diction had succeeded in making poetry, in some particulars, more plain
spoken. But Taylor also remarked that in effect a new poetic
diction had covertly replaced the old. If Romantic poets no
longer refer to the nightingale by the Greek name, Philomel,
some of them refer to it by the Persian name, Bulbul; Taylor
cites one reader who said "he had learnt, for the first time,
from Lord Byron's poetry, that two bulls make a nightingale." Worse still are the stock terms scattered through poetry
"with a sort of feeling senselessness," such as "wild," "bright,"
"lonely," and "dream," and especially the variant forms of
the word "breathing"; "to breathe," Taylor says, has become
"a verb poetical which [means] anything but respiration."[1]

To this shrewd observation I would add that "breathing"
is only one aspect of a more general component in Romantic
poetry. This is air-in-motion, whether it occurs as breeze or
breath, wind or respiration—whether the air is compelled into
motion by natural forces or by the action of the human lungs.
That the poetry of Coleridge, Wordsworth, Shelley, Byron

should be so thoroughly ventilated is itself noteworthy; but the surprising thing is how often, in the major poems, the wind is not only a property of the landscape, but also a vehicle for radical changes in the poet's mind. The rising wind, usually linked with the outer transition from winter to spring, is correlated with a complex subjective process: the return to a sense of community after isolation, the renewal of life and emotional vigor after apathy and a deathlike torpor, and an outburst of creative power following a period of imaginative sterility.

Coleridge's *Dejection: An Ode,* written in 1802, provides the earliest inclusive instance of this symbolic equation. The poetic meditation is set in April, which turns out, as in Eliot's *Waste Land,* to be the cruelest month because, in breeding life out of the dead land, it painfully revives emotional life in the observer, mixing memory and desire. And as the poem opens, a desultory breeze makes itself audible on a wind-harp—an instrument whose eerie modulations sound through most of the writings with which we are concerned.

James Bowyer, Coleridge's schoolmaster and a pre-Wordsworthian reformer of poetic diction, had vigorously proscribed the traditional lyre as an emblem for poetizing. "Harp? Harp? Lyre? Pen and ink, boy, you mean!"[2] But by the process already noted—we might call it Taylor's principle—the lyre of Apollo was often replaced in Romantic poetry by the Aeolian lyre, whose music is evoked not by art, human or divine, but by a force of nature. Poetic man, in a statement by Shelley which had close parallels in Coleridge and Wordsworth, is an instrument subject to impressions "like the alternations of an ever-changing wind over an Aeolian lyre which move it by their motion to ever-changing melody."[3] The wind-harp has become a persistent Romantic analogue of the poetic mind, the figurative mediator between outer motion and inner emotion. It is possible to speculate that, without this plaything of the eighteenth century, the Romantic poets would have lacked a conceptual model for the way the mind and imagination respond to the wind, so that some of their most characteristic passages might have been, in a literal sense, inconceivable.

In Coleridge's *Dejection* the moaning wind-harp foretells a storm which the lyric speaker in his lethargy awaits in the hope that, as in the past, it may send "my soul abroad" and release the

> stifled, drowsy, unimpassioned grief,
> Which finds no natural outlet, no relief.

The speaker reviews the afflictions that have made him take refuge in "abstruse research," and have destroyed his inner joy and any possibility of emotional commerce with the outer scene. Worst of all is the attendant paralysis of his poetic power, the "shaping spirit of Imagination." But even as the speaker inventories the conditions of his death-in-life, the outer wind mounts to a storm of driving rain and compels the wind-harp into loud and violent music. In implicit parallel with the harp, the poet responds to the storm with mounting vitality—what he calls "the passion and the life, whose fountains are within," once more break out—until, in a lull of the wind, the poem rounds on itself and ends where it began, with a calm both of nature and of mind. But the poet has moved from the calm of apathy to one of peace after passion. By the agency of the wind storm it describes, the poem turns out to contradict its own premises: the poet's spirit awakens to violent life even as he laments his inner death, achieves release in the despair at being cut off from all outlet, and demonstrates the power of imagination in the process of memorializing its failure.

That the poem was grounded in experience is evident from Coleridge's many letters testifying to his delight in wind and storms, which he watched "with a total feeling worshipping the power & 'eternal Link' of Energy," and through which he had walked, "stricken . . . with barrenness" in a "deeper dejection than I am willing to remember," seeking the inspiration for completing *Christabel*.[4] In one passage, written some nine months after he had completed *Dejection,* we find a symbolic wind again involving the revival of feeling and imagination, and leading to the sense of the one life within us and abroad:

In simple earnest, I never find myself alone within the embracement of rocks & hills, a traveller up an alpine road, but my spirit courses, drives, and eddies, like a Leaf in Autumn: a wild activity, of thoughts, imaginations, feelings, and impulses of motion, rises up from within me—a sort of *bottom-wind*, that blows to no point of the compass, & comes from I know not whence, but agitates the whole of me. . . . Life seems to me then a universal spirit, that neither has, nor can have, an opposite. . . . where is there *room* for Death?[5]

Similarly with Coleridge's friend, Wordsworth: "Winter winds," Dorothy wrote, "are his delight—his mind I think is often more fertile in this season than any other."[6] Of this phenomenon Wordsworth himself gave remarkable testimony in the autobiographical *Prelude*. From the beginning of this work, in fact, the recurrent wind serves unobtrusively as a leitmotif, representing the chief theme of continuity and interchange between outer motions and the interior life and powers, and providing the poem with a principle of organization beyond chronology.

Earlier poets had launched their epics by invoking for inspiration a muse, Apollo, or the Holy Spirit. Wordsworth's opening lines, which have an identical function, are:

> Oh there is blessing in this gentle breeze
> That blows from the green fields and from the clouds
> And from the sky.

Released at last from the city and the oppressive weight of the past, the poet says "I breathe again"; but so, we find, is nature breathing, in a passage where the wind becomes both the stimulus and outer correspondent to a springlike revival of the spirit after a wintry season, and also to a revival of poetic inspiration which Wordsworth, going beyond Coleridge, equates with the inspiration of the prophets when touched by the Holy Spirit. There is even a glancing metaphoric parallel between the resulting poetic creation and the prototypal creation by divine utterance—for "Nature's self," as Wordsworth says later, "is the breath of God" (*The Prelude*, 1805 text, V, 222).

For I, methought, while the sweet breath of heaven
Was blowing on my body, felt within
A corresponding mild creative breeze,
A vital breeze which travelled gently on
O'er things which it had made, and is become
A tempest, a redundant energy,
Vexing its own creation. 'Tis a power
That does not come unrecognised, a storm
Which, breaking up a long-continued frost,
Brings with it vernal promises . . .
The holy life of music and of verse. . . .

> To the open fields I told
A prophesy; poetic numbers came
Spontaneously, and clothed in priestly robe
My spirit, thus singled out, as it might seem,
For holy services.

And a bit farther on comes the remaining element of the Romantic complex, the analogy between poetic mind and Aeolian harp:

It was a splendid evening, and my soul
Did once again make trial of the strength
Restored to her afresh; nor did she want
Eolian visitations—but the harp
Was soon defrauded.   (1805 text, I, 1–105)

Later Wordsworth parallels Milton's reinvocations of his divine guides by recalling the "animating breeze" which had made a "glad preamble to this verse," and now, made visible by the tossing boughs of his favorite grove, once again

Spreads through me a commotion like its own,
Something that fits me for the poet's task.   (VII, 1–56)

Wordsworth's account of his mental breakdown in *The Prelude* runs broadly parallel to the autobiographical passages in Coleridge's *Dejection*. And at the nadir of his apathy, when he felt "utter loss of hope itself / And things to hope for," Wordsworth signalized his recovery by addressing again the correspondent breeze:

> Not with these began
> Our song, and not with these our song must end.
> Ye motions of delight, that through the fields
> Stir gently, breezes and soft airs that breathe
> The breath of paradise, and find your way
> To the recesses of the soul.   (XI, 7–12)

"Spring returns,—/ I saw the spring return"; and even the influence of Dorothy is apprehended as a revivifying spring breeze:

> Thy breath,
> Dear sister, was a kind of gentler spring
> That went before my steps. (XI, 23–24; XIII, 244–46)

Time and again Wordsworth's most arcane statements similarly involve, as he put it in *The Excursion* (IV, 600), "the breeze of nature stirring in his soul."[7] In the *Ode: Intimations of Immortality,* "The winds come to me from the fields of sleep"; and in *The Prelude,* the poet listens to sounds that

> make their dim abode in distant winds.
> Thence did I drink the visionary power;

or asserts that

> visionary power
> Attends the motions of the viewless winds,
> Embodied in the mystery of words.

The shell of the Arab, in Wordsworth's dream, which utters "a loud prophetic blast of harmony,"

> Had voices more than all the winds, with power
> To exhilarate the spirit.   (1850 text, II, 310–11;
>   V, 595–97, 92–108)

Of the two "spots of time"—the indelible memories by which his imagination, having, like Coleridge's, been "impaired," was "nourished and invisibly repaired"—one incorporated a woman with "her garments vexed and tossed / By the strong wind," and the other "the wind and sleety rain" evoking "the bleak music of that old stone wall." The result is that to this very time, whether in winter storm and rain or when the summer trees rock

> In a strong wind, some working of the spirit,
> Some inward agitations thence are brought.
>   (1850 text, XII, 208–332)

Wordsworth read his completed masterpiece to Coleridge in 1807, five years after the writing of *Dejection,* and when Coleridge's spirits were at their lowest ebb. In his memorial on that occasion, *To William Wordsworth,* Coleridge duly noted that Wordsworth had described the quickening effect within his mind of the springtime wind: of "vital breathings secret as the soul / Of vernal growth." Then, as he listened to those passages in which Wordsworth expressed his love and hope for Coleridge himself, suddenly the poet's solemn voice seized upon his friend as though it were itself a great wind which, like the literal storm in *Dejection,* fanned his torpid spirit, "whose hope had seem'd to die," into a momentary and painful rebirth. The episode is one of the most moving in literature:

> The storm
> Scatter'd and whirl'd me, till my thoughts became
> A bodily tumult. . . .
> Ah! as I listened with a heart forlorn,
> The pulses of my being beat anew:
> And even as Life returns upon the drowned,
> Life's joy rekindling roused a throng of pains—
> Keen pangs of Love, awakening as a babe
> Turbulent, with an outcry in the heart.[8]

It is easy to multiply similar quotations, from these and other Romantic writers. Childe Harold, for example, found his spirit participating in the violence of an Alpine tempest, and drew a parallel with the violent explosion of his mind in poetry (Canto III, xcii–xcvii). And while De Quincey, a child

of six, stood secretly and alone by the deathbed of a beloved
sister, "a solemn wind began to blow"; as his "ear caught this
vast Aeolian intonation" and his eye turned from "the golden
fulness of life" outdoors in the midsummer noon to settle
"upon the frost which overspread my sister's face, instantly a
trance fell upon me. . . . I, in spirit, rose as if on billows."[9]

One poet, the most visionary and vatic of all these, demands
special attention. Shelley's best known poem is addressed
directly to the wind, in the form of a sustained invocation
and petition. In the opening stanzas the wild West Wind is at
once destroyer and preserver because in the autumn it tears
down the dead leaves and the seeds, but only so that in a later
season another west wind—"thine azure sister of the Spring"—
may blow the clarion of resurrection, revive the seeds, and
call out the buds to feed, like flocks of sheep, on the moving
air, the wind itself. In the last stanza Shelley, like Coleridge
in *Dejection*, cries out to the wind, in the autumn of his spirit,
to blow through him as through a wind-harp—"Make me thy
lyre, even as the forest is"—and to drive the withered leaves
of his dead thoughts over the universe "to quicken a new
birth." And in the coda, to the blast of the wind sounding
this time the apocalyptic trumpet of the general destruction
and resurrection, the immense analogy is consummated
between the effect of the wind on the unawakened earth, the
singer's inspiration to poetry and prophecy, and the springtime of the human spirit everywhere:

> Be thou, Spirit fierce,
> My spirit! Be thou me, impetuous one! . . .
>
> Be through my lips to unawakened earth
>
> The trumpet of a prophecy! O, Wind,
> If Winter comes, can Spring be far behind?

Elsewhere the wind served Shelley repeatedly as a stimulus
and symbol of inspiration, in his prose essays as well as his
verse. *Alastor* opens with an invocation to the "Mother of this
unfathomable world!"

> Serenely now
> And moveless, as a long-forgotten lyre . . .
> I wait thy breath, Great Parent, that my strain
> May modulate with murmurs of the air.[10]

Shelley's use of the wind in *Adonais* is of particular interest. This poem follows the classic elegiac pattern—consonant also with the evolution of earlier Romantic poems of dejection—from despair to consolation, although Shelley's consolation involves a death wish:

> Die,
> If thou wouldst be with that which thou dost seek! . . .
> Why linger, why turn back, why shrink, my Heart?

The conclusion, however, is astonishing. Most of these poems begin with a literal wind which transforms itself into the metaphorical wind of inspiration. Shelley reverses the sequence. At the end of *Adonais* the inspiration he had evoked "in song" (that is, in his *Ode to the West Wind*) actually descends upon him; and what he feels is a tangible breath which rises to the violence of a literal storm of wind:

> The breath whose might I have invoked in song
> Descends on me; my spirit's bark is driven,
> Far from the shore, far from the trembling throng
> Whose sails were never to the tempest given;
> The massy earth and spherèd skies are riven!
> I am borne darkly, fearfully, afar. . . .[11]

II

Taken singly the symbolic equations between breeze, breath, and soul, respiration and inspiration, the reanimation of nature and of the spirit, are not peculiarly Romantic, nor in any way recent. All are older than recorded history; they are inherent in the constitution of ancient languages, are widely current in myth and folklore, and make up some of the great commonplaces of our religious tradition.

When Shelley, for example, made the West Wind the breath of autumn's being and a spirit which became his breath and his spirit and blew, through him, the trumpet prophesying a universal resurrection, he may seem radically innovative. But from a philological point of view Shelley was reactionary; he merely revived and exploited the ancient undivided meanings of these words. For the Latin *spiritus* signified wind and breath, as well as soul. So did the Latin *anima*, and the Greek *pneuma*, the Hebrew *ruach*, the Sanskrit *atman*, as well as the equivalent words in Arabic, Japanese, and many other languages, some of them totally unrelated. In myth and religion, moreover, wind and breath often play an essential part in the creation both of the universe and of man. In the beginning the spirit, or breath, or wind *(ruach)* of God moved upon the face of the waters; and after forming man, God "breathed into his nostrils the breath of life; and man became a living soul." Even in the Old Testament breath and wind were given the added power of renewing life after death, as in Ezekiel 37:9: "Prophesy, son of man, and say to the wind, . . . Come from the four winds, O breath, and breathe upon these slain, that they may live." Similarly Jesus said (John 3:7–8): "Marvel not that I said unto thee, Ye must be born again. The wind bloweth where it listeth . . . so is every one that is born of the Spirit." But God's breath in the Bible could also be a destroying storm (as in I Kings 19:11; Ezekiel 13:13), symbolizing the explosion of God's wrath as well as the gift of life or grace. In parallel fashion the Wind Gods of Greek and Roman myth were regarded as destructive, requiring propitiation; but they also—especially the West Wind, "Zephyrus," or "Favonius"—were held to possess an animating or impregnating power, a fact noted by medieval encyclopedists, and by Chaucer, in the opening passage of *The Canterbury Tales:*

> Whan Zephyrus eek with his swete breeth
> Inspired hath in every holt and heeth
> The tendre croppes.

Shelley thus had ample precedent, pagan and Christian, for his West Wind, both breath and spirit, destroyer as well as preserver, which is equally the revitalizing Zephyrus of the Romans and the trumpet blast of the Book of Revelation, announcing the simultaneous destruction of the present world and a new life in a world re-created. The additional connection between wind and inspiration is, of course, implicit in the latter term, for "to inspire" once meant "to blow or breathe into," and when a man received the divine "afflatus" he received, literally, the breath or wind of a god or muse. According to classical belief, this supernatural breath stimulated the visionary utterances of religious oracles and prophetic poets. Eliphaz the Temanite, in the Book of Job (4:13–16), expressed a similar view: "In thoughts from the visions of the night . . . a spirit [or breeze: *ruach*] passed before my face. . . . there was silence, and I heard a voice." And on the day of Pentecost, in the Acts of the New Testament (2:1–4), "suddenly there came a sound from heaven as of a rushing mighty wind. . . . And they were all filled with the Holy Ghost, and began to speak with other tongues, as the Spirit gave them utterance."

One other historical item is pertinent. The Stoic concept of the World-Soul—of the *Pneuma,* or *Spiritus Sacer,* or *Anima Mundi*—originally involved, in the literal sense of these names, the concept of a kind of breath, a divine gas, which infuses the material world and constitutes also the individual human psyche. The poet Lucan said that Apollo founded the Delphic oracle at a huge chasm where "the earth breathed forth divine truth, and . . . gave out a wind that spoke"; and he suggested that the Pythian priestess stationed there is inspired by inhaling the very breath of the World-Soul.[12] It is noteworthy that the familiar Romantic Soul of Nature, or Spirit of the Universe, sometimes retained its primitive airy essence, homogeneous with the soul of man, as well as its power of quasi-literal inspiration. In *The Eolian Harp* Coleridge speculated that all animated nature may be but organic wind-harps, diversely framed, through which sweeps "one intellectual breeze, / At once the Soul of each, and God of all." Wordsworth in *The Prelude* invoked the "Wisdom," "spirit," and "soul" of the Universe,

> That giv'st to forms and images a breath
> And everlasting motion,

and also the "Soul of things," that in its love renews

> Those naked feelings which when thou wouldst form
> A living thing thou sendest like a breeze
> Into its infant being.[13]

Shelley called upon the West Wind, the "breath of Autumn's being," to blow through him: "Be thou, spirit fierce, / My spirit!" The Soul of the worlds, Emerson later declared in "The Over-Soul," "can inspire whom it will, and behold! their speech shall be lyrical and sweet, and universal as the rising of the wind."

III

In the biblical commentaries of the Church Fathers it was commonly recognized that the moving air, the breath of the Lord, the Holy Spirit, the life and spiritual rebirth of man, and the inspiration of the prophets in the Old and New Testaments were connected, if not literally, then allegorically, or by a system of correspondence, or by some other exegetical relation. Before the end of the fourth century, Saint Augustine had imported the spiritual breeze into the context of autobiography that is common to all the Romantic writings I have cited. In the central passage of his *Confessions* (VIII, xi–xii), Augustine described his tortured state as he hesitated at the brink of conversion, "soul-sick . . . and tormented," as he said, "hesitating to die to death and live to life." Then one day he retired into the garden next his lodging, and "when a deep consideration had from the secret bottom of my soul drawn together and heaped up all my misery in my heart, there arose a mighty wind, bringing a mighty shower of tears"; with the result that "by a light as it were of serenity infused into my heart, all the darkness of doubt vanished away."

Even the typical procedure in Romantic wind-poems of beginning with the description of a natural scene and then moving to inner correspondences had precedents in prose and verse. During the Middle Ages the mode of self-inquisition and spiritual inventory, of which Augustine's *Confessions* became a prime exemplar, led to the identification of a standard condition of apathy and spiritual torpor called "acedia," or "aridity," or "interior desolation," closely related, according to Cassian, to another state of the soul called "dejection" *(tristitia)*.[14] The descriptions of this interior condition and of its relief were sometimes couched in natural and seasonal metaphors: winter, drought, and desert, as against spring, the coming of rain, and the burgeoning plant or garden. Coleridge echoed the technical language of theology when, in a letter of 25 March 1801 which was a prose rehearsal for *Dejection*, he described his "intellectual *exsiccation*," a state in which "the Poet is dead in me," his imagination "lies, like a Cold Snuff on the circular Rim of a Brass Candle-stick," and he remains "squat and square on the earth amid the hurricane."[15]

In the later Renaissance the alternation of aridity and freshness, in which spiritual and imaginative death and rebirth are equated with aspects of the natural scene, became a frequent topic in the meditations of the religious poets. An instance in George Herbert is the pair of poems called *Employment*, which inspired Coleridge's *Work Without Hope;* another is *The Flower*, also a favorite of Coleridge, in which we find a complex interplay between the death-in-life and revival of the soul, of the poetic faculty, and of a perennial plant.

> How fresh, O Lord, how sweet and clean
> Are thy returns! Ev'n as the flowers in spring,
> To which, besides their own demean,
> The late-past frosts tributes of pleasure bring. . . .

> And now in age I bud again,
> After so many deaths I live and write;
>   I once more smell the dew and rain,
> And relish versing. O my only light,
>   It cannot be
>   That I am he
> On whom thy tempests fell all night.

Henry Vaughan at times approximates still more closely the familiar Romantic pattern of inner depression and revival, paralleled to changes in the landscape in diverse weathers and seasons. And the role of the wind is made explicit in poems such as *The Storm* and the second *Mount of Olives,* but above all in *Regeneration.* "One day," he says in that poem, "I stole abroad." "It was high spring. . . . Yet was it frost within." After traversing a spiritual landscape and toiling up a purgatorial mountain, he entered a flowery grove reminiscent of several earlier pleasances, all of them wind-blown: Dante's Earthly Paradise, the garden which had been the setting of Augustine's conversion, and that favorite medieval symbol, the *hortus conclusus,* the closed garden, of the Song of Songs:[16]

> Here musing long, I heard
>   A rushing wind
> Which still increased, but whence it stirred
>   Nowhere I could not find. . . .
>
> But while I list'ning sought
>   My mind to ease
> By knowing where 'twas, or where not,
>   It whispered: Where I please.
>
> Lord, then said I, on me one breath,
> And let me die before my death!

The Romantic wind, then, is remote in kind from the pleasingly horrific storm dear to eighteenth-century connoisseurs of the natural sublime; and the confessional lyrics of dejection and recovery in which this wind plays its part are not (as common report would have it) in the tradition of the eighteenth-century poems of melancholy and spleen. These lyrics are rather secularized versions of an older devotional poetry, employed in the examination of the soul's condition as it approaches and retreats from God. Secularized—yet the religious element remains as at least a formal parallel, or a verbal or rhetorical echo. Coleridge's finest odes, including *Dejection* and *To William Wordsworth,* use theological language and end in the cadence of a prayer. Wordsworth's poetic meditations commonly involve a presence whose dwelling is the light of setting suns. And even the pagan Shelley's *Ode to the West Wind* is a formal orison addressed to the Spirit and Breath of Autumn's Being.

IV

And now the question: What are we to make of the phenomenon of the correspondent breeze in Romantic poetry? These days the answer seems obvious enough, and it may have occasioned surprise that I have so long resisted calling the wind an "archetypal image." I should not hesitate to use so convenient a term, if it were merely a neutral way of identifying a persistent material symbol for a psychological condition. In the context of present criticial theory, however, the term "archetypal" commits the user to implications which are equally unnecessary and undesirable. For example, in order to explain the origin and currency of the correspondent wind it would seem adequate to point to the inescapable conditions of the human endowment and of its physical milieu. That breath and wind are both instances of air in motion, and that breathing is a sign of life and its cessation a sign of death, are matters evident to casual observation, as are the alternations of inhalation and exhalation, despair and elation, imaginative energy and torpor, birth and death, in the constant environmental rhythms of calm and storm, drought and rain, winter and spring. If a connection between a universal inner experience and an omnipresent outer analogue has been made once, it will be made again, and may readily become a commonplace of oral and written tradition; there is no rational need to assume, as Jung does, that after leaving its mark on the nervous system the image goes underground, to emerge sporadically from the racial unconscious. But of course if we neutralize the archetype by eliminating dark allusions to "primordial images," or "the racial memory," or "timeless depths," archetypal criticism is drained of the mystique or pathos which is an important condition of its present vogue.

For literary criticism, moreover, the ultimate criterion is not whether a doctrine is a justifiable psychological hypothesis, but what it does when put to work interpreting a text. And from this point of view standard archetypal criticism can be charged with blurring, if it does not destroy, the properties of the literary products it undertakes to explicate. A mode of reading that persists in looking through the literal, particular, and artful qualities of a poem in order to discover a more important ulterior pattern of primitive, general, and unintended meanings eliminates its individuality, and threatens to nullify even its status as a work of art. For the result of such reading is to collapse the rich diversity of individual works into one, or into a very limited number, of archetypal patterns, which any one poem shares not only with other poems, but with such unartful phenomena as myth, dreams, and the fantasies of psychosis.

Maud Bodkin's influential book, *Archetypal Patterns in Poetry* (1934), intelligent and extremely suggestive though it is, provides a radical illustration of this process. Miss Bodkin begins her study by considering the significance of the wind in Coleridge's *Ancient Mariner,* and of the contrast between the becalmed ship and, after the blessing of the water snakes, the storm which drives the ship into violent motion. In the Romantic poems I have discussed, the rising wind was explicitly paralleled to a change in the inner state of the lyric speaker. *The Ancient Mariner,* on the other hand, is explicitly a narrative about the actions and sufferings of an unfortunate sailor; yet Miss Bodkin has no hesitation in reading the change from calm to storm as a symbolic projection—by the author—of the mental states that Jung calls "progression and regression." This psychic sequence constitutes the "Rebirth archetype," which is also manifested by the vegetation god of ritual and myth, is echoed in the resurrection of Christ, reappears in dreams, and in literature constitutes the basic pattern, among other works, of *Oedipus, Hamlet,* the Book of Jonah, the *Aeneid,* the *Divine Comedy, Paradise Lost, Kubla Khan,* and *Women in Love.* Once unleashed, indeed, the archetype proves insatiable, and goes on to devour even subhuman phenomena: Miss Bodkin (page 75) detects the characteristic pattern of the Night Journey and Rebirth in the behavior of Wolfgang Köhler's experimental apes, who passed through a period of baffled bewilderment before the flash of insight which enabled them to reach their banana.

These are astonishing equations, but the logical procedure by which they were achieved is simple enough. It consists in treating loose analogy as though it were identity. This strategy, to be sure, has a singular virtue; it cannot fail. Only leave out enough of the qualities that make a poem, or any complex experience, distinctive, and it can be reduced to an abstract pattern—almost any abstract pattern, including, if that is our inclination, the pattern of the vegetational cycle of death and rebirth. But by what a prodigious abstraction of everything that matters is a literary ballad, *The Ancient Mariner,* shown to be identical in ultimate significance with tragedies, epics, novels, and lyrics, together with the basic formulas of myth and religion!

A procedure which ingeniously contrives to reduce all—or at least a great many—serious poems to variations upon a timeless theme is not much to the purpose of the literary critic, whose chief concern is with the particularity of a work; nor is it more useful to the literary historian, despite his greater interest in establishing literary types and the general qualities of a literary period. For example, we know that the use of the wind in Romantic poetry had ample precedent in myth, religion, and the poetry of religious meditation. Yet the correspondent breeze, like the guilt-haunted wanderer and the Promethean or Satanic figure of the heroic rebel, can justly be identified as a distinctively Romantic image, or icon. For one thing, there is no precedent for the way in which the symbolic wind was called upon by poet after poet, in poem after poem, all within the first few decades of the nineteenth century. For another, the fact that they explored the literary possibilities of myth and primitive thinking, and played secular variations on ancient devotional patterns, is itself characteristic of the Romantic poets. But above all, these writers exploited attributes of the wind which rendered it peculiarly apt for the philosophical, political, and aesthetic preoccupations of the age.

Thus Wordsworth's are, specifically, "viewless winds," which are "unseen though not inaudible,"[17] and Shelley's wind is an "unseen presence." When Blake denounced "single vision & Newton's sleep," and Coleridge warned repeatedly against "the despotism of the eye," and Wordsworth, recalling his joy "before the winds, / And roaring waters, and in lights and shades," decried the "bodily eye" as "the most despotic of our senses," all attributed to an obsession with what is materially visible the diverse shortcomings of the eighteenth century, from its sensationist philosophy to its theory and practice of the arts.[18] The wind, as an invisible power known only by its effects, had an even greater part to play than water, light, and clouds in the Romantic revolt against the world-view of the Enlightenment. In addition, the moving air lent itself preeminently to the aim of tying man back into the environment from which, Wordsworth and Coleridge felt, he had been divorced by post-Cartesian dualism and mechanism. For not only are nature's breezes the analogue of human respiration; they are themselves inhaled into the body and assimilated to its substance—the "breezes and soft airs," as Wordsworth said, "find [their] way / To the recesses of the soul," and so fuse materially, as well as metaphorically, the "soul" of man with the "spirit" of nature. Lastly, the Romantic wind is typically a wild wind and a free one—Shelley's "thou uncontrollable"—which, even when gentle, holds the threat of destructive violence. Wordsworth's "gentle breeze," greeted as messenger and friend by a captive "coming from a house / Of bondage, from yon City's walls set free," soon, like the breeze in Coleridge's *Dejection,* mounts to "a tempest . . . Vexing its own creation." These traits made the wind storm, as it had been earlier, a ready counterpart for the prophetic furor of the inspired poet. But they also rendered it a most eligible model for Romantic activism, as well as an emblem of the free Romantic spirit; and in an era obsessed with the fact and idea of revolution, they sanctioned a parallel, manifest in Shelley, with a purifying revolutionary violence which destroys in order to preserve.[19]

The Romantic ideal, it should be added, is that of a controlled violence, of a self-ordering impetus of passion, which Coleridge described in *To Matilda Betham,* and once again by analogy to the wind:

> Poetic feelings, like the stretching boughs
> Of mighty oaks, pay homage to the gales,
> Toss in the strong winds, drive before the gust,
> Themselves one giddy storm of fluttering leaves;
> Yet, all the while self-limited, remain
> Equally near the fixed and solid trunk
> Of Truth and Nature in the howling storm,
> As in the calm that stills the aspen grove.

This sovereign order in rage is, I think, characteristic of the longer Romantic lyric at its best. The tide of the systematic derogation of that achievement seems to be receding, but it may still be worth registering the judgment that the Romantic lyric at its best is equal to the greatest.

THREE

English Romanticism: The Spirit of the Age

M<small>Y TITLE</small> echoes that of William Hazlitt's remarkable book of 1825, which set out to represent what we now call the climate of opinion among the leading men of his time. In his abrupt way Hazlitt did not stay to theorize, plunging into the middle of things with a sketch of Jeremy Bentham. But from these essays emerges plainly his view that the crucial occurrence for his generation had been the French Revolution. In that event and its repercussions, political, intellectual, and imaginative, and in the resulting waves of hope and gloom, revolutionary loyalty and recreancy, he saw both the promise and the failures of his violent and contradictory era.

The span covered by the active life of Hazlitt's subjects—approximately the early 1790s to 1825—coincides with what literary historians now call the Romantic period; and it is Hazlitt's contention that the characteristic poetry of the age took its shape from the form and pressure of revolution and reaction. The whole "Lake school of poetry," he had said seven years earlier, "had its origin in the French revolution, or rather in those sentiments and opinions which produced that revolution."[1] Hazlitt's main exhibit is Wordsworth (the "head" of the school), whose "genius," he declares, "is a pure emanation of the Spirit of the Age." The poetry of Wordsworth in the period of *Lyrical Ballads* is "one of the innovations of the time."

> It partakes of, and is carried along with, the revolutionary movement of our age: the political changes of the day were the model on which he formed and conducted his poetical experiments. His Muse (it cannot be denied, and without this we cannot explain its character at all) is a levelling one.[2]

Neither the concept that the age had an identifying "spirit," nor the view that this spirit was one of revolutionary change, was unique with Hazlitt. Just after the revolution of July 1830, John Stuart Mill wrote a series of essays on *The Spirit of the Age* in which he said that the phrase, denoting "the dominant idea" of the times, went back only some fifty years, and resulted from the all but universal conviction "that the times are pregnant with change"—a condition "of which the first overt manifestation was the breaking out of the French Revolution."[3] Shelley, in *A Philosophical View of Reform* (1819), after reviewing the European outbreaks of liberty against tyranny which culminated in the American and French revolutions, asserted that the related crisis of change in England had been accompanied by a literary renascence, in which the poets displayed "a comprehensive and all-penetrating spirit" that was "less their own spirit than the spirit of their age."[4] Conservative critics, like the radical Shelley, recognized the fact of a great new poetry and associated its genesis with political events. "The revolution in our literature," Francis Jeffrey claimed in 1816, had as one of its primary causes "the agitations of the French revolution, and the discussions as well as the hopes and terrors to which it gave occasion."[5] And De Quincey said (1839) that the almost "miraculous" effect of the "great moral tempest" of the Revolution was evident "in all lands . . . and at the same time." "In Germany or England alike, the poetry was so entirely regenerated, thrown into moulds of thought

and of feeling so new, that the poets everywhere felt themselves . . . entering upon the dignity and the sincere thinking
of mature manhood."[6]

It seems to me that Hazlitt and his contemporary viewers
of the literary scene were, in their general claim, manifestly
right: the Romantic period was eminently an age obsessed
with the fact of violent and inclusive change, and Romantic
poetry cannot be understood, historically, without awareness
of the degree to which this preoccupation affected its substance and form. The phenomenon is too obvious to have
escaped notice, in monographs devoted to the French Revolution and the English poets, singly and collectively. But when
critics and historians turn to the general task of defining the
distinctive qualities of "Romanticism," or of the English
Romantic movement, they usually ignore its relations to the
revolutionary climate of the time. For example, in an anthol-
ogy of "the 'classic' statements" on Romanticism, especially in
England, which came out in 1962, the few essays which give
more than passing mention to the French Revolution do so
to reduce the particularity of Romantic poems mainly to a
distant reflection of an underlying economic reality, and to
an unconscious rationalization of the bourgeois illusion of
"freedom."[7]

It may be useful, then, to have a new look at the obvious
as it appeared, not to post-Marxist historians, but to intelligent observers at the time. I shall try to indicate briefly some
of the ways in which the political, intellectual, and emotional
circumstances of a period of revolutionary upheaval affected
the scope, subject-matter, themes, values, and even language
of a number of Romantic poems. I hope to avoid easy and
empty generalizations about the *Zeitgeist,* and I do not propose the electrifying proposition that "le romantisme, c'est la
révolution." Romanticism is no one thing. It is many very
individual poets, who wrote poems manifesting a greater
diversity of qualities, it seems to me, than those of any preceding age. But some prominent qualities a number of these
poems share, and certain of these shared qualities form a
distinctive complex which may, with a high degree of prob-
ability, be related to the events and ideas of the cataclysmic

coming-into-being of the world to which we are by now becoming fairly accustomed.

I. THE SPIRIT OF THE 1790S

By force of chronological habit we think of English Romanticism as a nineteenth-century phenomenon, overlooking how many of its distinctive features had been established by the end of the century before. The last decade of the eighteenth century included the complete cycle of the Revolution in France, from what De Quincey called its "gorgeous festival era"[8] to the *coup d'état* of November 10, 1799, when to all but a few stubborn sympathizers it seemed betrayed from without and within, and the portent of Napoleon loomed over Europe. That same decade was the period in which the poets of the first Romantic generation reached their literary maturity and had either completed, or laid out and begun, the greater number of what we now account their major achievements. By the end of the decade Blake was well along with *The Four Zoas;* only *Milton* and *Jerusalem* belong to the nineteenth century. By the end of the year 1800 Wordsworth had already announced the overall design and begun writing the two great undertakings of his poetic career; that is, he had finished most of the first two books and a number of scattered later passages of *The Prelude,* and of *The Recluse* he had written *Home at Grasmere* (which included the extraordinary section he later reprinted as the "Prospectus of the design and scope of the whole poem") as well as the first book of *The Excursion.* Coleridge wrote in the 1790s seven-tenths of all the nondramatic material in his collected poems.

"Few persons but those who have lived in it," Southey reminisced in his Tory middle age, "can conceive or comprehend what the memory of the French Revolution was, nor what a visionary world seemed to open upon those who were just entering it. Old things seemed passing away, and nothing was dreamt of but the regeneration of the human race."[9] The early years of the Revolution, a modern commentator has remarked, were "perhaps the happiest in the memory of civilized man,"[10] and his estimate is justified by the ecstasy described by Wordsworth in *The Prelude*—"bliss was it in that dawn to be alive"—and expressed by many observers of France in its glad dawn. Samuel Romilly exclaimed in May 1792: "It is the most glorious event, and the happiest for mankind, that has ever taken place since human affairs have been recorded." Charles James Fox was less restrained in his evaluation: "How much the greatest event it is that ever happened in the world! and how much the best!"[11] A generation earlier Dr. Johnson had written a concluding passage for Goldsmith's *The Traveller* which summed up prevailing opinion:

> How small, of all that human hearts endure,
> That part which laws or kings can cause or cure!
> Still to ourselves in every place consigned,
> Our own felicity we make or find.

But now it seemed to many social philosophers that the revolution against the king and the old laws would cure everything and establish felicity for everyone, everywhere. In 1791 Volney took time out from his revolutionary activities to publish *Les Ruines, ou méditations sur les révolutions des empires,* in which a supervisory Genius unveils to him the vision of the past, the present, and then the "New Age," which had in fact already begun in the American Revolution and was approaching its realization in France. "Now," cries the author, "may I live! for after this there is nothing which I am not daring enough to hope."[12] Condorcet wrote his *Outlines . . . of the Progress of the Human Mind* as a doomed man hiding from the police of the Reign of Terror, to vindicate his unshaken faith that the Revolution was a breakthrough in man's progress; he ends with the vision of mankind's imminent perfection both in his social condition and in his intellectual and moral powers.[13] The equivalent book in England was Godwin's *Political Justice,* written under impetus of the Revolution in 1791–93, which has its similar anticipation of mankind morally transformed, living in a state of total economic and political equality.[14]

The intoxicating sense that now everything was possible was not confined to systematic philosophers. In 1793, Hazlitt said, schemes for a new society "of virtue and happiness" had been published "in plays, poems, songs, and romances—made their way to the bar, crept into the church . . . got into the hearts of poets and the brains of metaphysicians . . . and turned the heads of almost the whole kingdom."[15] Anyone who has looked into the poems, the sermons, the novels, and the plays of the early 1790s will know that this is not a gross exaggeration. Man regenerate in a world made new; this was the theme of a multitude of writers notable, forgotten, or anonymous. In the Prologue to his highly successful play *The Road to Ruin* (1792), Thomas Holcroft took the occasion to predict that the Revolution in France had set the torrent of freedom spreading,

> To ease, happiness, art, science, wit, and genius to give birth;
> Ay, to fertilize a world, and renovate old earth![16]

"Renovate old earth," "the regeneration of the human race"—the phrases reflect their origin, and indicate a characteristic difference between French and English radicalism. Most French philosophers of perfectibility (and Godwin, their representative in England) were anticlerical skeptics or downright atheists, who claimed that they based their predictions on an inductive science of history and a Lockian science of man. The chief strength and momentum of English radicalism, on the other hand, came from the religious Nonconformists who, as true heirs of their embattled ancestors in the English civil wars, looked upon contemporary politics through the perspective of biblical prophecy. In a sermon on the French Revolution preached in 1791 the Reverend Mark Wilks proclaimed: "Jesus Christ was a Revolutionist; and the Revolution he came to effect was foretold in these words, 'He hath sent me to proclaim liberty to the captives.' "[17] The Unitarians—influential beyond their numbers because they included so large a proportion of scientists, literary men, and powerful pulpit orators—were especially given to projecting on the empirical science of human progress the pattern and detail of biblical prophecies, Messianic, millennial, and apocalyptic.

"Hey for the New Jerusalem! The millennium!" Thomas Holcroft cried out, in the intoxication of first reading Paine's *The Rights of Man* (1791);[18] what this notorious atheist uttered lightly was the fervent but considered opinion of a number of his pious contemporaries. Richard Price, in 1785, had viewed the American Revolution as the most important step, next to the introduction of Christianity itself, in the fulfillment of the "old prophecies" of an empire of reason, virtue, and peace, when the wolf will "dwell with the lamb and the leopard with the kid." "May we not see there the dawning of brighter days on earth, and a new creation rising?" In the sermon of 1789 which evoked the hurricane of Burke's *Reflections on the French Revolution,* he sees that event capped by one even greater and more immediately promising: "I am thankful that I have lived to [see] it: and I could almost say, *Lord, now lettest thou thy servant depart in peace, for mine eyes have seen thy salvation.*"[19] By 1793 the increasingly violent course of the Revolution inspired the prophets to turn from Isaiah's relatively mild prelude to the peaceable kingdom and the "new heavens and a new earth" to the classic text of apocalyptic violence, the Book of Revelation. In February of that year Elhanan Winchester's *The Three Woe Trumpets* interpreted the Revolution in France as the precise fulfillment of those prophecies, with the seventh trumpet just about to sound (Revelation 11) to bring on the final cataclysm and announce the Second Advent of Christ, in a Kingdom which should be "the greatest blessing to mankind that ever they enjoyed, or even found an idea of."[20] In 1791 Joseph Priestley, scientist, radical philosopher, and a founder of the Unitarian Society, had written his *Letters* in reply to Burke's *Reflections,* in which he pronounced the American and French revolutions to be the inauguration of the state of universal happiness and peace "distinctly and repeatedly foretold in many prophecies, delivered more than two thousand years ago." Three years later he expanded his views in *The Present State of Europe Compared with Antient Prophecies.* Combining philosophical empiricism with biblical fundamentalism, he related the convulsions of the time to the Messianic prophecies in Isaiah and Daniel, the apocalyptic passages in various books of the New Testa-

ment, and especially to the Book of Revelation, as a ground
for confronting "the great scene, that seems now to be opening upon us . . . with tranquillity, and even with satisfaction,"
in the persuasion that its "termination will be glorious and
happy," in the advent of "the millennium, or the future
peaceable and happy state of the world."[21] Wordsworth's Solitary, in *The Excursion,* no doubt reflects an aspect of Wordsworth's own temperament, but the chief model for his earlier
career was Joseph Fawcett, famous Unitarian preacher at the
Old Jewry, and a poet as well. In Wordsworth's rendering,
we find him, in both song and sermon, projecting a dazzling
vision of the French Revolution which fuses classical myth
with Christian prophecy:

> I beheld
> Glory—beyond all glory ever seen,
> Confusion infinite of heaven and earth,
> Dazzling the soul. Meanwhile, prophetic harps
> In every grove were ringing, "War shall cease."
> . . . I sang Saturnian rule
> Returned,—a progeny of golden years
> Permitted to descend, and bless mankind.
> —With promises the Hebrew Scriptures teem:
> . . . the glowing phrase
> Of ancient inspiration serving me,
> I promised also,—with undaunted trust
> Foretold, and added prayer to prophecy.[22]

The formative age of Romantic poetry was clearly one of
apocalyptic expectations, or at least apocalyptic imaginings,
which endowed the promise of France with the form and
impetus of one of the deepest rooted and most compelling
myths in the culture of Christian Europe.

II. THE VOICE OF THE BARD

In a verse-letter of 1800 Blake identified the crucial influences in his spiritual history as a series beginning with Milton

and the Old Testament prophets and ending with the American War of Independence and the French Revolution.[23] Since Blake is the only major Romantic old enough to have published poems before the Revolution, his writings provide a convenient indication of the effects of that event and of the intellectual and emotional atmosphere that it generated.

As Northrop Frye has said in his fine book on Blake, his *Poetical Sketches* of 1783 associate him with Collins, Gray, the Wartons, and other writers of what Frye later called "The Age of Sensibility."[24] As early as the 1740s this school had mounted a literary revolution against the acknowledged tradition of Waller-Denham-Pope—a tradition of civilized and urbane verse, controlled by "good sense and judgment," addressed to a closely integrated upper class, in which the triumphs, as Joseph Warton pointed out, were mainly in "the didactic, moral, and satyric kind."[25] Against this tradition, the new poets raised the claim of a more daring, "sublime," and "primitive" poetry, represented in England by Spenser, Shakespeare, Milton, who exhibit the supreme virtues of spontaneity, invention, and an "enthusiastic" and "creative" imagination—by which was signified a poetry of inspired vision, related to divinity, and populated by allegorical and supernatural characters such as do not exist "in nature."[26]

Prominent in this literature of revolt, however, was a timidity, a sense of frustration very different from the assurance of power and of an accomplished and continuing literary renascence expressed by a number of their Romantic successors: Coleridge's unhesitating judgment that Wordsworth's genius measured up to Milton's, and Wordsworth's solemn concurrence in this judgment; Leigh Hunt's opinion that, for all his errors, Wordsworth was "at the head of a new and great age of poetry"; Keats's conviction that "great spirits now on earth are sojourning"; Shelley's confidence that "the literature of England . . . has arisen, as it were, from a new birth."[27] The poets of sensibility, on the contrary, had felt that they and all future writers were fated to be epigones of a tradition of unrecapturable magnificence. So Collins said in his *Ode on the Poetical Character* as, retreating from "Waller's myrtle shades," he tremblingly pursued Milton's "guiding steps":

> In vain . . .
> . . . Heaven and Fancy, kindred powers,
> Have now o'erturned the inspiring bowers,
> Or curtained close such scene from every future view.

And Gray:

> But not to one in this benighted age
> Is that diviner inspiration given,
> That burns in Shakespeare's or in Milton's page,
> The pomp and prodigality of Heaven.

So, in 1783, Blake complained to the Muses:

> How have you left the antient love
> That bards of old enjoy'd in you!

Besides *Poetical Sketches,* Blake's main achievements before the French Revolution were *Songs of Innocence* and *The Book of Thel,* which represent dwellers in an Eden trembling on the verge of experience. Suddenly in 1790 came *The Marriage of Heaven and Hell,* boisterously promulgating "Energy" in opposition to all inherited limits on human possibilities; to point the contemporary relevance, Blake appended a "Song of Liberty," which represents Energy as a revolutionary "son of fire," moving from America to France and crying the advent of an Isaian millennium:

EMPIRE IS NO MORE! AND NOW THE LION & WOLF SHALL CEASE.

In 1791 appeared Blake's *The French Revolution,* in the form of a Miltonic epic. Of the seven books announced, only the first is extant, but this is enough to demonstrate that Blake, like Priestley and other religious radicals of the day, envisioned the Revolution as the portent of apocalypse. After five thousand years "the ancient dawn calls us / To awake," and the Abbé de Sieyès pleads for a peace, freedom, and equality which will effect a regained Eden—"the happy earth sing in its course, / The mild peaceable nations be opened to heav'n, and men walk with their fathers in bliss"; when his plea is ignored, there are rumblings of a gathering Armageddon, and the book ends with the portent of a first resurrection: "And the bottoms of the world were open'd, and the graves of arch-angels unseal'd."

The "Introduction" to *Songs of Experience* (1794) calls on us to attend the voice which will sing all Blake's poems from now on: "Hear the voice of the Bard! / Who Present, Past, & Future, sees," who calls to the lapsèd Soul and enjoins the earth to cease her cycle and turn to the eternal day. This voice is that of the poet-prophets of the Old and New Testaments, now descending to Blake from its specifically British embodiment in that "bard of old," John Milton. In his "minor prophecies," ending in 1795, Blake develops, out of the heroic-scaled but still historical agents of his *French Revolution*, the Giant Forms of his later mythical system. The Bard becomes Los, the "Eternal Prophet" and father of "red Orc," who is the spirit of Energy bursting out in total spiritual, physical, and political revolution; the argument of the song sung by Los, however, remains that announced in *The French Revolution*. As David Erdman has said, *Europe: A Prophecy* (1794) was written at about the time Blake was illustrating Milton's *On the Morning of Christ's Nativity*, and reinterprets that poem for his own times.[28] Orc, here identified with Christ the revolutionary, comes with the blare of the apocalyptic trumpet to vex nature out of her sleep of 1,800 years, in a cataclysmic Second Coming in "the vineyards of red France" which, however, heralds the day when both the earth and its inhabitants will be resurrected in a joyous burst of unbounded and lustful energy.[29]

By the year 1797 Blake launched out into the "strong heroic Verse" of *Vala, or The Four Zoas*, the first of his three full-scale epics, which recounts the total history of "the Universal Man" from the beginning, through "his fall into Division," to a future that explodes into the most spectacular and sustained apocalyptic set-piece since the Book of Revelation; in this holocaust "the evil is all consum'd" and "all things are chang'd, even as in ancient times."[30]

III. ROMANTIC ORACLES

No amount of historical explanation can make Blake out to be other than a phoenix among poets; but if we put his work into its historical and intellectual context, and alongside that of his poetic contemporaries of the 1790s, we find at least that he is not a freak without historical causes but that he responded to the common circumstances in ways markedly similar, sometimes even to odd details. But while fellow poets soon left off their tentative efforts to evolve a system of "machinery" by which to come to terms with the epic events of their revolutionary era, Blake carried undauntedly on.

What, then, were the attributes shared by the chief poets of the 1790s, Blake, Wordsworth, Southey, Coleridge?—to whom I shall add Shelley. Byron and Keats also had elements in common with their older contemporaries, but these lie outside the immediate scope of my paper. Shelley, however, though he matured in the cynical era of Napoleon and the English Regency, reiterated remarkably the pattern of his predecessors. By temperament he was more inclusively and extremely radical than anyone but Blake, and his early "principles," as he himself said, had "their origin from the discoveries which preceded and occasioned the revolutions of America and France." That is, he had formed his mind on those writers, from Rousseau through Condorcet, Volney, Paine, and Godwin, whose ideas made up the climate of the 1790s—and also, it should be emphasized, on the King James Bible and *Paradise Lost*.[31]

1. First, these were all centrally political and social poets. It is by a peculiar injustice that Romanticism is often described as a mode of escapism, an evasion of the shocking changes, violence, and ugliness attending the emergence of the modern industrial and political world. The fact is that to a degree

without parallel, even among major Victorian poets, these writers were obsessed with the realities of their era. Blake's wife mildly complained that her husband was always in Paradise; but from this vantage point he managed to keep so thoroughly in touch with mundane reality that, as David Erdman has demonstrated, his epics are hardly less steeped in the scenes and events of the day than is that latter-day epic, the *Ulysses* of James Joyce. Wordsworth said that he "had given twelve hours thought to the conditions and prospects of society, for one to poetry";[32] Coleridge, Southey, and Shelley could have made a claim similarly extravagant; all these poets delivered themselves of political and social commentary in the form of prose pamphlets, essays, speeches, editorials, or sermons; and all exhibit an explicit or submerged concern with the contemporary historical and intellectual situation in the greater part of their verses, narrative, dramatic, and lyric, long and short.

2. What obscures this concern is that in many poems the Romantics do not write direct political and moral commentary but (in Schorer's apt phrase for Blake) "the politics of vision," uttered in the persona of the inspired prophet-priest. Neoclassic poets had invoked the muse as a formality of the poetic ritual, and the school of sensibility had expressed nostalgia for the "diviner inspiration" of Spenser, Shakespeare, and Milton. But when the Romantic poet asserts inspiration and revelation by a power beyond himself—as Blake did repeatedly, or Shelley in his claim that the great poets of his age are "the priests of an unapprehended inspiration, the mirrors of gigantic shadows which futurity casts upon the present"[33]—he means it. And when Wordsworth called himself "a youthful Druid taught . . . Primeval mysteries, a Bard elect . . . a chosen Son," and Coleridge characterized *The Prelude* as "more than historic, that prophetic Lay," "an Orphic song" uttered by a "great Bard,"[34] in an important sense they meant it too, and we must believe that they meant it if we are to read them aright.

The Romantics, then, often spoke confidently as elected members of what Harold Bloom calls "The Visionary Company," the inspired line of singers from the prophets of the

Old and New Testaments through Dante, Spenser, and above all Milton. For Milton had an exemplary role in this tradition as the native British (or Druidic) Bard who was a thorough political, social, and religious revolutionary, who claimed inspiration both from a Heavenly Muse and from the Holy Spirit that had supervised the creation and inspired the biblical prophets, and who, after the failure of his millennial expectations from the English Revolution,[35] had kept his singing voice and salvaged his hope for mankind in an epic poem.

3. Following the Miltonic example, the Romantic poet of the 1790s tried to incorporate what he regarded as the stupendous events of the age in the suitably great poetic forms. He wrote, or planned to write, an epic, or (like Milton in *Samson Agonistes*) emulated Aeschylean tragedy, or uttered visions combining the mode of biblical prophecy with the loose Pindaric, the "sublime" or "greater Ode," which by his eighteenth-century predecessors had been accorded a status next to epic, as peculiarly adapted to an enthusiastic and visionary imagination. Whatever the form, the Romantic Bard is one "who present, past, and future sees"; so that in dealing with current affairs his procedure is often panoramic, his stage cosmic, his agents quasi-mythological, and his logic of events apocalyptic. Typically this mode of Romantic vision fuses history, politics, philosophy, and religion into one grand design, by asserting Providence—or some form of natural teleology—to operate in the seeming chaos of human history so as to effect from present evil a greater good; and through the mid-1790s the French Revolution functions as the symptom or early stage of the abrupt culmination of this design, from which will emerge a new man on a new earth which is a restored paradise.

To support these large generalizations I need to present a few particulars.

Robert Southey, the most matter-of-fact and worldly of these poets, said that his early adoration of Leonidas, hero of Thermopylae, his early study of Epictetus, "and the French Revolution at its height when I was just eighteen—by these my mind was moulded."[36] The first literary result came a year later, in 1793, when during six weeks of his long vacation from Oxford he wrote *Joan of Arc: An Epic Poem*,[37] which along with Blake's *French Revolution* is the first English epic worth historical notice since Glover's *Leonidas*, published in 1737. Southey's Joan has been called a Tom Paine in petticoats; she is also given to trances in which "strange events yet in the womb of Time" are to her "made manifest." In the first published version of 1796, Book IX consists of a sustained vision of the realms of hell and purgatory, populated by the standard villains of the radicals' view of history. To Joan is revealed the Edenic past in the "blest aera of the infant world," and man's fall, through lust for gold and power, to this "theatre of woe"; yet "for the best / Hath he ordained all things, the ALL-WISE!" because man, "Samson-like," shall "burst his fetters" in a violent spasm not quite named the French Revolution,

> and Earth shall once again
> Be Paradise, whilst WISDOM shall secure
> The state of bliss which IGNORANCE betrayed.
> "Oh age of happiness!" the Maid exclaim'd,
> "Roll fast thy current, Time, till that blest age
> Arrive!"[38]

To the second book of *Joan*, Coleridge (then, like Southey, a Unitarian, and like both Southey and Wordsworth, considering entering the clergy) contributed what he called an "Epic Slice," which he soon patched up into an independent poem, *The Destiny of Nations: A Vision*. The vision, beamed "on the Prophet's purgèd eye," reviews history, echoes the Book of Revelation, and ends in the symbolic appearance of a bright cloud (the American Revolution) and a brighter cloud (the French Revolution) from which emerges "a dazzling form," obviously female, yet identified in Coleridge's note as an Apollo-figure, portending that "soon shall the Morning struggle into Day."[39] With the epomania of the age, Coleridge considered writing an epic of his own, laid out plans which would take twenty years to realize, and let it go at that.[40] His ambition to be the Milton of his day was, in practice, limited to various oracular odes, of which the most interesting for our purpose is *Religious Musings,* his first long poem in blank verse; on this, Coleridge said, "I build all my poetic pretensions."[41] The poem as published bore the title "Religious Musings on Christmas Eve. In the year of Our Lord, 1794," and Coleridge had earlier called it "The Nativity."[42] The year is precisely that of Blake's *Europe: A Prophecy,* and like that poem, *Religious Musings* is clearly a revision for the time being of Milton's *On the Morning of Christ's Nativity,* which had taken the occasion of memorializing Christ's birth to anticipate "the wakefull trump of doom" and the universal earthquake which will announce His Second Coming:

> And then at last our bliss
> Full and perfect is.

There is never any risk of mistaking Coleridge's voice for that of Blake, yet a reading of Coleridge's poem with Blake's in mind reveals how remarkably parallel were the effects of the same historical and literary situation, operating simultaneously on the imagination of the two poets.

Coleridge's opening, "This is the time," echoes "This is the Month," with which Milton begins his Prologue, as Blake's "The deep of winter came" reflects "It was the Winter wild," with which Milton begins the Hymn proper. (Blake's free verse is also at times reminiscent of the movement of Milton's marvelous stanza.) Musing on the significance of the First Advent, Coleridge says, "Behold a VISION gathers in my soul"; the vision provides him, among other things, a survey of human history since "the primeval age" in the form of a brief theodicy, "all the sore ills" of "our mortal life" becoming "the immediate source / Of mightier good." The future must bring "the fated day" of violent revolution by the oppressed masses, but happily "Philosophers and Bards" exist to mold the wild chaos "with plastic might" into the "perfect forms" of their own inspired visions. Coleridge then presents an interpretation of contemporary affairs which, following his Unitarian mentor, Joseph Priestley, he neatly summarizes in his prose Argument as: "The French Revolution. Millennium. Universal Redemption. Conclusion." His procedure is to establish a parallel (developed in elaborate footnotes) between current revolutionary events and the violent prophecies of the Book of Revelation. The machinery of apocalypse is allegorical, with the "Giant Frenzy" given the function of Blake's Orc in "uprooting empires with his whirlwind arm." In due course the "blest future rushes on my view!" in the form of human-kind as a "vast family of Love" living in a communist economy. "The mighty Dead" awaken, and

> To Milton's trump
> The high groves of the renovated Earth
> Unbosom their glad echoes,

in the adoring presence of three English interpreters of mil-lennial prophecy, Newton, Hartley, and Priestley, "patriot, and saint, and sage."[43] (In Blake's *Europe*, not Milton but Newton had "siez'd the trump & blow'd the enormous blast"; as in Coleridge's poem, however, he seemingly appears not in his capacity as scientist but as author of a commentary on the Book of Revelation.)

Wordsworth thought the concluding section of *Religious Musings* on "the renovated Earth" to be the best in Cole-ridge's *Poems* of 1796. On this subject Wordsworth was an expert, for a year prior to the writing of the poem, in 1793, he had concluded his own *Descriptive Sketches* with the proph-ecy (precisely matching the prophecy he attributed to the Wanderer in his *Excursion*) that the wars consequent on the French Revolution would fulfill the predictions both of the Book of Revelation and of Virgil's fourth eclogue:

> —Tho' Liberty shall soon, indignant, raise
> Red on his hills his beacon's comet blaze . . .
> Yet, yet rejoice, tho' Pride's perverted ire
> Rouze Hell's own aid, and wrap thy hills in fire.
> Lo! from th' innocuous flames, a lovely birth!
> With its own Virtues springs another earth:
> Nature, as in her prime, her virgin reign
> Begins, and Love and Truth compose her train. . . .
> No more . . .
> On his pale horse shall fell Consumption go.

"How is it," Blake was to ask in his conclusion of *The Four Zoas*, "we have walk'd thro' fires & yet are not consum'd? / How is it that all things are chang'd, even as in ancient times?"[44]

Some two decades later Shelley recapitulated and expanded these poetic manifestations of the earlier 1790s. At the age of nineteen he began his first long poem, *Queen Mab*, in the mode of a vision of the woeful past, the ghastly present, and the blissful future, and although the concepts are those of the French and English *philosophes,* and the Spirit of Necessity replaces Providence as the agent of redemption, much of the imagery is imported from biblical millennialism. The prophecy is that "a garden shall arise, in loveliness / Surpassing fabled Eden"; when it eventuates, "all things are recreated," the lion sports "in the sun / Beside the dreadless kid," and man's intellectual and moral nature participates in "the gradual renovation" until he stands "with taintless body and mind" in a "happy earth! reality of Heaven!" the "consummation of all mortal hope!"[45]

If I may just glance over the fence of my assigned topic: in Germany, as in England, a coincidence of historical, religious, and literary circumstances produced a comparable imaginative result. In the early 1790s the young Hölderlin was caught up in the intoxication of the revolutionary promise; he was at the time a student of theology at Tübingen, and immersed in the literary tradition of *Sturm und Drang* libertarianism, Schiller's early poems, and Klopstock's *Messias* and allegoric odes. A number of Hölderlin's odes of that decade (the two *Hymnen an die Freiheit,* the *Hymne an die Menschheit, Der Zeitgeist*) are notably parallel to the English form I have been describing; that is, they are visionary, oracular, panoramic, and see history on the verge of a blessed culmination in which the French Revolution is the crucial event, the Book of Revelation the chief model, and the agencies a combination of Greek divinities, biblical symbols, and abstract personifications of his own devising. In the *Hymne an die Freiheit* of 1792, for example, the rapt poet chants a revelation of man's first pastoral innocence, love, and happiness; this "Paradise" is destroyed by a "curse"; but then in response to a call by the Goddess Liberty, Love "reconciles the long discord"

and inaugurates "the new hour of creation" of a free, fraternal, abundantly vital, and radiant century in which "the ancient
infamy is cancelled" and "der Erndte grosser Tag beginnt"—
"there begins the great day of the harvest."[46]

IV. THE APOCALYPSE OF IMAGINATION

The visionary poems of the earlier 1790s and Shelley's earlier prophecies show imaginative audacity and invention, but
they are not, it must be confessed, very good poems. The
great Romantic poems were written not in the mood of revolutionary exaltation but in the later mood of revolutionary
disillusionment or despair. Many of the great poems, however, do not break with the formative past, but continue to
exhibit, in a transformed but recognizable fashion, the scope,
the poetic voice, the design, the ideas, and the imagery developed in the earlier period. This continuity of tradition converts what would otherwise be a literary curiosity into a matter
of considerable historical interest, and helps us to identify
and interpret some of the strange but characteristic elements
in later Romantic enterprises.

Here is one out of many available instances. It will have
become apparent even from these brief summaries that certain terms, images, and quasi-mythical agents tend to recur
and to assume a specialized reference to revolutionary events
and expectations: the earthquake and the volcano, the purg-
ing fire, the emerging sun, the dawn of glad day, the awakening earth in springtime, the Dionysian figure of
revolutionary destruction and the Apollonian figure of the
promise of a bright new order. Prominent among these is a
term which functions as one of the principal leitmotifs of
Romantic literature. To Europe at the end of the eighteenth
century the French Revolution brought what Saint Augustine said Christiantiy had brought to the ancient world: hope.
As Coleridge wrote, on first hearing Wordsworth's *Prelude*

read aloud, the poet sang of his experience "amid the tremor of a realm aglow,"

> When from the general heart of human kind
> Hope sprang forth like a full-born Deity!

and afterward, "of that dear Hope afflicted and struck down. . . ."[47] This is no ordinary human hope, but a universal, absolute, and novel hope which sprang forth from the revolutionary events sudden and complete, like Minerva. Pervasively in both the verse and prose of the period, "hope," with its associated term "joy" and its opposites "dejection," "despondency," and "despair," are used in a special application, as shorthand for the limitless faith in human and social possibility aroused by the Revolution, and its reflex, the nadir of feeling caused by its seeming failure—as Wordsworth had put it, the "utter loss of hope itself / And things to hope for" (*The Prelude,* 1805 text, XI, 6–7).

It is not irrelevant, I believe, that many seemingly apolitical poems of the later Romantic period turn on the theme of hope and joy and the temptation to abandon all hope and fall into dejection and despair; the recurrent emotional pattern is that of the key books of *The Excursion,* labeled "Despondency" and "Despondency Corrected," which apply specifically to the failure of millennial hope in the Revolution. But I want to apply this observation to one of those passages in *The Prelude* where Wordsworth suddenly breaks through to a prophetic vision of the hidden significance of the literal narrative. In the sixth book Wordsworth describes his first tour of France with Robert Jones in the summer of 1790, the brightest period of the Revolution. The mighty forms of Nature, "seizing a youthful fancy," had already "given a charter to irregular hopes," but now all Europe

> was thrilled with joy,
> France standing on the top of golden hours,
> And human nature seeming born again.

Sharing the universal intoxication, "when joy of one" was "joy for tens of millions," they join in feasting and dance with a "blithe host / Of Travellers" returning from the Federation Festival at Paris, "the great spousals newly solemnised / At their chief city, in the sight of Heaven." In his revisions of the 1805 version of *The Prelude*, Wordsworth inserted at this point a passage in which he sees, with anguished foreboding, the desecration by French troops of the Convent of the Chartreuse (an event which did not take place until two years later, in 1792). The travelers' way then brings them to the Simplon Pass.

Wordsworth's earlier account of this tour in the *Descriptive Sketches,* written mainly in 1791–92, had ended with the prophecy of a new earth emerging from apocalyptic fires, and a return to the golden age. Now, however, he describes a strange access of sadness, a "melancholy slackening." On the Simplon road they had left their guide and climbed ever upward, until a peasant told them that they had missed their way and that the course now lay downwards.

> Loth to believe what we so grieved to hear,
> For still we had hopes that pointed to the clouds,
> We questioned him again, and yet again;

but every reply "ended in this,—*that we had crossed the Alps.*"

> Imagination . . .
> That awful Power rose from the mind's abyss
> Like an unfathered vapour that enwraps,
> At once, some lonely traveller. I was lost;
> Halted without an effort to break through;
> But to my conscious soul I now can say—
> "I recognize thy glory."

Only now, in retrospect, does he recognize that his imagination had penetrated to the emblematic quality of the literal climb, in a revelation proleptic of the experience he was to recount in all the remainder of *The Prelude*. Man's infinite hopes can never be matched by the world as it is and man as he is, for these exhibit a discrepancy no less than that between

his "hopes that pointed to the clouds" and the finite height
of the Alpine pass. But in the magnitude of the disappoint-
ment lies its consolation; for the flash of vision also reveals
that infinite longings are inherent in the human spirit, and
that the gap between the inordinacy of his hope and the limits of possibility is the measure of man's dignity and greatness:

> Our destiny, our being's heart and home,
> Is with infinitude, and only there;
> With hope it is, hope that can never die,
> Effort, and expectation, and desire,
> And something evermore about to be.

In short, Wordsworth evokes from the unbounded and
hence impossible hopes in the French Revolution a central
Romantic doctrine, one which reverses the cardinal neoclassic ideal of setting only accessible goals, by converting what
had been man's tragic error—the inordinacy of his "pride"
that persists in setting infinite aims for finite man—into his
specific glory and his triumph. Wordsworth shares the recognition of his fellow Romantics, German and English, of the
greatness of man's infinite *Sehnsucht,* his saving insatiability,
Blake's "I want! I want!"[48] and Shelley's "the desire of the
moth for the star"; but with a characteristic and unique difference, as he goes on at once to reveal:

> Under such banners militant, the soul
> Seeks for no trophies, struggles for no spoils
> That may attest her prowess, blest in thoughts
> That are their own perfection and reward.

The militancy of overt political action has been transformed
into the paradox of spiritual quietism: under such militant
banners is no march, but a wise passiveness. This truth having been revealed to him, Wordsworth at once goes on to his
apocalypse of nature in the Simplon Pass, where the *coincidentia oppositorum* of its physical attributes become the symbols of the biblical Book of Revelation:

> Characters of the great Apocalypse,
> The types and symbols of Eternity,
> Of first, and last, and midst, and without end.[49]

This and its companion passages in *The Prelude* enlighten the orphic darkness of Wordsworth's "Prospectus" to *The Recluse,* drafted as early as 1800, when *The Prelude* had not yet been differentiated from the larger poem. Wordsworth's aim, he there reveals, is still that of the earlier period of millennial hope in revolution, still expressed in a fusion of biblical and classical imagery. Evil is to be redeemed by a regained paradise, or Elysium: "Paradise," he says, "and groves / Elysian, Fortunate Fields . . . why should they be / A history only of departed things?" And the restoration of paradise, as in the Book of Revelation, is still symbolized by a sacred marriage. But the hope has been shifted from the history of mankind to the mind of the single individual, from militant external action to an imaginative act; and the marriage between the Lamb and the New Jerusalem has been converted into a marriage between subject and object, mind and nature, which creates a new world out of the old world of sense:

> For the discerning intellect of Man,
> When wedded to this goodly universe
> In love and holy passion, shall find these
> A simple produce of the common day.
> —I, long before the blissful hour arrives,
> Would chant, in lonely peace, the spousal verse
> Of this great consummation . . .
> And the creation (by no lower name
> Can it be called) which they with blended might
> Accomplish:—this is our high argument.[50]

In the other Romantic visionaries, as in Wordsworth, naive millennialism produced mainly declamation, but the shattered trust in premature political revolution and the need to reconstitute the grounds of hope lay behind the major achievements. And something close to Wordsworth's evolution—the shift to a spiritual and moral revolution which will transform our experience of the old world—is also the argument of a number of the later writings of Blake, Coleridge, Shelley, and, with all his differences, Hölderlin. An example from Shelley must suffice. Most of Shelley's large enterprises after *Queen Mab*—*The Revolt of Islam, Prometheus Unbound, Hellas*—were inspired by a later recrudescence of the European revolutionary movement. Shelley's view of human motives and possibilities became more and more tragic, and, like Blake after his *French Revolution,* he moved from the bald literalism of *Queen Mab* to an imaginative form increasingly biblical, symbolic, and mythic; but the theme continues to be the ultimate promise of a renovation in human nature and circumstances. In *Prometheus Unbound* this event is symbolized by the reunion of Prometheus and Asia in a joyous ceremony in which all the cosmos participates. But this new world is one which reveals itself to the purged imagination of Man when he has reformed his moral nature at its deep and twisted roots; and the last words of Demogorgon, the inscrutable agent of this apocalypse, describe a revolution of spirit whose sole agencies are the cardinal virtues of endurance, forgiveness, love, and, above all, hope—though a hope that is now hard to distinguish from despair:

> To suffer woes which Hope thinks infinite . . .
> To love, and bear; to hope till Hope creates
> From its own wreck the thing it contemplates . . .
> This is alone Life, Joy, Empire, and Victory!

V. WORDSWORTH'S OTHER VOICE

"Two voices are there: . . . And, Wordsworth, both are thine." I have as yet said nothing about Wordsworth's *Lyrical Ballads* and related poems, although Hazlitt regarded these as the inauguration of a new poetic era and the close poetic equivalent to the revolutionary politics of the age. Yet the *Ballads* seem in every way antithetical to the poetry I have just described: instead of displaying a panoramic vision of present, past, and future in an elevated oracular voice, these poems undertake to represent realistic "incidents and situations from common life" in ordinary language and to employ "humble and rustic life" as the main source of the simple characters and the model for the plain speech.

Here are some of the reasons Hazlitt gives for his claim that "the political changes of the day were the model on which [Wordsworth] formed and conducted his poetical experiments":

> His Muse (it cannot be denied, and without this we cannot explain its character at all) is a levelling one. It proceeds on a principle of equality, and strives to reduce all things to the same standard. . . .
>
> His popular, inartificial style gets rid (at a blow) of all the trappings of verse, of all the high places of poetry. . . . We begin *de novo,* on a tabula rasa of poetry. . . . The distinctions of rank, birth, wealth, power . . . are not to be found here. . . . The harp of Homer, the trump of Pindar and of Alcaeus, are still.[51]

Making due allowance for his love of extravagance, I think that Hazlitt sets out a very plausible case. He shrewdly recognizes that Wordsworth's criteria are as much social as literary, and that by their egalitarianism they subvert the foundations of a view of poetry inherited from the Renaissance. This view assumed and incorporated a hierarchical structure of social classes. In its strict form, it conceived poetry as an order of well-defined genres, controlled by a theory of decorum whereby the higher poetic kinds represent primarily kings and the aristocracy, the humbler classes (in other than a subsidiary function) are relegated to the lowlier forms, and each poem is expressed in a level of style—high, middle, or low—appropriate, among other things, to the social status of its characters and the dignity of its genre. In England after the sixteenth century, this system had rarely been held with continental rigor, and eighteenth-century critics and poets had carried far the work of breaking down the social distinctions built into a poetic developed for an aristocratic audience. But Wordsworth's practice, buttressed by a strong critical manifesto, carried an existing tendency to an extreme which Hazlitt regarded as a genuine innovation, an achieved revolution against the *ancien régime* in literature. He was, Hazlitt said, "the most original poet now living, and the one whose writings could least be spared: for they have no substitute elsewhere." And Wordsworth had not only leveled, he had transvalued Renaissance and neoclassic aesthetics, by deliberately seeking out the ignominious, the delinquent, and the social outcast as subjects for serious or tragic consideration— not only, Hazlitt noted, "peasants, pedlars, and village-barbers," but also "convicts, female vagrants, gipsies . . . ideot boys and mad mothers."[52] Hence the indignation of Lord Byron, who combined political liberalism with a due regard for aristocratic privilege and traditional poetic decorum:

> "Peddlers," and "Boats," and "Wagons"! Oh! ye shades
> Of Pope and Dryden, are we come to this?

In his Preface to *Lyrical Ballads* Wordsworth justified his undertaking mainly by the ultimate critical sanctions then available, of elemental and permanent "nature" as against the corruptions and necessarily short-lived fashions of "art." But Wordsworth also dealt with the genesis and rationale of *Lyrical Ballads* in several other writings, and in terms broader than purely critical, and these passages clearly relate his poems of humble lives in the plain style to his concept and practice of poetry in the grand oracular style.

In the crucial thirteenth book of *The Prelude* Wordsworth describes how, trained "to meekness" and exalted by "humble faith," he turned from disillusionment with the "sublime / In what the Historian's pen so much delights / To blazon," to "fraternal love" for "the unassuming things that hold / A silent station in this beauteous world," and so to a surrogate for his lost revolutionary hopes:

> The promise of the present time retired
> Into its true proportion; sanguine schemes,
> Ambitious projects, pleased me less; I sought
> For present good in life's familiar face,
> And built thereon my hopes of good to come.

He turned, that is, away from Man as he exists only in the hopes of naive millennialists or the abstractions of the philosophers of perfectibility to "the man whom we behold / With our own eyes"; and especially to the humble and obscure men of the lower and rural classes, "who live / By bodily toil," free from the "artificial lights" of urban upper-class society, and utter the spontaneous overflow of powerful feelings ("Expressing liveliest thoughts in lively words / As native passion dictates"). "Of these, said I, shall be my song." But, he insists, in this new subject he continues to speak "things oracular," for though he is "the humblest," he stands in the great line of the "Poets, even as Prophets, each with each / Connected in a mighty scheme of truth," each of whom possesses "his own peculiar faculty, / Heaven's gift, a sense that fits him to perceive / Objects unseen before." And chief among the prophetic insights granted to Wordsworth is the discovery that Nature has the power to "consecrate" and "to breathe / Grandeur upon the very humblest face / Of human life," as well as upon the works of man, even when these are "mean, have nothing lofty of their own."[53]

We come here to a central paradox among the various ones that lurk in the oracular passages of Wordsworth's major period: the oxymoron of the humble-grand, the lofty-mean, the trivial-sublime—as Hazlitt recognized when he said that Wordsworth's Muse "is distinguished by a proud humility," and that he "elevates the mean" and endeavors "(not in vain) to aggrandise the trivial."[54] The ultimate source of this concept is, I think, obvious, and Wordsworth several times plainly points it out for us. Thus in *The Ruined Cottage* (1797–98) the Pedlar (whose youthful experiences parallel Wordsworth's, as the poet showed by later transferring a number of passages to *The Prelude*) had first studied the Scriptures, and only afterward had come to "*feel* his faith" by discovering the corresponding symbol-system, "the writing," in the great book of nature, where "the least of things / Seemed infinite," so that (as a "chosen son") his own "being thus became / Sublime and comprehensive. . . . Yet was his heart / Lowly"; he also learned to recognize in the simple people of rural life what Wordsworth in a note called "the aristocracy of nature."[55] The ultimate source of Wordsworth's discovery, that is, was the Bible, and especially the New Testament, which is grounded on the radical paradox that "the last shall be first," and dramatizes that fact in the central mystery of God incarnate as a lowly carpenter's son who takes fishermen for his disciples, consorts with beggars, publicans, and fallen women, and dies ignominiously, crucified with thieves. This interfusion of highest and lowest, the divine and the base, as Erich Auerbach has shown, had from the beginning been a stumbling block to readers habituated to the classical separation of levels of subject-matter and style, and Robert Lowth in the mid-eighteenth century still found it necessary to insist, as had Augustine and other theologians almost a millennium and a half earlier, that the style of the Bible had its special propriety and was genuinely sublime, and not, as it seemed to a cultivated taste, indecorous, vulgar, barbarous, grotesque.[56] Wordsworth, it should be recalled, had had a pious mother, attended a church school at Hawkshead, and was intended for the clergy. In this aspect his poetic reflects a movement in eighteenth-century Pietism and envangelicalism which had emphasized, in the theological term, God's "condescension" or "accommodation" in revealing his immense divinity to the limited human mind through the often trivial events of Scripture, as well as in sending his son to be born as the lowliest among men. The archetypal figure, among Wordsworth's many numinous solitaries, is the humble shepherd magnified in the mist, "glorified" by the setting sun, and "descried in distant sky,"

> A solitary object and sublime,
> Above all height! like an aerial cross
> Stationed alone upon a spiry rock
> Of the Chartreuse, for worship. Thus was man
> Ennobled outwardly before my sight—

apotheosized, rather, as *figura Christi,* the Good Shepherd himself; for by such means Wordsworth learned, he says, to see Man "as, more than anything we know, instinct / With godhead," while yet "acknowledging dependency sublime."[57]

An important document connecting the religious, political, and aesthetic elements in his poetic theory is Wordsworth's neglected "Essay, Supplementary to the Preface" of 1815, in which he undertakes to explain at length why his *Lyrical Ballads* had been met with almost "unremitting hostility" ever since they appeared. The argument is extraordinarily contorted, even for Wordsworth's prose; but this, I believe, is the gist of it. "The higher poetry," especially when it "breathes the spirit of religion," unites "grandeur" and "simplicity," and in consequence is apt to evoke dislike, contempt, suspicion from the reader.

> For when Christianity, the religion of humility, is founded upon the proudest faculty of our nature [imagination], what can be expected but contradictions? . . . The commerce between Man and his Maker cannot be carried on but by a process where much is represented in little, and the Infinite Being accommodates himself to a finite capacity. In all this may be perceived the affinity between religion and poetry.

(In the sentence before the last, Wordsworth defines exactly the theological concept of "accommodation" or "condescension.") Wordsworth then puts himself at the end of a long list of great poets who had been neglected or misunderstood; necessarily so, for original genius consists in doing well "what was never done before," and so introducing "a new element into the intellectual universe"; hence such an author has "the task of *creating* the taste by which he is to be enjoyed." Wordsworth's originality, he says (Hazlitt made essentially the same claim), lies in producing a revolutionary mode of sublimity in poetry. Can it, then,

> be wondered that there is little existing preparation for a poet charged with a new mission to extend its kingdom [i.e., of sublimity], and to augment and spread its enjoyments?

The "instinctive wisdom" and "heroic" (that is, epic) "passions" of the ancients have united in his heart "with the meditative wisdom of later ages" (that is, of the Christian era) to produce the imaginative mode of "sublimated humanity," and "*there*, the poet must reconcile himself for a season to few and scattered hearers." For he must create the taste by which his innovation is to be enjoyed by stripping from the reader's literary responses their ingrained class-consciousness and social snobbery—what Wordsworth calls "the prejudices of false refinement," "pride," and "vanity"—so as to establish "that dominion over the spirits of readers by which they are to be humbled and humanised, in order that they may be purified and exalted."[58] Having given up the hope of revolutionizing the social and political structure, Wordsworth has discovered that his new calling, his divine "mission," condemning him to a period of inevitable neglect and scorn, is to effect through his poetry an egalitarian revolution of the spirit (what he elsewhere calls "an entire regeneration" of his upper-class readers)[59] so that they may share his revelation of the equivalence of souls, the heroic dimensions of common life, and the grandeur of the ordinary and the trivial in Nature.

In his account of this same discovery in *The Prelude*, Book XIII, Wordsworth says that in his exercise of a special power, unprecedented in literature, "upon the vulgar forms of present things, / The actual world of our familiar days,"

> I remember well
> That in life's every-day appearances
> I seemed about this time to gain clear sight
> Of a new world,

capable of being made visible "to other eyes," which is the product of "a balance, an ennobling interchange," between "the object seen, and eye that sees."[60] This carries us back to the "Prospectus" to *The Recluse*, for it is clear that this "new world" is an aspect of the re-created universe there represented as "a simple produce of the common day," if only we learn to marry our mind to nature "in love and holy passion." And if we put the "Prospectus" back into its original context in the concluding section of *Home at Grasmere*, we find that this document, written precisely at the turn of the century, gathers together the various themes with which we have been dealing: the sense of divine mission and illumination, the conversion of his aspiration for millennial achievements beyond possibility into its spiritual equivalent in a militant quietism, and the replacement of his epic schemes by a new poetic enterprise, to communicate his transforming visions of the common man and the ordinary universe.

In the seclusion of Grasmere vale, Wordsworth has dismissed "all Arcadian dreams, / All golden fancies of the golden Age" that is "to be / Ere time expire," yet finds remaining a "sufficient hope." He proclaims that "yet to me I feel / That an internal brightness is vouchsafed," something that "is shared by none," which impels him, "divinely taught," to speak "of what in man is human or divine." The voice of Reason sanctions the lesson which Nature has stealthily taught him:

> Be mild and cleave to gentle things,
> Thy glory and thy happiness be there.
> Nor fear, though thou confide in me, a want
> Of aspirations that *have* been, of foes
> To wrestle with, and victory to complete,
> Bounds to be leapt, darkness to be explored . . .
> All shall survive—though changed their office.

Therefore he bids "farewell to the Warrior's schemes," as well as to "that other hope, long mine, the hope to fill / The heroic trumpet with the Muse's breath!" But having given up his ambition for a Miltonic epic, he at once finds that his new argument exceeds in its scope the height of Milton's "heaven of heavens" and the depths of Milton's hell, and that it presents its imaginative equivalent of a restored paradise. Hence he will need, he claims—in that union of arrogance with humility which characterizes all poet-prophets who know they are inspired, but by a power for which they are not responsible—a Muse that will outsoar Milton's, just as Milton had claimed that his Muse would outsoar "th' Aonian Mount" of the pagan Homer. "Urania," Wordsworth says,

> I shall need
> Thy guidance, or a greater Muse, if such
> Descend to earth or dwell in highest heaven![61]

Wordsworth, then, in the period beginning about 1797, came to see his destiny to lie in spiritual rather than in overt

action and adventure, and to conceive his radical poetic vocation to consist in communicating his unique and paradoxical,
hence inevitably misunderstood, revelation of the more-than-
heroic grandeur of the humble, the contemned, the ordinary, and the trivial, whether in the plain style of direct bal-
lad-like representation, or in the elevated voice in which he
presents himself in his office as recipient of this gift of vision.
In either case, the mode in which Wordsworth conceived his
mission evolved out of the ambition to participate in the renovation of the world and of man which he had shared with
his fellow poets during the period of revolutionary enthusiasm. Both the oracular and the plain poetry, in the last analysis, go back beyond Milton, to that inexhaustible source of
radical thought, the Bible—the oracular poetry to the Old
Testament prophets and their descendant, the author of the
Book of Revelation, and the plain poetry to the story of Christ
and to His pronouncements on the exaltation of the lowly
and the meek. For the Jesus of the New Testament, as the
Reverend Mark Wilks had said in 1791, was indeed "a Revolutionist," though not a political one; and Wordsworth, in
his long career as apologist for the Anglican Establishment,
never again came so close to the spirit of primitive Christianity as in the latter 1790s, when, according to Coleridge, he
had been still "a Republican & at least a *Semi*-atheist."[62]

FOUR

Structure and Style in the Greater Romantic Lyric

THERE is no accepted name for the kind of poem I want to talk about, even though it was a distinctive and widely practiced variety of the longer Romantic lyric and includes some of the greatest Romantic achievements in any form. Coleridge's *The Eolian Harp*, *Frost at Midnight*, *Fears in Solitude*, and *Dejection: An Ode* exemplify the type, as does Wordsworth's *Tintern Abbey*, his *Ode: Intimations of Immortality*, and (with a change in initial reference from scene to painting) his *Elegiac Stanzas Suggested by a Picture of Peele Castle, in a Storm*. Shelley's *Stanzas Written in Dejection* follows the formula exactly, and his *Ode to the West Wind* is a variant on it. Of Keats's odes, that to a nightingale is the one which approximates the pattern most closely. Only Byron, among the major poets, did not write in this mode at all.

These instances yield a paradigm for the type. Some of the poems are called odes, while the others approach the ode in having lyric magnitude and a serious subject, feelingfully meditated. They present a determinate speaker in a particularized, and usually a localized, outdoor setting, whom we overhear as he carries on, in a fluent vernacular which rises easily to a more formal speech, a sustained colloquy, some-

times with himself or with the outer scene, but more frequently with a silent human auditor, present or absent. The
speaker begins with a description of the landscape; an aspect
or change of aspect in the landscape evokes a varied but integral process of memory, thought, anticipation, and feeling
which remains closely intervolved with the outer scene. In
the course of this meditation the lyric speaker achieves an
insight, faces up to a tragic loss, comes to a moral decision,
or resolves an emotional problem. Often the poem rounds
upon itself to end where it began, at the outer scene, but with
an altered mood and deepened understanding which is the
result of the intervening meditation.

What shall we call this Romantic genre? To label these poems
simply nature lyrics is not only inadequate, but radically misleading. We have not yet entirely recovered from the earlier
critical stress on Wordsworth's statement that "I have at all
times endeavoured to look steadily at my subject," to the
neglect of his repeated warnings that accurate natural
description, though a necessary, is an inadequate condition
for poetry. Like Blake and Coleridge, Wordsworth manifested wariness, almost terror, at the threat of the corporeal
eye and material object to tyrannize over the mind and imagination, in opposition to that normative experience in which

> The mind is lord and master—outward sense
> The obedient servant of her will.[1]

In the extended lyrics we are considering, the visual report
is invariably the occasion for a meditation which turns out to
constitute the *raison d'être* of the poem. Romantic writers,
though nature poets, were humanists above all, for they dealt
with the nonhuman only insofar as it is the occasion for the
activity which defines man: thought, the process of intellection.

"The descriptive-meditative poem" is a possible, but a clumsy
term. *Faute de mieux*, I shall call this poetic type "the greater
Romantic lyric," intending to suggest, not that it is a higher
achievement than other Romantic lyrics, but that it displaced
what neoclassical critics had called "the greater ode"—the

elevated Pindaric, in distinction to "the lesser ode" modeled chiefly on Horace—as the favored form for the long lyric poem.

The repeated out-in-out process, in which mind confronts nature and their interplay constitutes the poem, is a remarkable phenomenon in literary history. If we don't find it strange, it is because our responses have been dulled by long familiarity with such a procedure not only in the Romantic poets, but in their many successors who played variations on the mode, from Matthew Arnold and Walt Whitman—both *Dover Beach* and *Crossing Brooklyn Ferry,* for example, closely follow the pattern of the greater Romantic lyric—to Wallace Stevens and W. H. Auden. But at the beginning of the nineteenth century this procedure in the lyric was part of a new and exciting poetic strategy, no less epidemic than Donne's in his day, or T. S. Eliot's in the period after the First World War. For several decades poets did not often talk about the great issues of life, death, love, joy, dejection, or God without talking at the same time about the landscape. Wordsworth's narrative of Michael emerges from a description of the scene around "the tumultuous brook of Green-head Ghyll," to which in the end it returns:

> and the remains
> Of the unfinished Sheep-fold may be seen
> Beside the boisterous brook of Green-head Ghyll.

Coleridge's great, neglected love poem, *Recollections of Love,* opens with a Quantock scene revisited after eight years have passed, and adverts suddenly to the river Greta at the close:

> But when those meek eyes first did seem
> To tell me, Love within you wrought—
> O Greta, dear domestic stream!
>
> Has not, since then, Love's prompture deep,
> Has not Love's whisper evermore
> Been ceaseless, as thy gentle roar?
> Sole voice, when other voices sleep,
> Dear under-song in clamor's hour.

Keats's first long poem of consequence, though it is his introduction to an *ars poetica,* represents what he saw, then what
he thought, while he "stood tip-toe upon a little hill." Shelley
treats the theme of permanence in change by describing the
mutations of a cloud, defines the pure Idea of joy in a meditation on the flight and song of a skylark, and presents his
ultimate concept of the secret and impersonal power behind
all process in a description of Mont Blanc and the Vale of
Chamouni. Wordsworth's *The Prelude* can be viewed as an
epic expansion of the mode of *Tintern Abbey,* in both overall
design and local tactics. It begins with the description of a
landscape visited in maturity, evokes the entire life of the
poet as a protracted meditation on things past, and presents
the growth of the poet's mind as an interaction with the natural milieu by which it is fostered, from which it is tragically
alienated, and to which in the resolution it is restored, with a
difference attributable to the intervening experiences; the
poem ends at the time of its beginning.

What I have called "the greater lyric," then, is only a special instance of a very widespread manner of proceeding in
Romantic poetry; but it is of great interest because it was the
earliest Romantic formal invention, and at once demonstrated the stability of organization and the capacity to
engender successors which define a distinct lyric species. New
lyric forms are not as plentiful as blackberries, and when one
turns up, it is worth critical attention. Suppose, therefore,
that we ask some questions about this one: about its genesis,
its nearest literary antecedents, and the reasons why this way
of proceeding, out of the alternatives in common lyric practice, should have appealed so powerfully to the Romantic
sensibility. Inquiry into some probable causes of the structure and style of the greater lyric will take us not only to the
evolution of certain descriptive genres in the seventeenth and
eighteenth centuries, but also to contemporary developments in philosophy and in theology, and to the spiritual
posture in which many poets, as well as philosophers, found
themselves at the end of the Enlightenment.

I. COLERIDGE AND WORDSWORTH

In this investigation Coleridge must be our central reference, not only because he had the most to say about these matters in prose, but because it was he, not Wordsworth, who inaugurated the greater Romantic lyric, firmly established its pattern, and wrote the largest number of instances. Wordsworth's first trial in the extended lyric was *Tintern Abbey*, which he composed in July 1798. Up to that time his only efforts in the long descriptive and reflective mode were the schoolboy effort, *The Vale of Esthwaite*, and the two tour-poems of 1793, *An Evening Walk* and *Descriptive Sketches*. The first of these was written in octosyllabic and the latter two in heroic couplets, and all differ in little but merit and the detail of single passages from hundreds of eighteenth-century predecessors.[2] Coleridge, however, as early as 20 August 1795, composed a short first version of *The Eolian Harp*, and in 1796—two years before *Tintern Abbey*—expanded it to fifty-six lines which established, in epitome, the ordonnance, materials, and style of the greater lyric.[3] It is in the dramatic mode of intimate talk to an unanswering auditor in easy blank-verse paragraphs. It begins with a description of the peaceful outer scene; this, in parallel with the vagrant sounds evoked from a wind-harp, calls forth a recollection in tranquillity of earlier experiences in the same setting and leads to a sequence of reflections which are suggested by, and also incorporate, perceptual qualities of the scene. The poem closes with a summary reprise of the opening description of "Peace, and this Cot, and Thee, heart-honour'd Maid!"

Between the autumn of 1796 and the spring of 1798 Coleridge composed a number of variations on this lyric type, including *Reflections on Having Left a Place of Retirement, This Lime-Tree Bower, Fears in Solitude,* and *The Nightingale.* To these writings G. M. Harper applied the term which Coleridge himself used for *The Nightingale*, "conversation poems"; very aptly, because they are written (though some of them only intermittently) in a blank verse which at its best captures remarkably the qualities of the intimate speaking voice, yet

remains capable of adapting without strain to the varying levels
of the subject-matter and feeling. And within this period, in
February of 1798, Coleridge produced one of the master-
pieces of the greater lyric, perfectly modulated and propor-
tioned, but so successful in the quiet way that it hides its art
that it has only recently attracted its meed of critical admiration. The poem is *Frost at Midnight,* and it follows, but greatly
enlarges and subtilizes, the pattern of *The Eolian Harp.* What
seems at first impression to be the free association of its central meditation turns out to have been called forth, qualified,
and controlled by the opening description, which evokes the
strangeness in the familiar surroundings of the solitary and
wakeful speaker: the "secret ministry" of the frost, the "strange
/ And extreme silentness" of "sea, and hill, and wood," the
life of the sleeping village "inaudible as dreams," and the film
that flutters on the grate "the sole unquiet thing." In consonance with these elements, and directed especially by the
rhythm of the seemingly unnoticed breathing of a sleeping
infant, the meditative mind disengages itself from the physical locale, moves back in time to the speaker's childhood, still
farther back, to his own infancy, then forward to express, in
the intonation of a blessing, the hope that his son shall have
the life in nature that his father lacked; until, in anticipating
the future, it incorporates both the present scene and the
results of the remembered past in the enchanting close—

> whether the eave-drops fall
> Heard only in the trances of the blast,
> Or if the secret ministry of frost
> Shall hang them up in silent icicles,
> Quietly shining to the quiet Moon.

  In the original version this concluding sentence trailed off
in six more verse-lines, which Coleridge, in order to emphasize the lyric rondure, later excised. Plainly, Coleridge worked
out the lyric device of the return-upon-itself—which he used
in *Reflections on Having Left a Place of Retirement* and *Fears in
Solitude,* as well as in *The Eolian Harp* and *Frost at Midnight*—
in a deliberate endeavor to transform a segment of experi-

ence broken out of time into a sufficient aesthetic whole. "The common end of all *narrative,* nay, of *all,* Poems," he wrote to Joseph Cottle in 1815, "is to convert a *series* into a *Whole:* to make those events, which in real or imagined History move on in a *strait* Line, assume to our Understandings a *circular* motion—the snake with it's Tail in its Mouth."[4] From the time of the early Greek philosophers, the circle had been the shape of perfection; and in occult philosophy the *ouroboros,* the tail-eating snake, had become the symbol for eternity and for the divine process of creation, since it is complete, self-sufficient, and endless. For Coleridge the perfect shape for the descriptive-meditative-descriptive poem was precisely the one described and exemplified in T. S. Eliot's *East Coker,* which begins, "In my beginning is my end," and ends, "In my end is my beginning"; another modern writer who knew esoteric lore designed *Finnegans Wake* so that the headless sentence which begins the book completes the tailless sentence with which it ends.

Five months after the composition of *Frost at Midnight,* Wordsworth set out on a walking tour with his sister. Reposing on a high bank of the River Wye, he remembered this among others of Coleridge's conversation poems—the dramatic mode of address to an unanswering listener in flexible blank verse; the opening description which evolves into a sustained meditation assimilating perceptual, personal, and philosophical elements; the free movement of thought from the present scene to recollection in tranquillity, to prayer-like prediction, and back to the scene; even some of Coleridge's specific concepts and phrases—and in the next four or five days' walk, worked out *Lines Composed a Few Miles above Tintern Abbey* and appended it forthwith to *Lyrical Ballads,* which was already in press.

To claim that it was Coleridge who deflected Wordsworth's poetry into a channel so entirely congenial to him is in no way to derogate Wordsworth's achievement, nor his powers of invention. *Tintern Abbey* has greater dimension and intricacy and a more various verbal orchestration than *Frost at Midnight.* In its conclusion Wordsworth managed Coleridge's specialty, the return-upon-itself, with a mastery of involuted reference without match in the poems of its begetter. *Tintern Abbey* also inaugurated the wonderfully functional device Wordsworth later called the "two consciousnesses": a scene is revisited, and the remembered landscape ("the picture of the mind") is superimposed on the picture before the eye; the two landscapes fail to match, and so set a problem ("a sad perplexity") which compels the meditation. Wordsworth played variations on this stratagem in all his later trials in the greater lyric, and in *The Prelude* he expanded it into a per-sisting double awareness of things as they are and as they were, and so anticipated the structural principle of the most influential masterpiece of our own century, Proust's *À la recherche du temps perdu.*

II. THE LOCAL POEM

What was the closest poetic antecedent of this controlled and shapely lyric genre? It was not the ancient lyric formula, going back to the spring-songs of the troubadors, which set forth an ideal spring scene (the *Natureingang*) and then presented a human experience in harmony or contrast—a formula which survived in Burns's

> Ye flowery banks o' bonnie Doon,
>   How can ye blume sae fair?
> How can ye chant, ye little birds,
>   And I sae fu' o' care?

Nor was it Thomson's *Seasons*, that omnibus of unlocalized description, episodic narration, and general reflection, in which the pious observer moves from Nature to Nature's God with the help of Isaac Newton's *Principia*. And certainly it was not the formal descriptive poem such as Collins' *Ode to Evening*, which adapted Pindar's ceremonial panegyric to land-scape mainly by the device of transforming descriptive and meditative propositions into a sequence of tableaux and brief allegories—a mode which Keats revitalized in his ode *To*

Autumn.[5] The clue to the provenience of the greater Romantic lyric is to be found in the attributes of the opening description. This landscape is not only particularized; it is in most cases precisely localized, in place, and sometimes in time as well. Critics have often remarked on Wordsworth's scrupulosity about specifying the circumstances for his poems, but his fellow poets were often no less meticulous in giving their greater lyrics an exact locality. We have "The Eolian Harp, Composed at Clevedon, Somersetshire" (the first versions also appended to the title a date, 20 August 1795); "This Lime-Tree Bower My Prison," with the headnote: "In the June of 1797 . . . the author's cottage . . . composed . . . in the garden-bower"; "Fears in Solitude written April, 1798. . . . The Scene, the Hills near Stowey";[6] "Lines Composed a Few Miles above Tintern Abbey . . . July 13, 1798"; "Elegiac Stanzas Suggested by a Picture of Peele Castle, in a Storm"; "Stanzas Written in Dejection, near Naples." Even when its setting is not named in the title, the poem usually has an identifiable local habitation, such as the milieu of Coleridge's cottage at Nether Stowey for *Frost at Midnight,* or the view from Coleridge's study at Keswick in *Dejection: An Ode.* To his *Ode to the West Wind,* Shelley was careful to add the note: "Written in a wood that skirts the Arno, near Florence. . . ."

There existed in the eighteenth century a well defined and immensely popular poetic type, in which the title named a geographical location, and which combined a description of that scene with the thoughts that the scene suggested. This was known as the "local" or "loco-descriptive" poem; Robert A. Aubin, in his compendious and amusing survey of *Topographical Poetry in XVIII-Century England,* lists almost two thousand instances of the form. "Local poetry," as Dr. Johnson concisely defined it in his life of John Denham, was

> a species of composition . . . of which the fundamental subject is some particular landscape to be poetically described, with the addition of such embellishments as may be supplied by historical restrospection or incidental meditation.[7]

The evidence, I think, makes it clear that the most characteristic Romantic lyric developed directly out of one of the most stable and widely employed of all the neoclassic kinds.

By general consent Denham, as Dr. Johnson said, was the "author" of the genre, in that excellent poem *Cooper's Hill,* of which the first version was written in 1642. In it the poet inventories the prospect of the Thames valley visible from the hilltop, with distant London on one side and Windsor Castle on the other. As Earl Wasserman has shown, the poem is a complex construction, in which the topographical elements are selected and managed so as to yield concepts which support a Royalist viewpoint on the eve of the civil wars.[8] But if, like Dr. Johnson, we abstract and classify Denham's incidental meditations, we find that some are historical and political, but that others are broadly sententious, and are achieved by the device of adducing to a natural object a correspondent moral idea. Thus the "aery Mountain" (lines 217–22), forced to endure the onslaught of winds and storms, instances "the common fate of all that's high or great," while the Thames (lines 163–64) hastens "to pay tribute to the Sea, / Like mortal life to meet Eternity."

This latter procedure is worth dwelling on for a moment, because for many of Denham's successors it displaced history and politics to become the sole meditative component in local poems, and it later evolved into the extended meditation of the Romantic lyric. The *paysage moralisé* was not invented as a rhetorical device by poets, but was grounded on two collateral and pervasive concepts in medieval and Renaissance philosophy. One of these was the doctrine that God has supplemented the Holy Scriptures with the *liber creaturarum,* so that objects of nature, as Sir Thomas Browne said, carry "in Stenography and short Characters, something of Divinity"[9] and show forth the attributes and providence of their Author. The second concept, of independent philosophic origin but often fused with the first, is that the divine Architect has designed the universe analogically, relating the physical, moral, and spiritual realms by an elaborate system of correspondences. A landscape, accordingly, consists of *verba visibilia* which enable pious interpreters such as Shakespeare's Duke in *As You Like It* to find "books in the running brooks, / Sermons in stones, and good in everything."

The metaphysic of a symbolic and analogical universe underlay the figurative tactics of the seventeenth-century metaphysical poets who were John Denham's predecessors and contemporaries. The secular and amatory poems exploited unexpected correspondences mainly as display rhetoric, positing the analogue in order to show the author's wit in supporting an argument and to evoke in the reader the shock of delightful discovery. In their devotional poems, however, the poets put forward their figures as grounded in the divine plan underlying the universe. Thus Henry Vaughan, musing over a waterfall, was enabled by the guidance of its Creator to discover its built-in correspondences with the life and destiny of man:

> What sublime truths and wholesome themes,
> Lodge in thy mystical deep streams!
> Such as dull man can never find
> Unless that spirit lead his mind
> Which first upon thy face did move,
> And hatched all with his quick'ning love.

In 1655, the year in which Vaughan published *The Waterfall,* Denham added to his enlarged edition of *Cooper's Hill* the famous pair of couplets on the Thames which link description to concepts by a sustained parallel between the flow of the stream and the ideal conduct of life and art:

> O could I flow like thee, and make thy stream
> My great example, as it is my theme!
> Though deep, yet clear, though gentle, yet not dull,
> Strong without rage, without o'erflowing, full.

The metaphysical device and ingenuity are still apparent, but we can see why this became the best known and most influential passage in the poetry of neoclassicism—a model not only for its versification, but also for some of its most characteristic ideas and rhetorical devices. In these lines the metaphysical wit has been tamed and ordered into the "true wit" which became the eighteenth-century ideal; Denham's "strength" (which Dr. Johnson defined as "much meaning in few words"), so universally admired, has replaced the "strong lines" (the compressed and hyperbolic ingeniousness) of John Donne; while the startling revelation of *discordia concors* between object and idea has been smoothed to a neoclassic decency, moulded to the deft play of antitheses around the caesura, and adapted to the presentation of the cardinal neo-classic ideal of a mean between extremes.[10]

In the enormous number of eighteenth-century local poems the organization of *Cooper's Hill* around a controlling political motif was soon reduced mainly to the procedure of setting up parallels between landscape and moral commonplaces. The subtitle of Richard Jago's long *Edge Hill* (1767) neatly defines the double function: "The Rural Prospect Delineated and Moralized"; while the title of an anonymous poem of 1790 reveals how monstrous this development could be: *An Evening's Reflection on the Universe, in a Walk on the Seashore*. The literal belief in a universe of divine types and correspon-dences, which had originally supported this structural trope, faded,[11] and the coupling of sensuous phenomena with moral statements came to be regarded as a rhetorical device partic-ularly apt to the descriptive poet's double aim of combining instruction with delight. John Dyer's *Grongar Hill* (1726) was justly esteemed as one of the most deft and agreeable of prospect-poems. Mounting the hill, the poet describes the widening prospect with a particularity beyond the call of the moralist's duty. Yet the details of the scene are duly equated with *sententiae;* and when he comes to moralize the river (always, after Denham's passage on the Thames, the favorite item in the topographic inventory), Dyer echoes the great theological concept of a typological universe lightly, as a pleasant conceit:

> And see the rivers how they run . . .
> Wave succeeding wave, they go
> A various journey to the deep,
> Like human life to endless sleep!
> Thus is nature's vesture wrought,
> To instruct our wand'ring thought;
> Thus she dresses green and gay,
> To disperse our cares away.

Thomas Gray's *Ode on a Distant Prospect of Eton College* (1747) provides significant evidence that the local poem evolved into the greater Romantic lyric. It is a hill-poem, and its setting—

Windsor heights and the Thames valley—is part of the very prospect which Denham had described. The topographical form, however, has been adapted to the Horatian ode, so that the focus of interest is no longer in the analogical inventory of scenic detail, but in the mental and emotional experience of a specific lyric speaker. The meditation becomes a coherent and dramatic sequence of thought, triggered by what was to become Wordsworth's favorite device of *déjà vu:* the scene is a scene revisited, and it evokes in memory the lost self of the speaker's youth:

> I feel the gales that from ye blow
> A momentary bliss bestow,
> As, waving fresh their gladsome wing,
> My weary soul they seem to soothe,
> And, redolent of joy and youth,
> To breathe a second spring.

As he watches the heedless schoolboys at their games, the speaker's first impulse is to warn them of the ambuscades which the "ministers of human fate" are even now laying for them: "Ah, tell them they are men!" But a new thought leads to a reversal of intention, for he suddenly realizes that since life's horrors are inescapable, forewarning is a needless cruelty.

We are a long way, however, from the free flow of consciousness, the interweaving of thought, feeling, and perceptual detail, and the easy naturalness of the speaking voice which characterize the Romantic lyric. Gray deliberately rendered both his observations and reflections in the hieratic style of a formal odic *oratio.* The poet's recollection of times past, for example, is managed through an invocation to Father Thames to tell him "who foremost now delight to cleave / With pliant arm thy glassy wave," and the language throughout is heightened and stylized by the apostrophe, exclamation, rhetorical question, and studied periphrasis which Wordsworth decried in Gray—"more than any other man curiously elaborate in the structure of his ... poetic diction."[12] Both reminiscence and reflection are depersonalized, and occur mainly as general propositions which are sometimes expressed as *sententiae* ("where ignorance is bliss / 'Tis folly to be wise"), and at other times as propositions which, in the standard artifice of the contemporary ode, are converted into the tableau-and-allegory form that Coleridge derogated as Gray's "translations of prose thoughts into poetic language."[13] Gray's poem is structurally inventive, and excellent in its kind, but it remains distinctly a mid-century period piece. We need to look elsewhere for the immediate occasion of Coleridge's invention of the greater Romantic lyric.

III. COLERIDGE AND BOWLES

I have quoted Coleridge's derogation of Gray from the first chapter of the *Biographia Literaria,* in which Coleridge reviewed his own early development as a poet. To Gray's style he opposed that of three poems, the only contemporary models he mentioned with approval; and all three, it is important to note, were of a type which combines local description with associated meditation. One was William Crowe's conventional prospect-poem *Lewesdon Hill* (1788) and another was Cowper's *The Task,* which incorporates a number of episodic meditations evoked by the environs of the river Ouse. Both these poems, however, he read later—*The Task,* he says, "many years" later—than a publication which at once seized irresistibly upon his sensibility, William Lisle Bowles's *Sonnets* of 1789. By these poems he was "year after year . . . enthusiastically delighted and inspired," and he worked zealously to win "proselytes" to his poetic divinity by buttonholing strangers and friends alike, and by sending out as gifts more than forty copies of Bowles's volume, which he had himself transcribed.[14]

Coleridge mentioned also Bowles's *Monody Written at Matlock* (1791), which is a long prospect-poem written in blank verse. But most of Bowles's poems of 1789 are obvious adaptations of this local-meditative formula to the sonnet form. As in both the local poems and the Romantic lyric, a number of Bowles's titles specify the place, and even the time: "To the

River Wensbeck"; "To the River Itchin, near Winton"; "On Dover Cliffs. July 20, 1787"; "Written at Ostend. July 22, 1787." The whole was "Written," as the title of 1789 points out, "Chiefly on Picturesque Spots, during a Tour," and constitutes a sonnet-sequence uttered by a latter-day wandering *penseroso* who, as the light fades from the literal day, images his life as a metaphoric tour from its bright morning through deepening shadow to enduring night. Within this overarching equation, the typical single poem begins with a rapid sketch of the external scene—frequently, as in so many of Denham's progeny, a river scene—then moves on to reminiscence and moral reflection. The transition is often managed by a connecting phrase which signalizes the shift from objects to concepts and indicates the nature of the relation between them: "So fares it with the children of the earth"; "ev'n thus on sorrow's breath / A kindred stillness steals"; "Bidding me many a tender thought recall / Of summer days"; "I meditate / On this world's passing pageant."

Bowles wrote in a Preface of 1805, when his poems had already achieved a ninth edition, that his sonnets "describe his personal feelings" during excursions taken to relieve "depression of spirits." They exhibit "occasional reflections which naturally rose in his mind" and were

> in general suggested by the scenes before them; and wherever such scenes appeared to harmonise with his disposition at the moment, the sentiments were involuntarily prompted.[15]

The local poem has been lyricized. That is, Bowles's sonnets present a determinate speaker, whom we are invited to identify with the author himself, whose responses to the local scene are a spontaneous overflow of feeling and displace the landscape as the center of poetic interest; hence the "occasional reflections" and "sentiments," instead of being a series of impersonal *sententiae* linked to details of the setting by analogy, are mediated by the particular temperament and circumstances of the perceiving mind, and tend to compose a single curve of feelingful meditation. *To the River Itchin, near Winton*—which so impressed Coleridge that he emulated it in

his sonnet *To the River Otter*—will represent Bowles's procedure, including his use of the recollection of an earlier visit
to stimulate the meditation:

> Itchin, when I behold thy banks again,
>   Thy crumbling margin, and thy silver breast,
>   On which the self-same tints still seem'd to rest,
> Why feels my heart the shivering sense of pain?
> Is it—that many a summer's day has past
>   Since, in life's morn, I carolled on thy side?
>   Is it—that oft, since then, my heart has sighed,
> As Youth, and Hope's delusive gleams, flew fast?
>   Is it—that those, who circled on thy shore,
>   Companions of my youth, now meet no more?
> Whate'er the cause, upon thy banks I bend,
>   Sorrowing, yet feel such solace at my heart,
> As at the meeting of some long-lost friend,
>   From whom, in happier hours, we wept to part.

Why Coleridge should have been moved to idolatry by so
slender, if genuine, a talent as that of Bowles has been an
enigma of literary history. It is significant, however, that
Bowles's *Sonnets* of 1789 had an impact on both Southey and
Wordsworth which was also immediate and powerful. As
Wordsworth later told Samuel Rogers:

> I bought them in a walk through London with my dear brother.
> . . . I read them as we went along; and to the great annoyance
> of my brother, I stopped in a niche of London Bridge to finish
> the pamphlet.[16]

And if we take into account Coleridge's intellectual preoccupations between the ages of seventeen and twenty-five, as well
as his growing discontent with current modes of poetry,
including his own, we find a sufficiency of reasons to explain
the power of Bowles over his sensibility and his practice as a
poet. Some of these are literary reasons, pertaining to Bowles's
characteristic subjects and style, while others concern the
philosophy of mind and its place in nature which, Coleridge
believed, was implicit in Bowles's habitual manner of proceeding.

Bowles's sonnets represent the lonely mind in meditation, and their *fin de siècle* mood of weary and self-pitying isolation—what Coleridge called their "lonely feeling"[17]—proved irresistible to a vigorous young newcomer to poetry. Of much greater and more enduring importance, however, as Coleridge emphasized in his *Biographia,* was the revelation to him of the possibility of a style "so tender and yet so manly, so natural and real, and yet so dignified and harmonious, as the sonnets etc. of Mr. Bowles!"[18] Even while he was absorbedly reading and tentatively imitating Bowles, Coleridge himself in his major efforts was primarily the poet "to turgid ode and tumid stanza dear," of Byron's unadmiring comment. In his poetic volume of 1796, as enlarged in 1797, the most ambitious undertakings were the *Religious Musings* and *Ode on the Departing Year.* Of this publication Coleridge said in the *Biographia* that though, even then, he clearly saw "the superiority of an austerer and more natural style" than his own obscure and turgid language, he failed to realize his ideal, partly out of "diffidence of my own comparative talent," and "partly owing to a wrong choice of subjects, and the desire of giving a poetic colouring to abstract and metaphysical truths, in which a new world then seemed to open upon me."[19] In the turbulence and crises of the early period of the French Revolution, he had been obsessed with the need to give public voice to his political, religious, and philosophical beliefs, and he had tried to poetize such materials in the fashion current in the 1790s.[20] That is to say, he had adopted a visionary and oracular persona—in accordance, as he said in the Dedication to his *Ode on the Departing Year,* with the practice of the ancients, when "the Bard and the Prophet were one and the same character"[21]—and had compounded biblical prophecy, the hieratic stance of Milton, and the formal rhetoric, allegorical tactics, and calculated disorder of what he called "the sublimer Ode" of Gray and Collins, in the effort to endow his subjects with the requisite elevation, passion, drama, and impact. As Coleridge wrote to Southey in December of 1794, while Bowles's poems were his "morning Companions," helping him, "a thought-bewilder'd Man," to discover his own defects, "I am so habituated to philosophizing, that I cannot divest myself of it even when my own Wretchedness is the subject."

> And I cannot write without a *body* of *thought*—hence my *Poetry* is crowded and sweats beneath a heavy burthen of Ideas and Imagery! It has seldom Ease.[22]

This "Ease" Coleridge had early discovered in Bowles. And as he said in the *Biographia,* the example of Bowles—together with Cowper, the first of the living poets who, in the style "more sustained and elevated" than in Percy's collection of popular ballads, "combined natural thoughts with natural diction; the first who reconciled the heart with the head"— rescued him from the unnatural division between intellect and feeling, and consonantly, from his use of "a laborious and florid diction"; but only, as he adds, "gradually."[23] The reason for the delay in making, as he put it, his "practice" conform to his "better judgment" is, I think, plain. Coleridge succeeded in emulating Bowles's ease only after he learned to adopt and commit himself to the lyric persona which demands such a style. That is, in place of philosophical, moral, and historical pronouncements translated into allegoric action by Pindaric artifice and amplified for public delivery in a ceremonious bardic voice, Bowles's sonnets opened out to Coleridge the possibilities in the quite ordinary circumstances of a private person in a specific time and place whose meditation, credibly stimulated by the setting, is grounded in his particular character, follows the various and seemingly random flow of the living consciousness, and is conducted in the intimate yet adaptive voice of the interior monologue. (Bowles's style, as Coleridge said, unites the possibilities of both colloquialism and elevation—it is "natural and real, and yet . . . dignified and harmonious.") It was in "the compositions of my twenty-fourth and twenty-fifth years," Coleridge goes on to say, including "the shorter blank verse poems"—that is, the poems of 1796–97, beginning with *The Eolian Harp,* which established the persona, idiom, materials, and ordonnance of the greater Romantic lyric—that he achieved his "present ideal in respect of the general tissue of the style."[24] No doubt the scholars are right who claim some influence on these poems of the relaxed and conversational blank verse of Cowper's *The Task*,[25] in the recurrent passages, within its mock-Miltonic manner, of serious description or meditation. I see no reason, however, to doubt Coleridge's repeated assertion that Bowles's sonnets and blank-verse poems were for him the prior and by far the preeminent models.

So much for the speaker and voice of Bowles's sonnets. Now what of their central structural trope, by which, as Coleridge described it in 1796, "moral Sentiments, Affections, or Feelings, are deduced from, and associated with, the scenery of Nature"? Even so early in his career Coleridge was an integral thinker for whom questions of poetic structure were inseparable from general philosophic issues, and he at once went on to interpret this device as the correlate of a mode of perception which unites the mind to its physical environment. Such compositions, he said,

> create a sweet and indissoluble union between the intellectual and the material world. . . . Hence the Sonnets of Bowles derive their marked superiority over all other Sonnets; hence they domesticate with the heart, and become, as it were, a part of our identity.[26]

This philosophical and psychological interpretation of Bowles's lyric procedure was not only, as Coleridge indicates, a cardinal reason for his early fascination with Bowles, but also the chief clue to his later disenchantment, and it merits attention.

IV. THE COALESCENCE OF SUBJECT AND OBJECT

In the opening chapter of his "Literary Life," Coleridge introduces Bowles's sonnets not on their own account, but as representing a stage in his total intellectual development—"as introductory to the statement of my principles in Politics, Religion, and Philosophy, and an application of the rules, deduced from philosophical principles, to poetry and criticism."[27] Hence he moves from his account of the shaping influence of Bowyer, Bowles, and Wordsworth into a summary review of the history of philosophy, as preliminary to establishing his own metaphysical and critical premises, of which the culmination was to be the crucial distinction between fancy and imagination.

In the course of his survey of the dominant philosophy of the preceding age, it becomes clear that Coleridge found intolerable two of its main features, common to philosophers in both the school of Descartes and the school of Locke. The first was its dualism, the absolute separation between mind and the material universe, which replaced a providential, vital, and companionable world by a world of particles in purposeless movement. The second was the method of reasoning underlying this dualism, that pervasive elementarism which takes as its starting point the irreducible element or part and conceives all wholes to be a combination of discrete parts, whether material atoms or mental "ideas."

Even in 1797, while Coleridge was still a Hartleian associationist in philosophy, he had expressed his recoil from elementarist thinking. The fault of "the Experimentalists," who rely only on the "testimony of their senses," is that "they contemplate nothing but *parts*—and all *parts* are necessarily little—and the Universe to them is but a mass of *little things*." "I can contemplate nothing but parts, & parts are all *little*—!— My mind feels as if it ached to behold & know something *great*—something *one & indivisible*. . . ."[28] And he wrote later in *The Friend* about that particular separation between part and part which divides mind from nature:

> The ground-work, therefore, of all true philosophy is the full apprehension of the difference between . . . that intuition of things which arises when we possess ourselves, as one with the whole . . . and that which presents itself when . . . we think of ourselves as separated beings, and place nature in antithesis to the mind, as object to subject, thing to thought, death to life.[29]

As to Coleridge, so to Wordsworth in 1797–98, "solitary objects . . . beheld / In disconnection" are "dead and spiritless," and division, breaking down "all grandeur" into successive "little-ness," is opposed to man's proper spiritual condition, in which "all things shall live in us and we shall live / In all things that surround us."[30] Absolute separation, in other words, is death-dealing—in Coleridge's words, it is "the philosophy of Death, and only of a dead nature can it hold good"[31]—so that the separation of mind from nature leads inevitably to the conception of a dead world in which the estranged mind is doomed to lead a life-in-death.

To the Romantic sensibility such a universe could not be endured, and the central enterprise common to many post-Kantian German philosophers and poets, as well as to Coleridge and Wordsworth, was to join together the "subject" and "object" that modern intellection had put asunder, and thus to revivify a dead nature, restore its concreteness, significance, and human values, and re-domiciliate man in a world which had become alien to him. The pervasive sense of estrangement, of a lost and isolated existence in an alien world, is not peculiar to our own age of anxiety, but was a common-place of Romantic philosophy. According to Friedrich Schelling, the most representative philosopher of that age, division from unity was the fall of man consequent upon his eating the fruit of the tree of knowledge in the Enlighten-ment. The guilt of modern men must be

> ascribed to their own will, which deviated from unity. . . . [This is] a truly Platonic fall of man, the condition in which man believes that the dead, the absolutely manifold and separated world which he conceives, is in fact the true and actual world.[32]

Long before he read Schelling, and while at the height of his enthusiasm for Bowles, Coleridge had included in his vision-ary *Religious Musings* (begun in 1794) an outline of human history in which mankind's highest good had been "to know ourselves / Parts and proportions of one wondrous whole"; the present evil was defined as a fall into an anarchic sepa-ration in which each man, "disherited of soul," feels "himself, his own low self the whole"; and man's redemption at the Second Coming was anticipated as a reintegration into his lost unity by a "sacred sympathy" which makes "the whole one Self! Self, that no alien knows! . . . all of all possessing!"[33] And in 1815 Coleridge recalled that the plan of Wordsworth's projected masterpiece, *The Recluse,* as he had understood it, had also been to affirm "a Fall in some sense, as a fact," to be redeemed by a

> Reconciliation from this Enmity with Nature . . . by the substitution of Life, and Intelligence . . . for the Philosophy of mechanism which in every thing that is most worthy of the human Intellect strikes *Death.*[34]

In the *Biographia Literaria,* when Coleridge came to lay down his own metaphysical system, he based it on a premise designed to overcome both the elementarism in method and the dualism in theory of knowledge of his eighteenth-century predecessors, by converting their absolute division between subject and object into a logical "antithesis," in order to make it eligible for resolution by the Romantic dialectic of thesis-antithesis-synthesis. The "primary ground" of his theory of knowledge, he says, is "the coincidence of an object with a subject" or "of the thought with the thing," in a synthesis, or "coalescence," in which the elements lose their separate identities. "In the reconciling, and recurrence of this contradiction exists the process and mystery of production and life."[35] And the process of vital artistic creation reflects the process of this vital creative perception. Unlike the fancy, which can only rearrange the "fixities and definites" of sense-perception without altering their identity, the "synthetic and magical power" of the secondary imagination repeats the primal act of knowing by dissolving the elements of perception "in order to recreate" them, and "reveals itself in the balance or reconciliation of opposite or discordant qualities"—including the reconciliation of intellect with emotion, and of thought with object: "the idea, with the image."[36]

In short, the reintegration of the divided self (of "head and heart") and the simultaneous healing of the breach between the ego and the alien other (of "subject and object") was for Coleridge a profound emotional need which he translated into the grounds of both his theory of knowledge and his theory of art. How pivotal the concept of human-nonhuman reconciliation came to be for Coleridge's aesthetics is apparent in his essay "On Poesy or Art," in which he specifically defined art as "the reconciler of nature and man . . . the power of humanizing nature, of infusing the thoughts and passions of man into every thing which is the object of his contemplation." It is "the union and reconciliation of that which is nature with that which is exclusively human."[37]

Perhaps now, to return at last to the sonnets of Bowles, we can understand better why those seemingly inconsequential poems made so powerful an impact on Coleridge, in their materials as well as their structure and style. Bowles's primary device by which sentiments and feelings "are deduced from, and associated with, the scenery of Nature" had seemed to Coleridge evidence of a poetry which not only "reconciled the heart with the head," but also united the mind with nature; in the terms available to him in 1796, it created "a sweet and indissoluble union between the intellectual and the material world." Through the next half-decade, however, Coleridge carried on his own experiments in the descriptive and meditative lyric, came to know the early poetry of Wordsworth, had his introduction to German metaphysics, and, in intense and almost fevered speculation, groped his way out of the mechanism and associationism of David Hartley and other English empiricists. Increasingly in the process he became dissatisfied with the constitution of Bowles's poems, and the reasons came sharply into focus in 1802, at about the time he was recasting his verse "Letter to [Asra]" into his highest achievement in the greater Romantic lyric, *Dejection: An Ode*. On 10 September he wrote a letter to William Sotheby which shows that his working his way through and beyond Bowles was an integral part of his working his way toward a new poetry, a new criticism, and a new world-view. The letter is a preliminary sketch for the *Biographia Literaria*, for like that work it moves from a critique of Bowles through a view of the relation of mind to nature in perception to a theory of poetic production, and it culminates in Coleridge's first explicit distinction between the elementaristic fancy and the synthetic imagination.

Bowles had just published a new edition of his sonnets, supplemented by several long poems in blank verse which reverted to a process of scenic inventory and incidental meditation very close to the eighteenth-century local poem. Bowles's second volume, Coleridge begins, "is woefully inferior to it's Predecessor."

> There reigns thro' all the blank verse poems such a perpetual trick of *moralizing* every thing—which is very well, occasionally—but never to see or describe any interesting appearance in nature, without connecting it by dim analogies with the moral world, proves faintness of Impression. Nature has her proper interest; & he will know what it is, who believes & feels, that every Thing has a Life of it's own, & that we are all *one Life*. A Poet's *Heart & Intellect* should be *combined, intimately* combined & *unified*, with the great appearances in Nature—& not merely held in solution & loose mixture with them, in the shape of formal Similes. . . . The truth is—Bowles has indeed the *sensibility* of a poet; but he has not the *Passion* of a great Poet. . . . he has no native Passion, because he is not a Thinker.[38]

Bowles's exaggeration in his later poems of his earlier devices has opened out to Coleridge his inherent failings. Bowles is able to reconcile the heart with the head, but only because of an equality of weakness in the antagonist powers of intellect and passion. And what Coleridge had earlier described as an "indissoluble union between the intellectual and the material world" now turns out to be no better than a "loose mixture," in which the separate parts, instead of being *"intimately* combined & *unified*," are merely held together by the rhetorical expedient of "formal Similes." In other words, what to Coleridge, the Hartleian associationist, had in 1796 appeared to be an adequate integration of mind and its milieu reveal itself—when he has learned to think of all higher mental processes in terms of a synthesis of contraries—to be what he later called the "conjunction-disjunctive" of neoclassic unity by a decorum of the parts.

In the letter to Sotheby, Coleridge goes on to draw a parallel distinction between the treatment of nature in Greek mythology and in the Hebrew poets, and ends by assigning the former type to the collocative process of the lower productive faculty, or Fancy. To the Greek poets

> all natural Objects were *dead*—mere hollow Statues—but there was a Godkin or Goddessling *included* in each. . . . At best, it is but Fancy, or the aggregating Faculty of the mind—not *Imagination,* or the *modifying,* and *co-adunating* Faculty. . . . In the Hebrew Poets each Thing has a Life of it's own, & yet they are all one Life.

Bowles's poems, it becomes apparent, remain in the mode of the Fancy because they fail to overcome the division between living mind and a dead nature by that act of the coadunating Imagination which fuses the two into "one Life"; for when Bowles joins the parts *a* and *b* they form an aggregate *ab,* instead of "interpenetrating" (in terms of Coleridge's critique of elementarist thinking) to "generate a higher third, including both the former," the product *c*.[39] For the "mystery of genius in the Fine Arts," as Coleridge said in "On Poesy or Art," is

> so to place these images [of nature] . . . as to elicit from, and to superinduce upon, the forms themselves the moral reflexions to which they approximate, to make the external internal, the internal external, to make nature thought, and thought nature.[40]

The shift in Coleridge's theory of descriptive poetry corresponded with a change in his practice of the form; and in the sequence of sonnets and conversation poems that he wrote under Bowles's influence we can observe him in the process of converting the conjunction of parts, in which nature stays on one side and thought on the other, into the Romantic interfusion of subject and object. W. K. Wimsatt has acutely remarked that Coleridge's sonnet *To the River Otter*—though written in express imitation of Bowles's *To the River Itchin,* perhaps so early as 1793—has begun to diverge from Bowles's "simple association . . . simply asserted" by involving the thought in the descriptive details so that the design "is latent

in the multiform sensuous picture."[41] *The Eolian Harp* (1795–
96) set the expanded pattern of the greater lyric, but in it the
meditative flight is a short one, while the thought is still at
times expressed in the mode of *sententiae* which are joined to
the details of the scene by formal similes. We sit

> beside our Cot, our Cot o'ergrown
> With white-flower'd Jasmin, and the broad-leav'd Myrtle,
> (Meet emblems they of Innocence and Love!)
> And watch the clouds, that late were rich with light,
> Slow saddening round, and mark the star of eve
> Serenely brilliant (such should Wisdom be)
> Shine opposite!

In *Frost at Midnight,* however, written two years later, the
images in the initial description are already suffused with an
unstated significance which, in Coleridge's terms, is merely
"elicited" and expanded by the subsequent reflection, which
in turn "superinduces" a richer meaning upon the scene to
which it reverts. *Fears in Solitude,* a few months after that,
exemplifies the sustained dialogue between mind and landscape which Coleridge describes in lines 215–20 of the poem:
the prospect of sea and fields

> seems like society—
> Conversing with the mind, and giving it
> A livelier impulse and a dance of thought!

And *Dejection: An Ode,* on which Coleridge was working in
1802 just as he got Bowles's poems into critical perspective,
is a triumph of the "co-adunating" imagination, in the very
poem which laments the severance of his community with
nature and the suspension of his shaping spirit of imagination. In unspoken consonance with the change of the outer
scene and of the responsive wind-harp from ominous quiet
to violent storm to momentary calm, the poet's mind,
momentarily revitalized by a correspondent inner breeze,
moves from torpor through violence to calm, by a process in
which the properties earlier specified of the landscape—the
spring rebirth, the radiated light of moon and stars, the clouds

and rain, the voice of the harp—reappear as the metaphors of the evolving meditation on the relation of mind to nature; these culminate in the figure of the one life as an eddy between antitheses:

> To her may all things live, from pole to pole,
> Their life the eddying of her living soul!

On Coleridge's philosophical premises, in this poem nature is made thought and thought nature, both by their sustained interaction and by their seamless metaphoric continuity.

The best Romantic meditations on a landscape, following Coleridge's examples, all manifest a transaction between subject and object in which the thought incorporates and makes explicit what was already implicit in the outer scene. And all the poets testify independently to a fact of consciousness which underlay these poems, and was the experiential source and warrant for the philosophy of cognition as an interfusion of mind and nature. When the Romantic poet confronted a landscape, the distinction between self and not-self tended to dissolve. Coleridge asserted that from childhood he had been accustomed to "unrealize . . . and then by a sort of transfusion and transmission of my consciousness to identify myself with the Object"; also that

> in looking at objects of Nature while I am thinking . . . I seem rather to be seeking, as it were *asking*, a symbolical language for something within me that already and forever exists, than observing any thing new.

So with Wordsworth: "I was often unable to think of external things as having external existence, and I communed with all that I saw as something not apart from, but inherent in, my own immaterial nature." Shelley witnessed to "the state called reverie," when men "feel as if their nature were dissolved into the surrounding universe, or as if the surrounding universe were absorbed into their being. They are conscious of no distinction." Even Byron's Childe Harold claimed that "I live not in myself," but that mountains, waves, and skies become "a part / Of me, and of my soul, as I of them." Keats's experience differs, but only in the conditions that, instead of assimilating the other to the self, the self goes out into the other, and that the boundary of self is "annihilated" when he contemplates, not a broad prospect, but a solid particular endowed with outline, mass, and posture or motion. That type of poet of which "I am a Member . . . has no self" but "is continually [informing] and filling some other Body"—a moving billiard ball, a breaking wave, a human form in arrested motion, a sparrow, an urn, or a nightingale.[42]

V. THE ROMANTIC MEDITATION

The greater Romantic lyric, then, as established by Coleridge, evolved from the descriptive-meditative structure of the eighteenth-century local poem, primarily through the inter-mediate stage of Bowles's sequence of sonnets. There remains, however, a wide disparity between the Romantic lyric and its predecessors, a disparity in the organization and nature of the meditation proper. In local poetry the order of the thoughts is the sequence in which the natural objects are observed; the poet surveys a prospect, or climbs a hill, or undertakes a tour, or follows the course of a stream, and he introduces memories and ideas intermittently, as the descriptive occasion offers. In Bowles's sonnets, the meditation, while more continuous, is severely limited by the straitness of the form, and consists mainly of the pensive commonplaces of the typical late-century man of feeling. In the fully developed Romantic lyric, on the other hand, the description is structurally subordinate to the meditation, and the meditation is sustained, continuous, and highly serious. Even when the initial impression is of the casual movement of a relaxed mind, retrospect reveals the whole to have been firmly organized around an emotional issue pressing for resolution. And in a number of the greatest lyrics—including Coleridge's *Dejection,* Wordsworth's *Intimations,* Shelley's *Stanzas Written in Dejection* and *West Wind,* Keats's *Nightingale*—the issue is one of a recurrent state often called by the specialized term "dejection." This is not the pleasing melancholy of the eighteenth-century poet of sensibility, nor Bowles's muted self-pity, but a profound sadness, sometimes bordering on the anguish of terror or despair, at the sense of loss, dereliction, isolation, or inner death, which is presented as inherent in the conditions of the speaker's existence.

In the English literary tradition these Romantic meditations had their closest analogue in the devotional poems of the seventeenth century. In his study *The Poetry of Meditation*, Louis Martz has emphasized the importance, for the religious poets we usually class as "metaphysical," of the numerous and immensely popular devotional handbooks which undertook to discipline the casual flow of ordinary consciousness by setting down a detailed regimen for evoking, sustaining, and ordering a process of meditation toward resolution. A standard sub-department was the "meditation on the creatures" (that is, on the created world) in order, as the title of Robert Bellarmine's influential treatise of 1615 put it, to achieve *The Ascent of the Mind to God by a Ladder of Things Created*. The recommended procedure, as this became stabilized at the turn of the century, tended to fall into three major divisions. The first involved what Loyola called the "composition of place, seeing the spot"; that is, envisioning in vivid detail the person, object, or scene which initiates the meditation. The second, the meditation proper, was the analysis of the relevance to our salvation of this scene, interpreted analogically; it often included a turn inward to a close examination of conscience. The last specified the results of this meditation for our affections and will, and either included, or concluded with, a "colloquy"—usually a prayer, or discourse with God, although as Saint Francis de Sales advises, "while we are forming our affections and resolutions," we do well to address our colloquy also "to ourselves, to our own hearts . . . and even to insensible creatures."[43]

Few seventeenth-century meditative poems accord exactly with the formulas of the Catholic or Anglican devotional manuals, but many of them unmistakably profited from that disciplining of fluid thought into an organized pattern which was a central enterprise in the spiritual life of the age. And those poetic meditations on the creatures which envision a natural scene or object, go on in sorrow, anguish, or dejection to explore the significance for the speaker of the spiritual signs built into the object by God, and end in reconciliation and the hope of rebirth, are closer to the best Romantic lyrics in meditative content, mood, and ordonnance than any poem by Bowles or his eighteenth-century predecessors. Good instances of the type are Vaughan's *The Waterfall, Regeneration, Vanity of Spirit,* and "I walkt the other day (to spend my hour,) / Into a field"—an hour being a standard time set aside for formal meditation. *Regeneration,* for example, begins with a walk through a spring landscape which stands in sharp contrast to the sterile winter of the poet's spirit, finds its resolution in a sudden storm of wind which, as *spiritus,* is the material equivalent both of the breath of God and the spirit of man, and ends in a short colloquy which is a prayer for a spiritual dying-into-life:

> Here musing long, I heard
>   A rushing wind
> Which still increased, but whence it stirred
>   Nowhere I could not find. . . .
>
> Lord, then said I, on me one breath,
> And let me die before my death!

The two key figures of the outer and inner seasons and of the correspondent, regenerative wind later served as the radical metaphors in a number of Romantic poems, including Coleridge's *Dejection* and Shelley's *Ode to the West Wind.*[44]

Or consider the meditation on a creature which—at least in his later life—was Coleridge's favorite poem by one of his favorite lyrists, George Herbert's *The Flower.*[45] Reflecting upon the annual death and rebirth of the plant, the poet draws a complex analogy with his own soul in its cycles of depression and joy, spiritual drouth and rain, death and springlike revival, alienation from God and reconcilement; in the concluding

colloquy he also (as Coleridge and Shelley were to do) incorporates into the analogy the sterility and revival of his poetic
powers:

> And now in age I bud again,
> After so many deaths I live and write;
>   I once more smell the dew and rain,
> And relish versing. O my only light,
>   It cannot be
>   That I am he
> On whom thy tempests fell all night.[46]

Herbert is describing the state of inner torpor through alienation from God known in theology as accidie, dejection, spiritual dryness, interior desolation; this condition was often
analogized to circumstances of the seasons and weather, and
was a matter of frequent consideration in the devotional
manuals. As Saint Francis de Sales wrote, in his section "Of
Spiritual Dryness and Sterility":

> Sometimes you will find yourself so deprived and destitute of
> all devout feelings of devotion that your soul will seem to be a
> fruitless, barren desert, in which there is no . . . water of grace
> to refresh her, on account of the dryness that seems to threaten
> her with a total and absolute desolation. . . . At the same time,
> to cast her into despair, the enemy mocks her by a thousand
> suggestions of despondency and says: "Ah! poor wretch, where
> is thy God? . . . Who can ever restore to thee the joy of His
> holy grace?"[47]

Coleridge, during the several years just preceding *Dejection*,
described in his letters a recurrent state of apathy and of the
paralysis of imagination in terms which seem to echo such
discussions of spiritual dryness: "My Imagination is tired,
down, flat and powerless . . . as if the *organs* of Life had been
dried up; as if only simple BEING remained, blind and stagnant!" "I have been . . . undergoing a process of intellectual
exsiccation. . . . The Poet is dead in me."[48]

The Romantic meditations, then, though secular meditations, often turn on crises—alienation, dejection, the loss of

a "celestial light" or "glory" in experiencing the created world—
which are closely akin to the spiritual crises of the earlier
religious poets. And at times Romantic lyrics become overtly
theological in expression. Some of them include not only col-
loquies with a human auditor, real or imagined, and with
what de Sales called "insensible creatures," but also with God
or with a Spirit of Nature, in the mode of a formal prayer
(*Reflections on Having Left a Place of Retirement, Ode to the West
Wind*), or else of a terminal benediction. Thus Coleridge's
Frost at Midnight falls into the ritual language of a blessing
("Therefore all seasons shall be sweet to thee")—a tactic which
Wordsworth at once picked up in *Tintern Abbey* ("and this
prayer I make. . . . Therefore let the moon / Shine on thee
in thy solitary walk") and which Coleridge himself repeated
in *Dejection* ("Visit her, gentle Sleep! with wings of heal-
ing. . . . To her may all things live, from pole to pole").

We must not drive the parallel too hard. There is little
external evidence of the direct influence of the metaphysical
poem upon the greater Romantic lyric; the similarity between
them may well be the result of a common tradition of meditations on the creatures—a tradition which continued in the
eighteenth century in so prodigiously popular a work as James
Hervey's *Meditations and Contemplations* (1746–47).[49] And there
is a very conspicuous and significant difference between the
Romantic lyric and the seventeenth-century meditation on
created nature—a difference in the description which initiates and directs the process of mind. The "composition of
place" was not a specific locality, nor did it need to be present
to the eyes of the speaker, but was a typical scene or object,
usually called up, as Saint Ignatius and other preceptors said,
before "the eyes of the imagination,"[50] in order to set off and
guide the thought by means of correspondences whose interpretation was firmly controlled by an inherited typology. The
landscape set forth in Vaughan's *Regeneration*, for example,
is not a particular geographical location, nor even a literal
setting, but the allegorical landscape common to the genre
of spiritual pilgrimages, from the *Divine Comedy* to *Pilgrim's
Progress*. And Herbert's flower is not a specified plant,
described by the poet with his eye on the object, but a generic

one; it is simply the class of all perennials, in which God has inscribed the invariable signatures of His providential plan. In the Romantic poem, on the other hand, the speaker merely happens upon a natural scene which is present, particular, and almost always precisely located; and though Coleridge occasionally alludes to it still as "that eternal language, which thy God / Utters,"[51] the primary meanings educed from the scene are not governed by a public symbolism, but have been brought to it by the private mind which perceives it. But we know already that these attributes also had a seventeenth-century origin, in a poet who inherited the metaphysical tradition yet went on, as Dryden and many of his successors commented,[52] to alter it in such a way as to establish the typical meter, rhetoric, and formal devices of neoclassic poetry. The crucial event in the development of the most distinctive of the Romantic lyric forms occurred when John Denham climbed Cooper's Hill and undertook to describe, in balanced couplets, the landscape before his eyes, and to embellish the description with incidental reminiscence and meditation.

FIVE

Coleridge, Baudelaire, and Modernist Poetics

I HAVE BEEN ASKED to say something about Coleridge, both as a representative Romantic critic of poetry and in relation to Symbolist and Modernist theories of poetry. An intimidating assignment! Yet clearly pertinent to the topic of this Conference, and timely as well. Although on the continent Coleridge as a critic has been important mainly to scholars, in England and America he has played not only a prominent, but a double role, as both villain and hero of the major literary movements of the last half-century. By participating in post-Kantian intellectual currents Coleridge, more than any other English writer of his time, represented the central tendencies of Romantic criticism in Europe. As a consequence he has been a key target in the general assault mounted against "Romanticism" more than a generation ago: F. R. Leavis, with characteristic briskness, declared in 1940 that the continued currency of Coleridge "as an academic classic is something of a scandal."[1] Yet excerpted elements in Coleridge's criticism—his exaltation of the imagination over the "understanding" of unenlightened scientism, his concept of "the balance or reconciliation of opposite or discordant qualities," his opposition of organic to mechanical form, his

discussions of the "symbol"—have been praised and assimilated to their own doctrines by such central personages in the
modern movement as T. E. Hulme, I. A. Richards, and T. S.
Eliot, as well as by the American New Critics; to an extent
which stimulated Stanley Edgar Hyman, in a survey of recent
English and American criticism, to the startling claim that
Coleridge, next to Aristotle, was the "most important pro-
genitor" and his *Biographia Literaria* "almost the bible of modern criticism."[2] However one may wish to qualify this
pronouncement, it is at any rate evident that the major
Romantic critic in England provided concepts with which
modern critics have attacked English Romantic poetry,
including some of Coleridge's own. On the other hand Coleridge's poems of magic and mystery, especially *The Ancient
Mariner*—as distinct from the great bulk of his lyrics, which
are concerned with what Coleridge called "things of every
day"—are often excepted from the modern indictment against
Romantic vagueness and emotional indulgence, because they
exhibit narrative impersonality and clarity of image, as well
as a seeming structural inconsequence which makes them
readily eligible for analysis as Symbolist poems *avant la lettre*.

Coleridge's traditional posture in literary history, with a
foot in both the Romantic and Modernist camps, makes him
especially relevant to our consideration of the origins of
modern poetics. But more than this, my assigned topic is a
timely one, because it provides an opportunity to examine a
recent tendency to revise the standard view of this development by controverting the claims of Hulme, Pound, Eliot,
and other founding fathers of the Modernist Anglo-American movements that they were counter-Romantic writers, and
by proposing instead that the new poetry and new criticism
which developed after the First World War, whether Imagist
or post-Symbolist, was essentially a continuation, in some ways
even a culmination, of early-nineteenth-century Romantic
innovations. Edmund Wilson, whose *Axel's Castle* (1936)
marked an epoch in the historical perspective on modern
English and American literature, was equivocal on this point.
The main movement of our day, he said, is "a counterpart"
to Romanticism, "a second flood of the same tide." But he

added that "even the metaphor of a tide is misleading: what we have today is an entirely distinct movement" which "must be dealt with in different terms."[3] The revisionist history of recent years can be represented by two books. In 1957 Frank Kermode wrote *Romantic Image* to demonstrate that two basic assumptions bind most of the major twentieth-century poets and critics in English with the French Symbolists and English Aestheticists of the latter nineteenth century: that the poem is an autonomous Image, insulated from social and human concerns, and that this poem is engendered by a poet who is necessarily and agonizingly estranged from his age. But the Image of the Moderns, Kermode maintains, together with "the Symbol of the French," is simply "the Romantic Image writ large"; and the entire aesthetic of the sufficient image and the poet-apart originated in Romantic poets and theorists, including in England Blake, Wordsworth, and Keats, as well as Coleridge.[4] And Richard Foster's *The New Romantics* (1962) proposes the thesis that the New Criticism, from Richards and Eliot through the reigning American group, whatever the overt claims to be anti-Romantic in the "principles of art and life," has in fact harbored a version of Romantic "aesthetics, epistemology, and metaphysics," and that "it is this romanticism of viewpoint or sensibility which most truly constitutes . . . the 'real' identity of the New Criticism as a literary movement."[5]

There are certainly some assumptions, ideas, and poetic practices which are shared by Romantic writers in England and innovative poets and critics of the last half-century. Nevertheless, attempts to assimilate Symbolist and Modernist literary tendencies to Romantic theory and practice in essentials rather than details are, I believe, mistaken; and I am the more concerned to put forward some important distinctions between these movements because in a book that I wrote more than a decade ago, I undertook to show that Romantic innovations included "many of the points of view and procedures which make the characteristic differences between traditional criticism and the criticism of our own time, including some criticism which professes to be anti-romantic."[6] Such an assertion, while not invalid, seems to me to need qualification if it is not to be misleading, and I should like in this paper to outline the kind of qualification I have in mind.

"What gives Romantic poetry as a whole its strong, deep and steady movement," Graham Hough has remarked, is that it participated in "a more inclusive movement in thought, politics and society," and that "the most living questions of the age were actually worked out in poetry."[7] In order to understand not only certain characteristic ideas in early Romantic writers in Germany and England, but also one important cause of later reactions against these writers, as well as some characteristic ideas which these reactions manifested, we must remember that Romantic poetics and poetry were not an isolated development. They were an integral part of radical changes in metaphysics, theology, morals, politics. And in their origins and early development, they were revolutionary, in the literal sense that these radical changes in inherited schemes of thought and values accompanied, and were in important ways stimulated and shaped by, the profound expectations and feelings aroused by the great and obsessive event of the age, the French Revolution, in its promise, its event, and its aftermath.

Their involvement with the liberal concepts and revolutionary events of their day was plainly evident to many participants in the movements of thought and literature in the 1790s and later. Fichte declared that the first presentiments of his *Wissenschaftslehre,* written in 1794–95, "surged up in me" while "I was writing a work on the Revolution," and that his system was the metaphysical equivalent of the French achievement of "tearing man loose from his chains."[8] At the Seminary in Tübingen, Schelling and Hegel, together with the poet Hölderlin, developed their early ideas under the same revolutionary impetus and enthusiasm. In England, Shelley, Hazlitt, Francis Jeffrey, and other commentators, radical and conservative alike, attributed the new literature to what they called "the Spirit of the Age," and explained that spirit as the consequence and literary counterpart to the ideas and events of the French Revolution—that "great moral tempest," as the Tory De Quincey wrote in retrospect (1839), which had an effect so nearly "miraculous" that "in Germany or England alike, the poetry was . . . entirely regenerated, thrown into moulds of thought and feeling" that were completely "new."[9] That this estimate, if exaggerated, is grounded on the historical facts is demonstrated by the life and early poetry of Hölderlin, Blake, Wordsworth, Coleridge, Southey, and Shelley; the belated Romantic movement in France was also related to liberal and revolutionary ideas and events, afterwaves of the first French Revolution. And when these poets lost their faith in the Utopian possibilities of radical social change, though a few recoiled into reaction, most of them did not simply turn against their earlier values and aims, but instead attempted so to reconstitute their views as to substitute a spiritual and imaginative base for hopes earlier grounded on radical political action.[10]

To a striking degree the various forms of Modernist poetics were formulated with persistent reference to Romantic precedents, so that these movements are patently post-Romantic. But when we judge them not by the retention of isolated elements and ideas, but by the premises and general directions of their thinking, we see that the various founders of Modernism who thought of themselves as anti-Romantic were not mistaken. Against Romantic views of poetry which, in their provenience, had been part of an inclusive political and intellectual radicalism, later critics opposed theories in which the aesthetic elements typically involved a philosophical world-view, and in many cases a political and theological stance as well; and these, in their totality, were antithetic to the basic prepossessions of the major Romantic writers about man, his world, his primary values, his hopes, and his aims in all lines of endeavor, including literature.

In this paper I have no intention of defining a Modernist poetic, but shall merely put forward a number of basic concepts which turn up repeatedly and prominently in many of the most influential theorists and poets of the last hundred years. To provide a focus for the discussion, I shall set beside Coleridge a French critic and poet, Charles Baudelaire. For the main development of these persistent modern ideas did not occur in England; it began in the ante-bellum American South, with Edgar Allan Poe, and was elaborated in France, in the mid-nineteenth century and later, by Baudelaire and his Symbolist and post-Symbolist successors. (T. S. Eliot spoke for many writers of his generation when he remarked that "the kind of poetry that I needed, to teach me the use of my own voice, did not exist in English at all; it was only to be found in French.")[11] There is no evidence that Baudelaire knew Coleridge's criticism except at second hand, through Poe, in whom Coleridge's ideas had already been drastically transformed. But as Coleridge, in his philosophical grasp and range, best represents central tendencies in Romantic thought and criticism, so Baudelaire—of whom T S. Eliot said that, despite "a good deal of romantic detritus," he was "the first counter-romantic in poetry," "far in advance of the point of view of his own time"[12]—has to an astonishing degree been the fountainhead of the most prominent ideas and view-points in post-Romantic criticism. To Rimbaud, Verlaine, Mallarmé, and Valéry, Baudelaire was an acknowledged master; members of the Decadent and Aesthetic groups developed elements from his writings into their own special-ized programs; and he continued to be both hero and exem-plar, no less outside of France than within it, to major writers in the Modernist modes, from 1910 to the recent past.[13]

I. THE ANALOGICAL UNIVERSE AND THE POETIC IMAGE

Beginning with his writings of the 1850s, when he had assim-ilated Poe's doctrines to his reading in Swedenborg and var-ious Illuminist writers, Baudelaire posited two worlds, one "naturel," "terrestre," and the other "surnaturel," "extrater-restre." The two are sharply differentiated, yet related by a "correspondence," or "universal symbolism," "une analogie réciproque, depuis le jour où Dieu a proféré le monde comme une complexe et indivisible totalité."[14] The artist operates in three modalities of analogy. There is an intercorrespon-dence among the senses in which "les parfums, les couleurs et les sons se répondent," and there is also an analogy between mind and the outer world, in which you can "contemplate yourself, to speak as the mystics do, in your own correspondence." Baudelaire most emphasizes, however, the third plane of analogy, that between the sensible and spiritual world, where "tout, forme, mouvement, nombre, couleur, parfum, dans le *spirituel* comme dans le *naturel,* est significatif, réciproque, converse, *correspondant.*"[15] Hence poetry, in rendering the hieroglyphs of this world, is that "qui n'est complètement vrai que dans un autre monde."[16] The artist, accordingly, does not "copy nature," as the "realist"—or rather, Baudelaire adds, "better to characterize his error, the 'positivist' "—would have it; instead, by the power of his imagination, "queen of the faculties," he repeats the act which produced the original world of correspondences, by decomposing the world in order to create it anew:

> [L'imagination] a créé, au commencement du monde, l'analogie et la métaphore. Elle décompose toute la création, et, avec les matériaux amassés et disposés suivant des règles dont on ne peut trouver l'origine que dans le plus profond de l'âme, elle crée un monde nouveau, elle produit la sensation du neuf.[17]

The poet is for us "un traducteur, un déchiffreur," because by his native clairvoyance he is able to detect the symbols and to render them in his images—"ces comparaisons, ces métaphores et ces épithètes [qui] sont puisées dans l'inépuisable fonds de *l'universelle analogie,* et . . . ne peuvent être puisées ailleurs."[18]

These and similar passages in Baudelaire were a frequent point of departure for the later theorists of Symbolism; and one cannot read them without being reminded of Coleridge's exposition of the role of the creative imagination. Indeed Baudelaire's description of the creative power of imagination is based on Coleridge, by way of a distant echo of Coleridge's distinction between fancy and imagination, together with his parallel between the divine and the poetic creativity, which Baudelaire himself quotes from Mrs. Catherine Crowe's *mélange* of spiritualist phenomena called *The Night Side of Nature, or Ghosts and Ghost Seers* (1848).[19] Moreover Coleridge, like Baudelaire, was fascinated by hermetic literature, and much concerned to define the nature of the symbol (though primarily in order to define the symbolic character, not of secular poetry, but of Scriptural narrative). Indeed the metaphysics underlying Coleridge's theory of the poetic imagination, based in large part on Schelling and other post-Kantian philosophers, is itself an elaborate doctrine of correspondences between levels of being. These similarities, however, overlie differences which sharply set off the poetic theory of Coleridge from that of Baudelaire and the Symbolists who succeeded him.

We can begin with Coleridge's essay "On Poesy or Art," in which he undertakes, like Baudelaire, to distinguish between the behest to copy nature and the procedure of the true artist:

> If the artist copies the mere nature, the *natura naturata,* what idle rivalry! . . . Believe me, you must master the essence, the *natura naturans,* which presupposes a bond between nature in the higher sense and the soul of man. . . . The artist must imitate that which is within the thing, that which is active through form and figure, and discourses to us by symbols—the *Naturgeist,* or spirit of nature. . . . The idea which puts the form together cannot itself be the form.[20]

Coleridge is not claiming here that the artist reproduces spiritual forms which he discerns behind the symbolic surface of nature. In context these passages turn out, instead, to be a way of saying that a genuine work of art does not reproduce fixed objects or forms, whether in nature or beyond it, but is the result of an evolving *process* of imagination which accords with the generative process going on within vital nature itself.[21] "Painful copying" produces "masks only, not forms breathing life"; the difference is "between form as proceeding, and shape as superinduced." Since the artist's "own spirit . . . has the same ground with nature," he can refer to that spirit to acquire, not "cold notions—lifeless technical rules—but living and life-producing ideas," which "contain their own evidence, the certainty that they are essentially one with the germinal causes in nature." "For of all we see, hear, feel and touch" we can be sure "that the life which is in us is in them likewise."[22]

We find in this essay the cardinal principle of all Coleridge's mature writings, one which he shares with most of the Romantic philosophers and critics in Germany after Herder. His great premise and paradigm, the invariable point of departure in his reasonings about both truth and value, is Life. From the attributes of living things he derives the categories for what is valid and excellent in all areas of human intellection and productivity, whether metaphysical, moral, political, or aesthetic. And for this way of thinking the prime character of a living thing is that it grows, by a self-starting process which assimilates diverse materials and organizes them by an inherent lawfulness into an organic whole: "It shapes," as Coleridge says, "as it develops itself from within, and the fullness of its development is one and the same with the perfection of its outward form. Such is the life, such the form."[23] The mode of this growth Coleridge translates, in philosophical terms, into the polar dialectic of successive and progressive antithesis and synthesis, opposition and reconciliation; as he says, "To the idea of life victory or strife is necessary. . . . So it is in beauty."[24]

In Coleridge's theory of poetry, accordingly, as he expounds it in his *Biographia Literaria,* the correspondence between planes of being is not, as it is in Baudelaire, a correspondence between component parts, whether sensations, objects, or forms, but a correspondent process of living, evolving growth and creativity, exhibited in an ascending order in nature, in man, and in Divinity. Thus "the primary Imagination" of man, "the living Power and prime Agent of all human Perception," parallels the living, creative principle in nature; the "secondary Imagination," which effects poetry, is "an echo" of the primary imagination, since "it dissolves, diffuses, dissipates, in order to recreate"; and both of these in turn can be said to correspond to the continuous generation of the universe in God—"a repetition in the finite mind of the eternal act of creation in the infinite I AM."[25] And in evolving the organic unity of a poem, that "synthetic and magical power," the secondary imagination, operates by the dialectic process which governs all growth; namely, by "the balance or reconciliation of opposite or discordant qualities: of sameness, with difference; of the general, with the concrete; the idea, with the image."[26]

I have dwelt on this matter because it is a key to a prime difference between Coleridge's view and a widely prevalent post-Romantic view of the elements and structure of a poem. What the Symbolists and post-Symbolists (however diverse among themselves) had in common with Anglo-American Imagists (who were themselves strongly indebted to Symbolist theories)[27] was the concept that the primary component of a poem is the image, which is "distinguished," as A. G. Lehmann has said, "by some special efficacy" from the elements of ordinary discourse.[28] For Symbolists this efficacy derives from the revelation by the image of an Idea or Essence; and whether this Idea subsists in its own superterrestrial realm, or in the mind and affects of the poet, or glows at the heart of the image itself, or is simply evoked by the incantation of a word, or (in Yeats's version) floats up from the racial memory, it is fixed, discrete, and (it is usually claimed) eternal. To Imagists, as Pound said, "the proper and perfect symbol is the natural object,"[29] so that the poetic image is not translucent, but opaque, owing its efficacy to a concreteness beyond abstract discursive language that enables it, as T. E. Hulme said, to "hand over sensations bodily," "to convey a physical thing";[30] but like the Symbol, the image is a static, isolated poetic entity.

"Glorifier le culte des images (ma grande, mon unique, ma primitive passion)," Baudelaire wrote in *Mon cœur mis à nu*.[31] The cult of the unitary image or symbol has been a prime legacy of Modernist poetics. In *The Poetic Image* (1948) C. Day Lewis, in stating his own views, neatly epitomizes the pervasive assumption: "The image is the constant in all poetry, and every poem is itself an image"; it is "an image composed from a multiplicity of images."[32] Such a premise has opened the way to a total revision in inherited concepts of the order and structure of poetry. Traditionally, the structure of a poem had been grounded on such matters as the representation of men whose interactions, in their complication and dénouement, constitute a plot; or on the marshalling of ideas to form a coherent and persuasive argument; or on the presentation of a meditation moving toward resolution. According to the new poetic, the poem is constructed of elemental images or symbols, or of the words evoking these elements. In the line of aesthetics inaugurated by Rimbaud, these images derive from a distortion of nature by means of "a systematic derangement of all the senses," and are put together by an irrational process of free fantasy. In the alternate and more influential view propounded by Mallarmé, the aim is to allow the structure to be entirely determined by inherent forces in the component elements themselves: the poet

> cède l'initiative aux mots, par le heurt de leur inégalité mobilisés. . . . Une ordonnance du livre de vers poind innée ou partout, élimine le hasard . . . ni le sublime incohérent de la mise en page romantique ni cette unité artificielle, jadis, mesurée en bloc au livre. Tout devient suspens, disposition fragmentaire avec alternance et vis-à-vis. . . . [33]

It has become a commonplace of modern criticism that the poem is a structure of dynamic images, ordered by such inherent principles as dissonance and harmony, disparity and conciliation, or irony, tension, paradox, or else by thematic and counter-thematic relevance. The sharp departure from traditional forms, in poems written in consonance with such theories, is patent, from the lyrics of Rimbaud and Mallarmé to *The Waste Land* of Eliot, *The Bridge* of Hart Crane, and the *Cantos* of Ezra Pound. By a number of New Critics, this modern principle of structure has been extended back to account for all good poetry, no matter when it was written. Shakespeare, for example, is made out to be essentially a Symbolist poet; so that in many modern explications of his plays, we find Macbeth, Lear, and Othello elbowed off the stage by images and symbols, protagonists in a drama which is a "symbolic action," or else (in an amalgam of Symbolist and Coleridgean theory) an "inherent dialectic," in which the initial oppositions between the component elements compel them toward an ultimate reconciliation.

For Coleridge, as we saw, the imaginative Idea was not a component image but a seed, or seminal principle—"living and life-producing ideas," he called them, "essentially one with the germinal causes in nature"—which controls the process of poetic development, and reveals itself only in the achieved fullness of that development. What Coleridge and like-minded contemporaries contributed to traditional poetics was the view of poetic structure as essentially process: an evolving organization, of which the key attributes are genesis and growth, and all parts lose their separate identities in an organic whole; as Coleridge said of Shakespeare's plays, "All is growth, evolution, *genesis*—each line, each word almost, begets the following."[34] To Coleridge a structure achieved by a combination of distinguishable images or symbols, in whatever relations of opposition and conciliation, would have been an instance, not of the imagination, but of the fancy, which he defined as having "no other counters to play with, but fixities and definites." And the difference between collocation and growth was to Coleridge—in the basic terms to which his philosophy invariably recurs—ultimately a matter of life and death. The imagination "is essentially *vital,* even as all objects (*as* objects) are essentially fixed and dead."[35] The mechanic system

> demanding for every mode and act of existence real or possible visibility . . . knows only of distance and nearness, composition . . . and decomposition, in short, the relations of unproductive particles to each other. . . . This is the philosophy of Death, and only of a dead nature can it hold good. In Life, and in the view of a vital philosophy, the two component counter-powers actually interpenetrate each other; and generate a higher third.[36]

II. ORIGINAL SIN AND FALLEN NATURE

"De Maistre et Edgar Poe," Baudelaire confided to his notebook, "m'ont appris à raisonner."[37] We can say, with an equivalent simplification, that Poe clarified for Baudelaire his incipient scheme of art in its relation to life, and that Joseph de Maistre provided that scheme with its principle and sanction—a theological sanction. In the middle and later 1840s, at the very time of his own brief overture at an artistic *rapprochement* with the *bourgeoisie* and short-lived attempt to combine Romanticism, progressivism, and revolutionary enthusiasm, Baudelaire found in Poe, with an extraordinary sense that he was reading in him his own secret heart and mind, a distinctive conjunction of ideas entirely opposed to these. For Poe posited the existence of two worlds, terrestrial and supernal, and attributed to poetry the struggle "to grasp *now*, wholly, here on earth . . . those divine and rapturous joys" which appertain only to the realm of "supernal Loveliness" and "eternity";[38] he expressed contempt for the theory and products of the American revolution—democracy, equality, social reform, progress—and proposed in their place a social order and aristocratic hierarchy in accordance with "the laws of *gradation* so visibly pervading all things in Earth and Heaven";[39] and he emphasized the night side of human nature with its "radical, primitive, irreducible sentiment" which he called "perverseness," the "unfathomable longing of the soul to *vex itself*," "the overwhelming tendency to do wrong for the wrong's sake."[40] Baudelaire found in de Maistre ("le grand génie de notre temps,—*un voyant!*" he called him)[41] a simple principle to reconcile and justify all these views: "le péché original," as de Maistre said, "qui explique tout et sans lequel on n'explique rien."[42] In his "Notes nouvelles sur Edgar Poe" (1857), Baudelaire brought together all these elements. "More important than anything else" in "a century infatuated with itself," Poe in his idea of perversity has affirmed "the natural wickedness of man" against all the humbugs who say "all of us are born good," when we are in fact "all born marked for evil!" Poe as a true poet "uttered the ardent sighs of *the fallen angel who remembers heaven;* he lamented the golden age and the lost Eden." And the admirable pages of Poe's anti-rational, anti-scientific, and anti-democratic fantasy, "The Colloquy of Monos and Una," "eussent charmé et troublé l'impeccable De Maistre."[43]

After this period Baudelaire's treatment of both man and his universe assumed the simplicity of an all-comprehensive dualism. His basic critical opposition between the "natural" and "supernatural" worlds is also a theological opposition between a fallen and an unfallen realm of being, for by primal inheritance not only man, but external nature as well, is radically corrupt: "La *nature* entière participe du péché originel."[44] The consequences Baudelaire draws from this premise are no less aesthetic than moral; in itself "la nature est laide," trivial, terrifying, shocking, "marécages de sang . . . abîmes de boue," producing only monsters and crime.[45] In it remain no more than vestiges and distorted reflections of the uncorrupted world, and it is only because he possesses the imaginative faculty that the artist is able "de saisir les parcelles du beau égarées sur la terre, de suivre le beau à la piste partout où il a pu se glisser à travers les trivialités de la nature déchue."[46]

If in these views, as it has become the fashion to say, Baudelaire is eminently a Christian moralist, his is an extraordinarily truncated Christianity. The kinds of things it leaves out are indicated by the full range of the doctrines of Saint Paul, who, if he founded the doctrine of original sin— "Wherefore, as by one man sin entered into the world, and death by sin; and so death passed upon all men, for that all have sinned" (Romans 5:12)—did so to emphasize the fact and magnitude of salvation—"much more the grace of God, and the gift by grace, which is by one man" (Romans 5:15)— and also proclaimed that "now abideth faith, hope, love, these three, but the greatest of these is love" (I Corinthians 13:13).

Christian millennialism and the cardinal virtues of faith, hope, and above all love, translated into non-theological equivalents, were the ultimate roots of the secular optimism and the belief in the fraternity of equal men which were at the heart both of the political theory of the French Revolution and of the humanism of revolutionary Romanticism. No doubt the extraordinary appeal to Baudelaire of the stark doctrine of inherited corruption, unqualified by the idea of love or redemption, inhered in part in his own inner division ("Il y a dans tout homme, à toute heure, deux postulations simultanées, l'une vers Dieu, l'autre vers Satan"), and in his love-hate ambivalence toward life ("Tout enfant, j'ai senti dans mon cœur deux sentiments contradictoires, l'horreur de la vie et l'extase de la vie").[47] But its appeal lay also in the fact that de Maistre had demonstrated the sweeping utility of the dogma of original sin as a political instrument, enabling him to attack the optimistic assumptions about the potentialities of political man of Rousseau and the theorists of the French Revolution, and to claim instead the indispensability of hereditary monarchy, papal supremacy, a strictly hierarchical social order, and an authoritarian government.

On the theological premise of fallen man and a fallen nature Baudelaire, combining the views of Poe and de Maistre, based the principles both of his counter-Revolutionary and anti-democratic politics and of his innovative poetics. And ever since Baudelaire there has been in Anglo-American, as well as French and German, letters the sporadic but persistent recurrence of a combination of dogmatic theological orthodoxy, political and social conservatism, and (through the continuing association of Romanticism with libertarian and egalitarian ideas) an anti-Romantic poetic, usually called "classical," but often used to justify an avant-garde art—all presented as mutually implicative positions. Thus in the 1890s, Charles Maurras, citing among his predecessors Joseph de Maistre and Poe,[48] conjoined the advocacy of absolutism in government and of an orthodox religious establishment to supply and enforce order, together with a total opposition to Rousseauism in thought, to the results of the French Revolution in society and politics, and to the associated movement of Romanticism—to which he also added Symbolism—in poetry. T. E. Hulme, identifying as his models "Maurras, Lassere and ... *L'Action Française*," charged that "it was romanticism that made the revolution" of 1789, that "romanticism both in England and France" continues to be "associated with certain political views," and that "the root of all romanticism" was the teaching of Rousseau "that man was by nature good." Hulme proposed instead "the sane classical dogma of original sin" as the sole possible base for order, tradition, limitation, impersonality, and control—the common elements in an authoritarian politics, a dogmatic religion, and a "classical" (which was in his case an Imagist) poetic.[49] The ideas of Ezra Pound paralleled those of his friend T. E. Hulme in politics and poetics, though not in religion. T. S. Eliot admired Poe and Baudelaire, praised and defended the views of Maurras, and joined some of those views with a number of poetic concepts derived from French writers in the Symbolist tradition. Eliot also supported the doctrines of Hulme—of whose ideas about original sin and discipline, ethical and political, he remarked, "Baudelaire would have approved";[50] propagated the opposition of tradition and a dogmatic theology against heterodoxy as a "more fundamental" equivalent for the standard opposition of classicism against Romanticism;[51] attributed much of the blame for the weakness of modern society, "worm-eaten with Liberalism," and of modern literature as well, to the "disappearance of the idea of *Original Sin*";[52] and in the famous phrase which is an echo of Maurras, identified his triple position as "classicist in literature, royalist in politics, and Anglo-Catholic in religion." With Allen Tate, a Southern Agrarian and one of the earliest exemplars of the American New Criticism, who drew upon both Hulme and Eliot, the line of development from Edgar Allan Poe returns to the place of its origin. In Tate the correlated positions, though qualified, recognizably recur: the deprecation of liberalism, progressivism, and the Romantic literary example; the return, in a search for authority and hierarchy, to a traditional social order and a revived religious orthodoxy; and the support, in the name of tradition, of the experimental new poetry and the post-Symbolist aesthetic of the autonomous, "autotelic" poem.

A few words about Coleridge in this connection. T. E. Hulme defined Romantics "as all who do not believe in the Fall of Man,"[53] but this definition does not apply to Coleridge. As early as March 1798 he wrote a letter to his brother George in which, recanting his earlier advocacy of the French revolutionaries, he also affirmed by way of corollary that "I believe most stedfastly in original Sin . . . that our organization is depraved, & our volitions imperfect."[54] A later statement is sufficiently sweeping to have charmed even the impeccable de Maistre:

> A fall of some sort or other . . . is the fundamental postulate of the moral history of man. Without this hypothesis, man is unintelligible; with it, every phenomenon is explicable.[55]

But Coleridge's differences from the de Maistre-Baudelaire-Maurras tradition are fundamental. He grounded his indictment of the course of the French Revolution not on man's innate corruption, nor on denial of the possibility and desirability of political and social progress, but on his basic philosophical antithesis between the mechanical attempt forcefully to impose a ready-made political scheme and the organic growth of living political institutions: valid meliorism in a state, Coleridge held, must work toward the better realization of its innate, evolving "Idea." And Coleridge repudiated the view that original sin is "Hereditary Sin—guilt inherited" as no other than a "monstrous fiction," proposing instead the interpretation that sin re-originates, inevitably, in the free will of each individual; this is not even, he says, an exclusively Christian tenet, but a "fact acknowledged in all ages, and recognized . . . in the Christian Scriptures."[56] And since the fall of man is thus a recurrent moral act, it cannot for Coleridge, as it does for Baudelaire, involve the primal fall of "la nature entière." Indeed Coleridge, like Schiller, Schelling, Hölderlin, and other German Romantic thinkers, tends to interpret the theological doctrine of the fall, in metaphysical terms, as a falling away, a fragmentation, of man from his primal unity with uncorrupted nature; and consonantly to think of "Redemption," as he wrote to Wordsworth, as a reintegration, a "Reconciliation from this Enmity with Nature."[57] When Coleridge looks upon the natural scene in a meditative mood, he finds in it, not ugly and monstrous reminders "du péché originel," but precisely the opposite: a surviving instance, in natural, living beauty, of man's simple and primal unity with himself and with nature before the fall, and a reminder of what man must strive deliberately to regain, but on the higher level of a complex and conscious reconciliation of the divided and conflicting elements:

> In the flowery meadow, on which my eye is now reposing . . . there is . . . no one character of guilt or anguish. For never can I look and meditate on the vegetable creation without a feeling similar to that with which we gaze at a beautiful infant. . . . It seems as if the soul said to herself: from this state hast *thou* fallen! Such shouldst thou still become. . . . But what the plant *is*, by an act not its own and unconsciously—*that* must thou *make* thyself to *become*.[58]

Coleridge's theological view of nature as unfallen, and of man as fallen away from a nature with which he must strive to be reconciled, has aesthetic consequences which are entirely opposed to those which follow from Baudelaire's view that nature is fallen, hence, until modified by art, no less ugly than it is evil. Thus, in his essay "On Poesy or Art," Coleridge describes nature as "to a religious observer the art of God," and posits as both the identifying attribute and chief value of art that it is "the mediatress between, and reconciler of, nature and man," "the union and reconciliation of that which is nature with that which is exclusively human."[59]

III. NATURE AND ART

It is already apparent that the conflict between Romantic and anti-Romantic theories of art was fought out in part on the traditional aesthetic battleground of "nature" as against "art," in the root sense in which nature signifies that within man which is spontaneous, emotional, instinctual, plus whatever external to man exists without human intervention; while art signifies that within man which is studied, deliberate, the turning of known means to foreseen ends, and whatever in the external world has been introduced or changed by human contrivance. In his early critical writings Wordsworth, like the eighteenth-century primitivists, tended to declare entirely for nature and "the spontaneous overflow of powerful feelings," as against art. Coleridge, however, while confirming the superior status of "nature," employed his ruling organic principle of the reconciliation of opposites to propose as norm a synthesis in which the element of conscious art is incorporated into a higher-order parallel to simple natural process: the imagination, as he says, "while it blends and harmonizes the natural and the artificial, still subordinates art to nature."[60] To Coleridge, as to many German theorists, great poems were thus indeed natural, but only in a sense which involves the contrary attributes of craft and artistic cunning, in "a union, an interpenetration . . . of *spontaneous* impulse and of *voluntary* purpose."[61] So Shakespeare "first studied patiently, meditated deeply, understood minutely, till knowledge [became] habitual and intuitive," and his process of composition became that of "a nature humanized, a genial understanding directing self-consciously a power and an implicit wisdom deeper than consciousness."[62]

In the theory of Baudelaire's maturity the term "nature," when used as an aesthetic norm in opposition to "art," no less than when it denominates this world in opposition to the supernatural world, usually connotes a theological, fallen nature. "La plupart des erreurs relatives au beau," he says,

> naissent de la fausse conception du dix-huitième siècle relative à la morale. La nature fut prise dans ce temps-là comme base, source et type de tout bien et de tout beau possibles. La négation du péché originel ne fut pas pour peu de chose dans l'aveuglement général de cette époque. . . . La nature ne peut conseiller que le crime. . . . [Dans] toutes les actions et les désirs du pur homme naturel, vous ne trouverez rien que d'affreux.[63]

In the later writings of Baudelaire, therefore, the beautiful and the good tend to be identified with art and the artificial; while the artificial, as the antithesis of the corrupt "natural," tends to fall into synonymity with the uncorrupted "supernatural."

> Tout ce qui est beau et noble est le résultat de la raison et du calcul. Le crime . . . est originellement naturel. La vertu, au

contraire, est *artificielle,* surnaturelle. . . . Le mal se fait sans effort, *naturellement,* par fatalité; le bien est toujours le produit d'un art. Tout ce que je dis de la nature comme mauvaise conseillère en matière de morale, et de la raison comme véritable rédemptrice et réformatrice, peut être transporté dans l'ordre du beau.[64]

Baudelaire thus responded to the Romantic ideal of an art reconciled with, but subordinate to, nature by the precisely opposite demand, on grounds that are at the same time religious, moral, and aesthetic, and in all the inherited senses in which art is the non-natural. In describing the process of poetic composition, Baudelaire derides what he says is the Romantic laudation of spontaneity, inspiration, and the expression of personal feelings, and makes poetry almost exclusively a matter of impersonal calculation and craft. He expresses contempt for the modern school of realistic landscape painting: "Dans ce culte niais de la nature, non épurée, non expliquée par l'imagination, je vois un signe d'abaissement général."[65] He recoils from the abundance, fecundity, and exuberance of living, vegetative nature. "Je suis incapable," says his letter of 1855 to Desnoyers, "de m'attendrir sur les végétaux. . . . Je ne croirai jamais que *l'âme des Dieux habite dans les plantes . . .* légumes sanctifiés. J'ai même toujours pensé qu'il y avait dans *la nature* florissante et rajeunie quelque chose d'affligeant, de dur, de cruel."[66] His taste is for "la majesté superlative des formes artificielles," and his dream is not mankind's immemorial dream of a natural, flourishing Eden-garden, but of "un vrai pays de Cocagne . . . supérieur aux autres, comme l'Art l'est à la Nature, où celle-ci est réformée par le rêve, où elle est corrigée, embellie, refondue."[67] This *paradis artificiel* is sometimes envisioned as a tropical or oriental setting, too exotic to seem "natural" to the European sensibility; more commonly, it is an urban dream—of a Lisbon of which "on dit qu'elle est bâtie en marbre, et que le peuple y a une telle haine du végétal, qu'il arroche tous les arbres . . . un paysage fait avec la lumière et le minéral, et le liquide pour les réfléchir";[68] or else of a Paris which has been denaturalized and devivified, "le végétal irrégulier" banished for the inorganic regularity of metal, stone, and imprisoned water: "L'enivrante monotonie / Du metal, du marbre et de l'eau."[69] Baudelaire shares the delight he ascribes to his friend Constantin Guys in civilized ceremony and in ritual behavior according to a strict code, *"la pompe de la vie,* telle qu'elle s'offre dans les capitales du monde civilisé, la pompe de la vie militaire, de la vie élégante, de la vie galante,"[70] which reaches its apogee in the pure ritualism of the dandy. And in the brilliant paradoxes of *Le Peintre de la vie moderne,* Baudelaire carries his systematic preference of art over nature to a laudation of cosmetics, of rouge and kohl, over the natural features and the living hue, as "une déformation sublime de la nature" which instances man's noble struggles for a "réformation de la nature" and of "tout ce que la vie naturelle y accumule de grossier, de terrestre et d'immonde."[71]

Baudelaire's anti-naturalism, in all its diverse aspects, has remained a persistent strain in post-Romantic aesthetics, which has tended—in fastidiousness, or luxuriousness, or horror, or perversity, or in a combination of these motives—to set both the artist and his art in opposition to instinctual and organic nature and the conditions of ordinary life. In the extreme form it took in the Decadent movement the aesthete, epitomized in Huysmans' Des Esseintes, isolated himself from life in order to live *à rebours,* systematically deranging his senses and flouting nature by every available device of artifice and perversity. Most Symbolists and post-Symbolists have, in various more moderate ways, proposed an art of anti-nature, in which the poet deliberately employs his craft to shape a superior alternative to this natural existence. Baudelaire's visions of the city of Lisbon or of Paris, in which all organic life is replaced by metal, marble, and geometric artifice, are echoed in the modern preoccupation with the city of Byzantium, persisting through Hulme, Pound, and Yeats. This city is viewed as the point in cultural history in which intellect and artifice triumphed over nature and organic life, and it is held to have fostered an art, as T. E. Hulme said, in which "there is nothing vital," which arises from "disgust with the trivial and accidental characteristics of living shapes" and seeks "a *perfection* and rigidity which vital things can never have,"

in anti-humanistic, life-alien, abstract and "geometric" forms.[72]
So, in order to escape "out of nature" and its "sensual music"
of generation, birth, and decay, Yeats represents himself as
an old man sailing (though very reluctantly) to Byzantium in
order to assume the "artifice of eternity"; it is a city of gold
and marble in which an artificial bird scorns aloud

> All that man is . . .
> The fury and the mire of human veins.[73]

Yeats's description in *Byzantium* of the flames burning away
the fleshly life,

> Dying into a dance,
> An agony of trance,

introduces an equally current modern emblem, the dance, a
subject on which Frank Kermode has written illuminatingly
in *Romantic Image*. Its unanalyzable fusion of dancer and dance
and its fluid fixity of ever altering but always perfect self-
containment made it a favored instance of life translated into
artifice, in which vital process is simulated, but perfected, by
turning control over to abstract, non-vital laws of rhythm and
form. The favorite dancer is Salome—a preoccupation of
Mallarmé, Flaubert, Yeats, no less than of the Decadents,
Moreau, Huysmans, and Wilde—the dancer who, feminine
but sterile, erotic yet passionless, with a beauty of feature
utterly masklike, weaves her remote and self-absorbed ara-
besque in a ritual dance of death.

The passage in which Coleridge represents a very similar
fusion of matter and form and of ceaseless motion in total
rest, is a description, not of an artificial simulacrum of life,
but of a natural thing exhibiting the essential processes of life
itself. Coleridge's instance is a growing plant, which is self-
evolving and self-contained, yet only by virtue of a ceaseless
reciprocation with an environment from which it takes in order
to give:

> Lo!—with the rising sun it commences its outward life and enters
> into open communion with all the elements, at once assimilat-

ing them to itself and to each other. At the same moment it strikes its roots and unfolds its leaves, absorbs and respires . . . and breathes a repairing spirit . . . into the atmosphere that feeds *it*. . . . Lo! . . . how it . . . effectuates its own secret growth. . . . Lo!—how upholding the ceaseless plastic motion of the parts in the profoundest rest of the whole it becomes the visible organismus of the whole *silent* or *elementary* life of nature.[74]

IV. "LA POÉSIE PURE" AND THE ABSOLUTE POEM

When Arthur Symons, in his influential exposition for English readers of *The Symbolist Movement in Literature* (1899), said of the new literature that "in speaking to us so intimately, so solemnly, as only religion had hitherto spoken to us, it becomes itself a kind of religion, with all the duties and responsibilities of the sacred ritual," he pointed to an obvious aspect of Symbolism, and one which has profoundly affected aesthetic theory. The Romantic writers of the 1790s and later had already begun the process of translating theological into aesthetic ideas. Hölderlin, Blake, Wordsworth, Shelley, Hugo, for example, reviving the ancient notion of the poet as *vates*, seriously represented themselves as inspired priests, in the great line of succession from the biblical poet-prophets through Dante and (for the English poets) Milton. So Wordsworth opened *The Prelude* by describing how, inspired by "the sweet breath of Heaven," he assumed the prophet's sacred mission:

> To the open fields I told
> A prophesy; poetic numbers came
> Spontaneously, and clothed in priestly robe
> My spirit, thus singled out, as it might seem,
> For holy services. . . .

In the writings of various French Symbolists, the infiltration of aesthetics by theology (though often a theology seen through Hermetic or Illuminist concepts) was carried to the point of constituting a fully formed religion of art. The resulting theories differed radically, however, from those of their Romantic predecessors, not only in the degree to which they assimilated religious ideas, but in their essential aesthetic perspective—the view they took of the nature of the work of art and its relation to the artist, the audience, and the world without.

The major Romantic poets had thought of themselves as poet-prophets because they felt they had been granted an illumination which desperately needed to be conveyed to mankind in a time of revolution and reaction, social disintegration, and a civilization in crisis. As Wordsworth had begun *The Prelude* by acknowledging his election to "holy services," so he closed it by calling on his fellow poet, Coleridge, in an age threatening to "fall back to old idolatry," "servitude," "to ignominy and shame," to carry on with him as

> joint labourers in the work . . .
> Of [men's] redemption, surely yet to come.
> Prophets of Nature, we to them will speak
> A lasting inspiration . . . teach them . . .
> Instruct them. . . . [75]

We can indicate the altered perspective of the post-Romantic religion of art by saying that the focus shifted from the poet, regarded in one of his functions as expressing a revelation to his fellow men, to the poem, regarded as existing in self-sufficiency as an end in itself. In the full development of this theological aesthetic, the poem, "l'œuvre pure," was envisioned as a sacred object, the embodied Idea, or Essence, or Absolute, existing in and for itself in a closed circle of perfection. To this work the poet was subordinated as the agent and ministrant who, in a painful renunciation of this world, has lost his life to find his art. And the work, veiled from the profane and vulgar, "la foule," by its sacred mystery, is accessible—insofar as it is accessible at all—only to an audience of the elect, initiates and communicants in the rites of art.

As Paul Valéry has noted, the "remarkable will to isolate Poetry once for all from every other essence than itself," "in its pure state," had been predicted by Poe; and "it is therefore not surprising to see in Baudelaire the beginnings of this striving toward a perfection that is concerned only with itself."[76] Baudelaire's theory, as we saw, rests on a distinction between fallen nature and the supernature which is evoked or reflected in the poem; the anomaly is that from this theological ground he develops, not the claim that poetry has a religious or moral purpose, but the opposite claim that a poem has no purpose beyond its own existence. In objecting, for example, to the fact that in Hugo's *Les Misérables* "la morale entre directement *à titre de but,*" Baudelaire raises the question "si l'œuvre d'art doit n'avoir d'autre but que *l'art,* si l'art ne doit exprimer d'adoration que pour *lui-même.*"[77] His own answer to this question he had often expressed: "teaching," "truth," and "morality" in poetry are "heresies." For

> la poésie . . . n'a pas d'autre but qu'elle-même; elle ne peut pas en avoir d'autre, et aucun poème ne sera si grand, si noble, si véritablement digne du nom de poème, que celui qui aura été écrit uniquement pour le plaisir d'écrire un poème.[78]

Baudelaire echoes Poe, who had said that "there neither exists nor *can* exist any work more thoroughly dignified—more supremely noble than . . . this poem *per se*—this poem which is a poem and nothing more—this poem written solely for the poem's sake."[79]

Statements of this type have become a staple of our critical discourse, and they carry for the modern reader a heavy weight of aesthetic pathos. But if we break out of the standard categories of modern poetics, the assertion seems by no means self-evident that a poem achieves not only its identity, but also its value, and indeed its supremacy over all other works of man, by the very fact that it is self-sufficient and self-bounded, free from any relation or aim outside the perfection of its own existence—as Baudelaire put it, without the need "to express adoration except for itself." Kant, following Baumgarten, had earlier made the limited claim that the work of art, as contemplated by the spectator, is an object whose value is intrinsic, without reference to its truth or utility. The unqualified assertion that the poem is a self-enclosed and utterly sufficient entity, however, moved against the full current of the European critical tradition; for even when an earlier critic had proposed that the *dulce* rather than the *utile* is the defining characteristic of poetry, he had asserted no more than that the poet alters and orders the materials he takes from this world with the aim of providing the maximum pleasure to his audience.

It seems clear that modern claims about the nature and superlative value of the autonomous work of art owe both their form and their persuasive force not to an aesthetic, but to a theological prototype. For in traditional Western thought, only one Being had possessed the attributes of absolute self-sufficiency; and post-Romantic theorists, following the direction indicated by Poe and Baudelaire, imported into aesthetics the concept of God's unique nature—*ipso facto* the apex of both reality and value—and applied it to the work of art. This concept made its appearance in Plato's description of the Idea of Ideas; this is the Idea of the Good, and the Good, Plato said, "differs from all other things . . . in that the being who possesses good always everywhere and in all things has the most perfect sufficiency, and is never in need of anything else."[80] Aristotle's God was an unmoved mover who, in his total sufficiency, is the criterion of goodness: "One who is self-sufficient can have no need of the service of others, nor of their affection, nor of social life, since he is capable of living alone. This is especially evident in the case of God. Clearly, since he is in need of nothing, God cannot have need of friends, nor will he have any."[81] In the Absolute of Plotinus, too, perfection was equivalent to self-sufficiency: "The One is perfect because it seeks for nothing, and possesses nothing, and has need of nothing."[82]

These thinkers were the most powerful classical influences on Christian theology, and they helped generate the strain of otherworldliness which, though among other and conflicting currents of ideas, became a durable element in the philosophy of Christendom. This is the view that the *ens perfectissimum*, the highest mode of existence and the supreme form of value, is alien to the categories of this world, and characterized by a timeless self-sufficiency; and that the

resultant ideal for mankind is to approximate such a severance from ordinary reality and experience, by a *contemptus
mundi* and *contemptus vitae* whose aim is a pure contemplation
(or else as nearly as possible, an imitation) of the perfect Being
who exists outside of this world. It is this persistent set of
ideas and attitudes which provided the paradigm for the otherworldly strain we have noted in much post-Romantic aesthetics.

The movement of *l'art pour l'art* had begun as a rebellion
against the triviality and ugliness of the present-day world
and the standards of its bourgeois and utilitarian society, in
the defiant declaration that the aim of a work of art is not to
be useful, but only to be beautiful. But the aesthetic ideas I
am describing, in their radical form, are more complex and
far-reaching than a defiance against an indifferent or hostile
contemporary milieu. The aim, in the English title of one of
Baudelaire's prose poems, is nothing less than to seek a way
"Anywhere out of the World"—"N'importe où! N'importe
où! pourvu que ce soit hors de ce monde!"[83] The tendency is
to undertake to disengage the poem from the ineradicable
conditions of human life in the natural world—regarded as
fallen, sordid, hideous, contemptible, or absurd—by defining the poem in categories alien to ordinary human experience and attributing to it a detached and self-enclosed
perfection of being. And as Baudelaire's pure work of art
takes on some of the attributes of a self-sufficient Deity, so
Baudelaire's "dandy" assimilates to the figure of the social
aristocrat the qualities of the Christian saint who emulates
God by substituting the detachment from life of the *vita con-
templativa* for the engagement with life of the *vita activa*. Dan-
dyism, says Baudelaire, is "a cult of oneself" which "borders
on spirituality" and, with its disciplines "to fortify the will and
to discipline the soul," constitutes "a kind of religion"; and
the dandy, by his "unshakable resolution never to be moved,"
cuts himself deliberately off from common humanity and—
detached, remote, imperturbable—devotes himself to the
utterly self-centered, and for that reason supreme, existence
of "cultivating the idea of beauty in his own person."[84] In a
parallel fashion Baudelaire's ideal poet undertakes to sever

himself from worldly and human relations in a self-sufficing existence, though in order to devote himself (in Yeats's later antithesis) to the perfection not of the life, but of the work:

> Goût invincible de la prostitution dans le cœur de l'homme, d'où naît son horreur de la solitude.—Il veut être *deux*. L'homme de génie veut être *un*, donc solitaire. . . .
>
> Foutre, c'est aspirer à entrer dans un autre, et l'artiste ne sort jamais de lui-même.[85]

That the modern concepts of the sufficient, impersonal image and of the dedicated, estranged artist are related, and that they are related because they derive from associated religious prototypes, comes out very clearly in James Joyce, who beyond most of his predecessors was systematic in constructing his aesthetics out of a secularized theology. "The esthetic image," explains Stephen Dedalus, "is first luminously apprehended as selfbounded and selfcontained. . . ." In drama, highest in the hierarchy of literary forms, "the esthetic image . . . is life purified in and reprojected from the human imagination," accomplishing "the mystery of esthetic like that of material creation," with "the artist, like the God of the creation," become "invisible, refined out of existence, indifferent, paring his fingernails." And when Stephen himself, at the end of *A Portrait of the Artist*, determines to embrace his artistic destiny in "silence, exile, and cunning," the poet-apart bears a patent likeness to Aristotle's self-sufficient deity who "cannot have need of friends":

> Cranly, now grave again, slowed his pace and said:
> —Alone, quite alone. You have no fear of that. And you know what that word means? Not only to be separate from all others but to have not even one friend.
> —I will take the risk, said Stephen.[86]

More than a generation before, however, Stéphane Mallarmé had explored the possibilities of aesthetic otherworldliness to their farthest consequences. Very early in life Mallarmé, expressing contempt for the world, had turned

his back on life and the sordid impurities of reality in order
to find in his art a purer self and world:

> Ainsi, pris du dégoût de l'homme à l'âme dure . . .
>
> Je fuis et je m'accroche à toutes les croisées
> D'où l'on tourne l'épaule à la vie et, béni,
> Dans leur verre, lavé d'éternelles rosées . . .
>
> Je me mire et me vois ange! et je meurs, et j'aime
> —Que la vitre soit l'art, soit la mysticité—
> À renaître, portant mon rêve en diadème,
> Au ciel antérieur où fleurit la Beauté![87]

By "la poésie pure" Baudelaire had signified a poetry unal-
loyed either by adaptation to a purpose beyond its own existence, or by exhibiting rhetorical awareness of an audience,
or by expressing the personal passion of the poet—"car la
passion est *naturelle,* trop naturelle pour ne pas introduire un
ton blessant, discordant, dans le domaine de la beauté pure"
in "les régions surnaturelles de la poésie."[88] Mallarmé's prose,
when put to the question, is no less elusive than his verse; but
it seems clear that he aimed at the ultimate purgation which
would free the poem from all earthly or human relations
whatever: not content with making it embody the Idea or
reflect the Absolute beyond reality, he undertook, with
unremitting single-mindedness, to transform the poem itself
into the Absolute. He aspired to ascend "la montagne sainte,"
on which Wagner's dramas are but a halfway house, to "cette
cime menaçante d'absolu" which haunts us all too lucidly,
"fulgurante, nue, seule: au-delà et que personne ne semble
devoir atteindre. Personne!"[89] And though Mallarmé's talk
of the Absolute was probably derived by hearsay from Hegel,
he means by it very much what Plotinus had meant: the One
that "is perfect because it seeks for nothing, and possesses
nothing, and has need of nothing." Mallarmé's aim was to
achieve the sufficient poem, absolute in its purity in the sense
that it is totally inhuman and unworldly, because independent not only of poet and audience, but even of reference to
anyone or anything outside itself.

In discussing the coming-into-being of a poem, Mallarmé
likes to replace the inherited terms "imitation," "representation," and "expression" (which imply a relation to the world
or to the poet) by metaphors taken from necromancy or the
occult, implying the conjuring up of a poem out of nothing
and nowhere. There is "une parité secrète" between poetry
and magic, and "évoquer . . . l'objet tu, comporte tentative
proche de créer: vraisemblable dans la limite de l'idée
uniquement mise en jeu par l'enchanteur de lettres."[90] The
poet like a mage utters the word and there rises up, not the
concrete object, but "la notion pure," a flower which is an
"idée même et suave, l'absente de tous bouquets."[91] As to the
author: "L'œuvre pure implique la disparition élocutoire du
poëte, qui cède l'initiative aux mots. . . . Encore la faut-il, pour
omettre l'auteur"; so that a work of art is "anonyme et par-
fait."[92] Nor does the pure poem require a reader: "Imper-
sonnifié, le volume, autant qu'on s'en sépare comme auteur,
ne réclame approche de lecteur. Tel, sache . . . il a lieu tout
seul: fait, étant."[93] And only "reportage," not literature, aims
to "narrate, instruct, even to describe"; the words of poetry
do not denote, but function beyond reference, like elements
in a dream, or an incantation, or (in a favorite analogue of
advocates of pure poetry) like the notes in the nonrepresen-
tational art of music. "Au contraire d'une fonction de
numéraire facile et représentatif," the speech of the poet,
"avant tout, rêve et chant," which "de plusieurs vocables refait
un mot total, neuf, étranger à la langue et comme incanta-
toire, achève cet isolement de la parole."[94] Poetry achieves its
purity by devouring and wearing away the reality it has no
recourse except to employ as its initial material. "Tout le
mystère est là: établir les identités secrètes par un deux à
deux qui ronge et use les objets, au nom d'une centrale pureté."[95] For although "la Nature a lieu, on n'y ajoutera pas" as
the source of poetry, yet to create poetically is to unrealize or
abolish it—"a l'égal de créer: la notion d'un objet, échappant,
qui fait défaut."[96]

Freed from the last bonds of worldly contingency and of
relationship to anything outside itself, the poem becomes an
isolated, introverted object constituted solely by the internal

relations of its words. "Le hasard n'entraîne pas un vers, c'est la grande chose. . . . Ce à quoi nous devons viser surtout est que, dans le poème, les mots—qui déjà sont assez eux pour ne plus recevoir d'impression du dehors—se reflètent les uns sur les autres jusqu'à . . . n'être que les transitions d'une gamme."[97] The absolute poem, then, in the perfection of its beauty, is self-contained, self-signifying, self-adoring; in describing it Mallarmé, like Joyce later, recalls Aristotle's claim that the self-sufficient deity needs no friends, and has none:

> Il n'y a que la Beauté,—et elle n'a qu'une expression parfaite: la Poésie. Tout le reste est mensonge—excepté pour ceux qui vivent du corps, l'amour, et cet amour de l'esprit, l'amitié. . . . Pour moi, la Poésie me tient lieu de l'amour, parce qu'elle est éprise d'elle-même et que sa volupté d'elle retombe délicieuse-ment en mon âme.[98]

Now, a self-bounded perfection of existence which neither expresses, communicates, nor describes, however it may suit the Deity, offers difficulties as the ideal for an art whose medium is language, the human instrument of expression, communication, and description. A. O. Lovejoy has raised the question with respect even to God whether, by positing an otherworldly Being who is defined exclusively by antithe-sis to the mode of existence of anything in this world, "many of the great philosophers and theologians have been occu-pied with teaching the worship of—nonentity."[99] This, at any rate, is what, seeking the absolute poem, Mallarmé seems very early in his career to have discovered:

> Malheureusement, en creusant le vers à ce point, j'ai rencontré deux abîmes, qui me désespèrent. L'un est le Néant . . . et je suis encore trop désolé pour pouvoir croire même à ma poé-sie.[100]

> Je te dirai que je suis depuis un mois dans les plus purs glaciers de l'Esthétique—qu'après avoir trouvé le Néant, j'ai trouvé le Beau,—et que tu ne peux t'imaginer dans quelles altitudes lucides je m'aventure.[101]

Pour garder une notion ineffaçable du néant pur, j'ai dû imposer
à mon cerveau la sensation du vide absolu. . . . Il me reste la
délimitation parfaite et le rêve intérieur de deux livres, à la
fois nouveaux et éternels, l'un tout absolu *Beauté,* l'autre per-
sonnel, les *Allégories somptueuses du Néant.* . . . Vraiment, j'ai bien
peur de *commencer* . . . par où notre pauvre et sacré Baudelaire
a fini.[102]

Pour moi, voici deux ans que j'ai commis le péché de voir le
Rêve dans sa nudité idéale. . . . Et maintenant arrivé à la vision
horrible d'une œuvre pure, j'ai presque perdu la raison et ce
sens des paroles les plus familières.[103]

In his pursuit of absolute purity Mallarmé exploited his
ingenious tactics of negating, eliminating, absenting, disem-
bodying, refining to the verge of nonentity the objects of this
world; and though he produced a slim body of extraordinary
verse, he was haunted by the apprehension that even his best
achievements, "d'une pureté que l'homme n'a pas atteinte,"
may in truth be of a purity that man "n'atteindra peut-être
jamais, car il se pourrait que je ne fusse le jouet que d'une
illusion, et que la machine humaine ne soit pas assez parfaite
pour arriver à de tels résultats."[104] "Mon art," Mallarmé once
said, "est une impasse." Of an art of language which aspires
to the condition of pure notation without denotation, the
inevitable result is—in that mode of *coincidentia oppositorum* to
which otherworldly theologians have always been reduced in
defining their Absolute—an eloquent silence. Mallarmé was
fascinated by the idea of the tacit poem—"l'écrit, envol tacite
d'abstraction," and "le poëme tu, aux blancs."[105]

From this extremity poetics had nowhere to go except back.
Mallarmé's successors, in the generation of Symbolists after
1890, typically felt the attraction of the ideal of a pure poetry
disengaged from the impurity of ordinary life, yet found it
necessary to bring poetry into some kind of relationship
with the world and mankind. "L'univers," Valéry wrote in
L'Ébauche d'un serpent, "n'est qu'un défaut / Dans la pureté
du Non-Être"; but his *Cimetière Marin* ends in the recognition
that "il faut tenter de vivre." And as Valéry acknowledged in
his retrospect of the Symbolist movement, the concept of the

absolute poem, as it developed after Poe and Baudelaire, turned out to be beyond existential possibility:

> À l'horizon, toujours, la poésie pure. . . . Là le péril; là, pré-cisément, notre perte; et là même, le but. . . . Rien de si pur ne peut coexister avec les conditions de la vie. . . . La poésie abso-lue . . . comme le vide parfait . . . ne se [laisse] même approcher qu'au prix d'une progression épuisante d'efforts . . . [et ne laisse] enfin que l'orgueil de n'être jamais satisfait.[106]

By and large, prominent modern theorists of art, from the Formalists through many of the New Critics, have inherited from the Symbolist doctrine of an absolute work their view of the nature of a poem and, in consequence, their central aesthetic problem. In maintaining the central insight of mod-ern aesthetics since Baumgarten and Kant—that a work of art has intrinsic values, to be contemplated independently of the state of mind in which it originated, or the truths it states, or the moral and other ends it effects—the modern theorist has usually, although needlessly, committed himself to the ontological claim that the work of art is "self-sufficient," "autonomous," "autotelic," "autarchic," "absolute," existing "for its own sake," "*per se*," as "an object in itself," in entire independence of any intent of its author, any reference to the outer world, any effects on an observer, and indeed, of any extra-poetic human concerns or values whatever. Such a view, since it appropriates to a poem the attributes originally assigned to an otherworldly deity, readily verges on poem-worship, and is often associated with the opinion that poetry has assumed the function which is no longer fulfilled by reli-gion, or else that art is itself a kind of religion, or intimately related to religious experience. This criticism continues to deploy other concepts preempted from theology; a phenom-enon visible, for example, in the claim that poetry provides a supreme and privileged knowledge immune from ordinary criteria or logic, and in the designation of competing views of poetry, not as products of error in aesthetic observation or reasoning, but as violations of a creed—that is (in the term introduced into aesthetics by Poe and Baudelaire) as "heresies." Consonantly, the central problem for Modernist theory has been to maintain the position that the work of art is a self-contained object, yet to relate the work once again to the world outside itself, and to reengage it with the emotional, intellectual, and moral concerns of common humanity.

An aesthetic of an otherworldly, self-sufficient poem is entirely remote from the views of the early and most influential Romantic philosophers and poets. They were all in some sense Idealists, but their critical theories were, in the final analysis, of this world, and their basic criteria humanistic. "Poetry," Coleridge wrote in "On Poesy or Art," "is purely human; for all its materials are from the mind, and all its products are for the mind"; it binds man with the objects of the external world, and these share his humanity, in that "the life which is in us is in them likewise."[107] On this issue the greatest statement was uttered by Wordsworth, in the Preface to *Lyrical Ballads,* which, Coleridge declared, whatever his exceptions to Wordsworth's theory of poetic diction, had been "half a child of my own Brain."[108] When Wordsworth says that "poetry is the first and last of all knowledge,"[109] he does not mean that it is an equivalent for the Deity, the *Alpha* and *Omega.* For "however exalted a notion we would wish to cherish of [his] character," what, Wordsworth asks, is a poet? "He is a man speaking to men," and his "poetry is the image of man and nature. . . . The Poet writes under one restriction only, namely, the necessity of giving immediate pleasure to a human Being possessed of that information which may be expected from him . . . as a Man"; and this condition is not demeaning, but "a homage paid to the native and naked dignity of man, to the grand elementary principle of pleasure, by which he knows, and feels, and lives, and moves." At the farthest extreme from the Modernist's alienated and sufficient poet, needing no friends, Wordsworth's poet expresses that which by "habitual and direct sympathy" connects "us with our fellow-beings," and is eminently "an upholder and preserver, carrying everywhere with him relationship and love," and uttering "the general passions and thoughts and feelings of men."[110]

Wordsworth's poet, then, deals with this world and universal human concerns, expresses those ideas and feelings which bind him to man and men to each other, and undertakes to appeal to the moral interests and springs of pleasure he shares with his audience. From other men he differs, not in kind, but only in the degree of his powers; and above all, he differs in his ready and joyous responsiveness to the very thing from which advocates of "l'œuvre pure" later sought, with ascetic zeal, to disengage both poet and poem entirely—namely, life itself. The poet, says Wordsworth, is a man "who rejoices more than other men in the spirit of life that is in him; delighting to contemplate similar volitions and passions as manifested in the goings-on of the Universe, and habitually impelled to create them where he does not find them."[111]

The differences between such views as these and characteristic Symbolist and post-Symbolist views of art derive from a radical cleavage in basic schemes of value. The early Romantics committed themselves on the side of life—life in this world. In their writings Life played a role equivalent to that of the Absolute in the otherworldly thinkers, functioning as the premise of their thinking and the residence and reference of their major values, including aesthetic values. This fact is epitomized by a passage in which Coleridge identifies as Absolute, not the state in which we disengage ourselves from this world, but on the contrary, that in which we reunite severed man and nature, subject and object, in an intuition which combines the central Romantic values of life, joy, and that total relationship for which Coleridge, like many of his contemporaries, used the term "love":

The ground-work, therefore, of all true philosophy is the full apprehension of the difference between . . . that intuition of things which arises when we possess ourselves, as one with the whole, which is substantial knowledge, and that which presents itself when . . . we think of ourselves as separated beings, and place nature in antithesis to the mind, as object to subject, thing to thought, death to life. . . . [The former] is an eternal and infinite self-rejoicing, self-loving, with a joy unfathomable, with a love all-comprehensive. It is absolute.[112]

For Coleridge, as for Wordsworth, such a full intuition of "the one Life within us and abroad," whose sign is the unison of all the faculties which he calls "joy,"[113] is the essential condition of the highest poetry. Shelley was not indulging in rhetoric, but putting forth a considered view he shared with his contemporaries, when he spoke of "the joy of the perception and still more of the creation of poetry," and described poetry as "the record of the best and happiest moments of the happiest and best minds."[114] In *Romantic Image* Frank Kermode has read back into Coleridge's *Dejection: An Ode* the Modernist concept of the poet-apart, whose estrangement and anguish are the inescapable price he pays for his ambiguous joy in accomplishing the self-sufficing image which is the poem.[115] The claim of Coleridge's poem, however, is precisely the opposite: that the severance of his responsive mind and feelings from the outer world is an unmitigated disaster which leaves him isolated in a nature that has been rendered dead and alien; that this state of "dejection," far from being necessary to creativity, has suspended his "shaping spirit of Imagination"; that the contrary state of "joy," attending full community with what is external to him, is the necessary condition for the imaginative recreation of the world in poetry; and that this new world is not a remote and purified otherworld or supernature, but merely the present and imperfect world, experientially transformed by the joyous power emanating from the poet's abundant sense of life. "Joy," he says, which is "Life, and Life's effluence,"

> Joy, Lady! is the spirit and the power,
> Which, wedding Nature to us, gives in dower
> A new Earth and new Heaven.

SIX

Two Roads to Wordsworth

THE FIRST CRITIC of Wordsworth's poetry was Wordsworth himself, and in his criticism, as in his poetry, he speaks with two distinct voices. The first voice is that of the Preface to *Lyrical Ballads*, in which Wordsworth powerfully applies to his poetry some humanistic values of the European Enlightenment. In his Preface the controlling and interrelated norms are the essential, the elementary, the simple, the universal, and the permanent. The great subjects of his poetry, Wordsworth says, are "the essential passions of the heart," "elementary feelings," "the great and simple affections," "the great and universal passions of men," and "characters of which the elements are simple . . . such as exist now, and will probably always exist," as these human qualities interact with "the beautiful and permanent forms of nature." His aim is a poetry written in a "naked and simple" style that is "well adapted to interest mankind permanently." And the poet himself, as "a man speaking to men," both affirms and effects the primal human values: the joy of life, the dignity of life and of its elemental moving force, the pleasure principle, and the primacy of the universal connective, love. The poet "rejoices more than other men in the spirit of life" both within him and without, pays homage "to the grand elementary principle of pleasure, by which he knows, and feels, and lives, and moves," and is "the rock of defence of human nature . . . carrying everywhere with him relationship and love."

Wordsworth's second critical voice has been far less heeded by his readers. It speaks out in the "Essay, Supplementary to the Preface" of his *Poems* of 1815, and reiterates in sober prose the claims he had made, years before, in the verse "Prospectus" to *The Recluse* (first printed with his Preface to *The Excursion)* and in the opening and closing passages of *The Prelude:* claims that it is his task to confront and find consolation in human suffering—whether the "solitary agonies" of rural life or the "fierce confederate storm / Of sorrow" barricadoed within the walls of cities—since he is a poet who has been singled out "for holy services" in a secular work of man's "redemption." In his "Essay" of 1815, Wordsworth addresses himself to explain and justify those aspects of novelty and strangeness in his poetry that have evoked from critics "unremitting hostility . . . slight . . . aversion . . . contempt." He does so by asserting that he, like every "truly original poet," has qualities that are "peculiarly his own," and in specifying his innovations, he does not now take his operative concepts from eighteenth-century humanism, but imports them from theology; that is, he deliberately adapts to poetry the idiom hitherto used by Christian apologists to justify the radical novelty, absurdities, and paradoxes of the Christian mysteries. For Wordsworth claims in this essay that there are "affinities between religion and poetry," "a community of nature," so that poetry shares the distinctive quality of Christianity, which is to confound "the calculating understanding" by its contradictions:

> For when Christianity, the religion of humility, is founded upon the proudest quality of our nature [the imagination], what can be expected but contradictions?

In the "Essay" of 1815, accordingly, Wordsworth does not represent poetry as elemental and simple, but stresses instead its "contradictions"—that is, its radical paradoxicality, its union of antitheses, its fusion of the sensuous and the transcendent, its violation of the customary, and its reversal of status between the highest and lowest. Poetry, for example, imitates the supreme contradiction of the Incarnation itself: it is "ethereal and transcendent, yet incapable to sustain [its] existence without sensuous incarnation." The higher poetry unites the "wisdom of the heart and the grandeur of imagination" and so achieves a "simplicity" that is "Magnificence herself." Wordsworth's own poems manifest "emotions of the pathetic" that are "complex and revolutionary." As for "the sublime"— he is specifically a poet "charged with a new mission to extend its kingdom, and to augment and spread its enjoyments." For as one of the poets who combine the "heroic passions" of pagan antiquity with Christian wisdom he has produced a new synthesis—an "accord of sublimated humanity." And his chief enterprise as a poet is expressed in a Christian paradox—he must cast his readers down in order to raise them up: their spirits "are to be humbled and humanized, in order that they may be purified and exalted."

Wordsworth as primarily the simple, affirmative poet of elementary feelings, essential humanity, and vital joy, and Wordsworth as primarily the complex poet of strangeness, paradox, equivocality, and dark sublimities—these diverse views, adumbrated by Wordsworth himself, were established as persistent alternative ways to the poet by Matthew Arnold and by A. C. Bradley. The cause of Wordsworth's greatness, Arnold said, taking his cue from Wordsworth's Preface to *Lyrical Ballads,* "is simple, and may be told quite simply. Wordsworth's poetry is great because of the extraordinary power" with which he feels and renders and makes us share "the joy offered to us in nature, the joy offered to us in the simple, primary affections and duties." And from the naturalness of his subject and the sincerity of his feeling, his characteristic and matchless style is that of "the most plain, first-hand, almost austere naturalness."[1] Wordsworth's great boon to us in "this iron time," Arnold says in his verses, is that he has restored our lost capacity for spontaneous and uncomplicated responsiveness, "the freshness of the early world." He adds, however, that Wordsworth achieved his "sweet calm" only by the expedient of averting his ken "from half of human fate."[2]

Although Bradley did not publish his great essay on Wordsworth until 1909, thirty years after Arnold's appeared, he set out explicitly to supplement what he regarded as Arnold's valid but incomplete view of the poet by specifying other qualities without which "Wordsworth is not Wordsworth." His challenge to Arnold's way to Wordsworth is direct and uncompromising: "The road into Wordsworth's mind must be through his strangeness and his paradoxes, and not round them." In pursuing this road Bradley follows the lead, not of Wordsworth's Preface, but of his vatic poetic pronouncements, which Arnold had noted only to derogate as the style "more properly . . . of eloquent prose." As Bradley's other essays make evident, his critical concepts, and his sensitiveness to negative and paradoxical elements in literature, also owe a great deal to the philosophy of Hegel. As Hegel himself had noted, however, his categories of negation, contradiction, and synthesis are (like Wordsworth's concept of the "contradictions" in the products of the modern poetic imagination) the conceptual equivalents of the paradoxes and the *coincidentia oppositorum* of the Christian mysteries. In the Hegelian cast of his critical concepts, then, Bradley is in broad accord with the spirit of Wordsworth's own "Essay, Supplementary to the Preface" of 1815.

In Bradley's view, that which is most distinctive in Wordsworth's poetry is "peculiar," "audacious," "strange," and Wordsworth's characteristic attitudes are a complex of contraries or contradictions. Although Wordsworth sang of joy and love, "he did not avert his eyes" from anguish or evil, but often represented "a dark world"; and though he undertook to show that suffering and misery can in fact be the conditions of happiness, strength, and glory, he did not pretend that this possibility solved "the riddle of the painful earth"— "the world was to him in the end 'this unintelligible world.' " Wordsworth is "preeminently the poet of soltitude," yet "no poet is more emphatically the poet of community." His native bent was not to simplicity, but to "sublimity"; and in this "mystic" or "visionary" strain "there is always traceable a certain hostility to 'sense,' " an intimation of something illimitable, eternal, infinite, that is "in some way a denial" of the limited sensible world, "contradicting or abolishing the fixed limits of our habitual view." As Bradley describes the paradoxical qualities of a Wordsworthian spot of time, using a portentous term, "Everything here is natural, but everything is apocalyptic."[3]

Twentieth-century critics of Wordsworth have tended to follow either Arnold's or Bradley's road to the poet, and the diverse approaches have yielded two Wordsworths. One Wordsworth is simple, elemental, forthright, the other is complex, paradoxical, problematic; one is an affirmative poet of life, love, and joy, the other is an equivocal or self-divided poet whose affirmations are implicitly qualified (if not annulled) by a pervasive sense of mortality and an ever-incipient despair of life; one is the great poet of natural man and the world of all of us, the other is a visionary or "mystic" who is ultimately hostile to temporal man and the world of sense and whose profoundest inclinations are toward another world that transcends biological and temporal limitations; one is the Wordsworth of light, the other the Wordsworth of chiaroscuro, or even darkness. Criticism since mid-century continues to manifest, and often to sharpen, this division, although the commentators who take either the one or the other of the old roads to Wordsworth have introduced new critical concepts that make their work seem, in the 1970s, distinctively "modern." I shall try to identify a few of the more conspicuous innovations within each of the traditional perspectives.

I. THE SIMPLE WORDSWORTH

In *The Poet Wordsworth* (1950) Helen Darbishire is an unqualified Arnoldian: Wordsworth is a poet whose motive power was "the depth and force of his feeling for humanity," who vindicated "sense-experience as the foundation of knowledge" and represented "simple men and women who are moved by the great emotions."[4] John F. Danby's poet, in a book published a decade later, is also, as his title asserts, *The*

Simple Wordsworth; the innovative element is Danby's view that Wordsworth is a craftsman whose simplicity has been achieved by "an alert and conscious artist," who controls the reader's responses by his management of the narrative personae, "tones of voice," and "masks." Danby's critique of *The Idiot Boy* is a belated recognition that Wordsworth is an accomplished comic poet. Its focus is on the interplay of the narrative voice, the voices of the characters, and the poet's own voice in sustaining the fine balance of humor and human warmth in the evolving story.[5]

Danby expressly opposes his treatment of Wordsworth as intentional artificer to the New Critical approach to a poem as a free-standing and autonomous structure of meanings, to be judged without recourse to the artist or his intention. Cleanth Brooks's essay on Wordsworth's *Ode: Intimations of Immortality* demonstrates what can be achieved by such a close reading of the poem "as an independent poetic structure," interrogated for what it "manages to say" entirely "in its own right" as a primarily ironic and paradoxical deployment of thematic imagery.[6] Having assimilated the insights made possible by this strict limitation of perspective in the New Criticism, many critics in the last decade or two have undertaken, like Danby, to rehumanize poetry by viewing the poet, in Wordsworth's phrase in the Preface, as "a man speaking to men," and by exploiting concepts such as "voice," "persona," "tone," and "point of view," which emphasize the poet's own involvement, as well as his management of the reader's participation, in the fictional process.

Such a revitalized rhetoric of poetry is prominent in many recent writings about Wordsworth. In the third chapter of *The Music of Humanity,* for example, Jonathan Wordsworth demonstrates the essential role, in *The Ruined Cottage,* of the interplay between Wordsworth's two "poetic selves," the Pedlar and the Poet, in effecting the reader's imaginative consent to the author's own attitudes toward the tragic story.[7] In an essay that has been much debated, Stephen Parrish reads *The Thorn* not as a quasi-supernatural story, but as an artful dramatic monologue, in which the controlling principle is the revelation of the mental workings of its credulous narrator, the old sea captain.[8] Neil Hertz's essay "Wordsworth and the Tears of Adam"—with a shift of emphasis from Wordsworth's rhetorical artistry to the characteristic disjunction of consciousness in his poetry—discriminates "the transformation of the voice" in a short verse passage, and details the interaction among three "aspects of Wordsworth's self" and a fourth subjectivity, that of the responding reader.[9]

II. THE PROBLEMATIC WORDSWORTH

In the 1960s there appeared a new mode of criticism in America whose appeal to younger critics presages its growing importance in studies of Romantic literature. The primary terms of this criticism are "consciousness" (or "self-consciousness") and the "dialectic" of its dealings with what is not-consciousness, and its characteristic procedure is to find something "problematic" in the surface meaning of single passages and to regard this as a clue to a deep structure manifesting an unspoken preoccupation of the poet. The proximate sources of this critical procedure are the diverse movements in European thought loosely classified as "phenomenology," "existentialism," and "structuralism," but its central idiom and concerns derive ultimately from Hegel; so that, when applied to Wordsworth, it can be regarded as a revived form of Bradley's neo-Hegelian approach to that poet. The focus, however, is much sharper than Bradley's, and the chief operative concepts are much more restricted. For as Hegel in his *Phenomenology of Spirit* translated the manifold particularities of human and individual history into diverse moments of the transactions between consciousness and its alienated other, so these critics view the manifold surface particularities of Romantic poems as generated primarily by a single submerged plot: the sustained struggle of the poet's consciousness (operating in the mode often called "imagination") to achieve "autonomy," or absolute independence from that adversary which is not itself—namely, "nature," the world of sensible objects.

In his influential essay "Intentional Structure of the Romantic Image," first published in 1960, Paul de Man sets out from the observation that there is a "dialectic" that is "paradoxical"—a "fundamental ambiguity" or "tension" that "never ceases to be problematic"—in Romantic attempts to link the polarities of consciousness, or imagination, and nature. De Man's paradigmatic instance is Mallarmé, who is represented as a revealing point of reference because he is a late Romantic who took over what had hitherto been an implicit tension of polar attitudes, "the alternating feeling of attraction and repulsion that the romantic poet experiences toward nature," and made it explicit as a "conscious dialectic of a reflective poetic consciousness." Mallarmé, unlike earlier Romantic poets, "always remained convinced of the essential priority of the natural object," so that his writings as an extreme "anti-natural poet" are a defiantly hopeless struggle by consciousness (or by the language in which consciousness manifests itself) to annihilate, by reducing to its own self, a nature that Mallarmé knows to be ultimately indefeasible. Wordsworth's poetry, on the other hand, with its "radical contradictions" in the representation of landscape (de Man's example is the passage on crossing the Alps in *The Prelude,* Book VI), puts into question "the ontological priority of the sensory object," by recourse to the faculty he calls "imagination," which "marks . . . a possibility for consciousness to exist entirely by and for itself, independently of all relationship with the outside world."[10]

Geoffrey Hartman also finds that Wordsworth's treatment of nature is "problematic," and that a number of passages in *The Prelude* which "overtly celebrate nature" in fact "share a motif opposed to the overt line of argument." Hartman's repeated reference, however, is not to Mallarmé but to Blake, the extreme representative of a deliberate commitment to a visionary and anti-natural imagination. "Blake," says Hartman, "would snap . . . that Wordsworth is of his party without knowing it." The difference is that Wordsworth, when he comes face to face with his "autonomous imagination," fears it, shies from it, or veils it. In consequence, his poetry constitutes "a series of evaded recognitions" of imagination and "an avoidance of apocalypse"—where imagination is defined by Hartman as "consciousness of self raised to apocalyptic pitch" and apocalypse signifies "any strong desire to cast out nature and to achieve an unmediated contact with the principle of things," hence as "involving a *death* of nature." It is this "unresolved opposition between Imagination and Nature"—through Wordsworth's "fear of the death of nature"—that "prevents him from becoming a visionary poet."[11]

Two other essays represent an approach to Wordsworth that emphasizes the duplicity and the strain between contradictions in his writings; the major operative concept, however, is not a revived Hegelian opposition between consciousness and an alien other, but the post-Freudian distinction between manifest and latent, conscious and unconscious content. The basic claim is that Wordsworth's overt or surface meaning often overlies a covert countermeaning that expresses what the poet profoundly felt and believed, as against what he rationalized himself into believing.

David Perkins' *The Quest for Permanence* undertakes to "go beneath the surface" of Wordsworth's poetry in order to explore the "negative implications" that are sometimes "contrary to his overt intentions and obiter dicta"; for any interpretation that concentrates on Wordsworth's obiter dicta "is not touching what is deepest in him." Under Wordsworth's overt claims that certitude and peace attend upon "the union of mind with nature," Perkins finds a contrary sense that there is a "gulf between human nature . . . and the rest of nature," and that man is doomed to be an isolated being, estranged from both nature and other men. There are symptoms also of "a kind of schizoid retreat" from situations that threaten the poet's composure, which in its extreme form manifests itself in Wordsworth as an attraction to the ultimate security of the grave.[12]

In *The Limits of Mortality*, published in the same year as Perkins' *Quest for Permanence* (1959), David Ferry's aim is to discover in Wordsworth "ideas and feelings which can in some way be related to our own deepest feelings and ideas." Ferry penetrates to this modern element, as he says, by "a special way of reading his poems." This way to Wordsworth is to strike a sharp dichotomy between the " 'surface' of his poems" and the "deeper" and "hidden" meanings which are in "tension" or "conflict" with the surface meanings, and to assert the prepotency of the hidden and antithetic meanings as constituting the "ultimate subject matter" of a poem. As Ferry formulates this semantic peripety:

> [The] apparent subject matter is a kind of cipher or hieroglyph for meanings which reject or devaluate the very experiences which express them. . . . The symbolic meanings of [Wordsworth's] poems tend to reject their sensuous, dramatic surfaces.

Like A. C. Bradley a half-century earlier, Ferry sets out, as he says, to correct Arnold's "tendency to take Wordsworth's vocabulary of feeling at face value," hence to evaluate him as "the poet of the primary affections and simple feelings." By Ferry's interpretative strategy, however, the paradoxical Wordsworth works free from Bradley's careful qualifications to become the polar opposite of Arnold's Wordsworth. The sophisticated modern reader is now enabled to look right through Wordsworth's surface assertions of reverence for a "sacramental" nature, love for elemental man, and esteem for the simple affections and ordinary experience, in order to discern a countermeaning of which the poet himself remained unaware—that is, a "mystical" yearning for an eternal and unchanging realm of being to which nature and man and even the articulations of poetry itself (since all are alike trapped in the conditions of time, space, and vicissitude) are an intolerable obstruction, an offense against the purity of eternity. Hence to the knowing reader Wordsworth's "sacramentalist" poems, far from being simple and natural in style, often turn out to be "contradictions of themselves" and to express a yearning "for their own destruction," and Wordsworth's "mystical imagination" is recognized to be "a hater of temporal nature" and "the enemy of poetry as of all distinctively human experience." Ferry's closing summation of the Wordsworth of the great decade is that "his genius was his enmity to man, which he mistook for love, and his mistake led him into confusions which he could not bear. But when he banished his confusions, he banished his distinctive greatness as well."[13]

Even the confirmed Arnoldian must admit the plausibility of some of the insights achieved by the recent critics who premise their reading of Wordsworth on the paradoxical strains and equivocal attitudes in his poetry. And it is a measure of the range and magnitude of Wordsworth's achievement that he continues to speak to us and our interests when interpreted by neo-Hegelian concepts, or when viewed as a proto-Mallarmé, or as a Blake manqué, or as, under the brave surface, really one of us in our age of alienation, anguish, and existential absurdity. An inveterate under-reading of the textual surface, however, turns readily into a habitual over-reading. The problem is, to what extent do these recent critical perspectives on Wordsworth simply bring into visibility what was always, although obscurely, there, and to what extent do they project upon his poems the form of their own prepossessions?

This is not the place to argue out the difficult issue. Instead, I shall cite some contemporary critics who, like A. C. Bradley, believe that Arnold described what is really there, but enlarge the scope of their vision to encompass the half of Wordsworth from which Arnold averted his ken. In their work, as in Bradley's essay, Wordsworth stands as a complex but integral poet, rather than as a radically divided one whose deepest inclinations, known to the modern critic but not to the poet himself, undercut or annul his repeated affirmations.

Like the recent explorers of the problematic Wordsworth, Lionel Trilling points to an aspect of his poetry that is strange, remote, even chilling to us. His account of it, however, is not psychoanalytic (Wordsworth's unconscious revulsion from life) but historical—Wordsworth's participation in a persistent strain of Hebrew and Christian culture which, at odds with the modern preoccupation with heroic struggle and apocalyptic violence, is committed to quietism, peace, and a wise passiveness. Wordsworth's quietism, however, "is not in the least a negation of life, but . . . an affirmation of life so complete that it needed no saying"; Trilling in fact uses Wordsworth as the positive standard by which to define the negatives of our adversary culture. Wordsworth has an "acute sense of his own being" that sharpens his awareness of other beings, and his intention is "to require us to acknowledge" the being of his narrative personae and so "to bring them within the range of conscience" and of "natural sympathy." It is not Wordsworth but we moderns who "do not imagine being . . . that it can be a joy" and who "are in love, at least in our literature, with the fantasy of death."[14] Writing also in the affirmative tradition of Arnold, Jonathan Wordsworth nonetheless identifies in *The Ruined Cottage* a dimension of poetic genius that Arnold had denied to Wordsworth: the power to reconcile us imaginatively with an instance of seemingly pointless suffering, futile courage, and meaningless death in a way that manifests both the poet's artistry and his "humanity"—"an insight into emotions not his own"—and with a success that places him "among the very few great English tragic writers."[15]

The position of Harold Bloom in the critical division about Wordsworth's poetry is a complex one. Citing Geoffrey Hartman, he concurs in the latter's distinction between surface and covert meaning and in the associated claim that, as Bloom puts it, "the inner problem of *The Prelude,* and of all the poetry of Wordsworth's great decade, is that of the autonomy of the poet's creative imagination," hence of a "hidden conflict between Poetry and Nature." But Bloom's reading of Wordsworth, taken overall, is different from Hartman's. He accepts Wordsworth's own statement, most notably in the "Prospectus" to *The Recluse,* that his high argument is the possibility of a union, by means of imagination, between mind and nature, in a reciprocity that redeems the world of ordinary experience. Instead of regarding Wordsworth as an all-but-Blake, he expressly differentiates his poetry from Blake's and parallels it instead to that of Wallace Stevens, as a "naturalistic celebration of the possibilities inherent in our condition here and now." Bloom accordingly reads *Tintern Abbey* as representing the poet in the act of discovering the theme of all his best poetry, a "reciprocity between the external world and his own mind" in which the two agents are equal in initiative and power. *The Old Cumberland Beggar,* in Bloom's analysis, registers a correlative aspect of Wordsworth's genius, his reverence for essential human life, seemingly alienated and "stripped to the nakedness of primordial condition," yet "still powerful in dignity, still infinite in value." And though he believes that Wordsworth's confidence in an imaginative communion of mind, nature, and man later weakened and failed, Bloom pays tribute to the novelty and magnitude of the enterprise. Wordsworth "personified a heroic mode of naturalism, which even he then proved unable to sustain." "No poet since," he declares, "has given us more."[16] Such a view is consonant with that of the present writer, who has explored *The Prelude,* and the opening book of *The Recluse* into which it leads, as Wordsworth's attempt to save the traditional design and values of human life, inherited from a Christian past, but to translate them to a naturalistic frame of reference—that is, to represent them as generated by a reciprocity between the natural world and the minds of men, "as natural beings in the strength of nature."[17]

Wordsworth criticism is in a flourishing condition these days, and its vigorous internal disputes testify to the poet's continuing vitality and pertinence. We are rediscovering what a number of Wordsworth's major contemporaries acknowledged—that he has done what only the greatest poets do. He has transformed the inherited language of poetry into a medium adequate to express new ways of perceiving the world, new modes of experience, and new relations of the individual consciousness to itself, to its past, and to other men. More than all but a very few English writers, Wordsworth has altered not only our poetry, but our sensibility and our culture.

SEVEN

Coleridge's "A Light in Sound": Science, Metascience, and Poetic Imagination

Iɴ the margin of *The Eolian Harp,* as printed in his *Poems* of 1797, Coleridge penciled, "This I think the most perfect poem I ever wrote"; with characteristic self-deprecation he added, "Bad may be the best perhaps."[1] Coleridge's first sentence is justified by the crucial part played by the poem not only in his own poetic development, but as the first and paradigmatic instance of the central Romantic form I have elsewhere called "the greater Romantic lyric" of description and meditation.

In the mid-1790s Coleridge's ambitious longer poems were in the genre he called "the sublimer Ode," in which he imitated the oracular manner and visionary matter of an earlier era when, as he said, "the Bard and the Prophet were one and the same character."[2] Writing amid the hopes and terrors engendered by the turbulent early years of the French Revolution, he had tried—emulating Milton in an earlier period of revolutionary crisis—to endow his poems with a resonant and authoritative public voice, like that of the biblical prophets, as the sanction for a philosophical, theological, and moral frame of reference that would help his contemporaries keep their bearings in a time of dereliction and dismay. These poems included passages of eloquence, but they manifested a borrowed and unconvincing stance, ill-digested Miltonisms, and a shrill falsetto voice; as Coleridge himself commented, in the effort to dramatize and give "a poetic colouring to abstract and metaphysical truths," his poetry "is crowded and sweats beneath a heavy burthen of Ideas and Imagery! It has seldom Ease."[3]

In *The Eolian Harp* Coleridge establishes the presence of a private person in a localized setting, speaking with a conversational voice in a fluent blank verse that conceals the intricacy of the structure, in which the counter-movements of description and meditation form a double helix. The poem begins with a description of observed details of the outer scene, then turns inward to the play of the observing consciousness; at the same time the consciousness, freed from time and space, moves out through a sustained evolution of memory, thought, and anticipation, which is controlled throughout by the seemingly casually chosen particulars of the physical setting, rises to a climactic moment of vision beyond sense, then turns again outward and also rounds back to end where it had begun, with a recapitulation of the details of the outer scene. *The Eolian Harp* is a flawed example of this remarkable poetic invention; there are instances of stock diction and standard moral parallels ("Meet emblems they of Innocence and Love!" "such should Wisdom be"), and the concluding verse-paragraph strikes the modern reader as a timid and ineptly managed retreat to religious orthodoxy from the bold speculation of the middle of the poem. Within a few years, however, Coleridge eliminated such weaknesses to achieve a perfection of the circuitous lyric of description and meditation in *Frost at Midnight* (1798).

The standard text of *The Eolian Harp* is usually dated 1795, but is in fact the version that Coleridge published in his collected poems, *Sibylline Leaves*, in 1817. Between 1795 and 1817 the poem was frequently altered and supplemented so that, although it was the first of his conversation poems to be undertaken, it was the last to be completed. The final version is thus a palimpsest that can serve as an index to Coleridge's evolving thought and imagination over a period of twenty-two years—the crucial years between his early and his mature views of the world. I shall sketch the four chief stages of the poem's development; references are to the line numbers in the standard text.

1. The first stage was a manuscript draft of seventeen lines entitled "Effusion 35. Clevedon, August 20th, 1795."[4] It corresponds, though with differences of detail, to the first sixteen and a half lines of the final version. "Effusion" connoted a spontaneous expression of personal circumstances and feelings. On 20 August Coleridge was engaged to marry Sara Fricker, and the poem represents the lovers on a visit to the cottage in Somersetshire that they were about to rent as their first home. The poet is seated by the cottage at evening, his bride leaning against his arm, receptive to the light and scents and sounds of the peaceful scene. In the partly opened window they have placed that favorite Romantic musical instrument, a wind-harp—that is, an oblong sounding box whose strings, in response to the variable touch of the breeze, vibrate into chords of altering pitch and loudness. The lover's consciousness invests the relations of the casement and the harp, the harp and the circumambient breeze, with the posture, languor, and guile of erotic dalliance. In the final rendering of these lines:

> And that simplest Lute,
> Placed length-ways in the clasping casement, hark!
> How by the desultory breeze caress'd
> Like some coy maid half yielding to her lover,
> It pours such sweet upbraiding, as must needs
> Tempt to repeat the wrong!

2. The second chief stage was the first published version, in Coleridge's *Poems on Various Subjects* of 1796. Although still called an "Effusion," the poem has been developed into an obviously artful construction of fifty-six lines; it corresponds to all of the final text except that it lacks lines 26–33. This

version is the one that justifies the usual description of *The Eolian Harp* as a wedding or honeymoon poem: Coleridge and Sara, having been married on 4 October 1795, are now living in the cottage at Clevedon.[5] Taking up where the earlier manuscript left off, Coleridge first continues the earlier sexual imagery (the sounds, at the bolder importunities of the masculine wind, "over delicious surges sink and rise"), then introduces a descriptive tour-de-force wherein the witchery of nature's music transforms, to the musing mind, the sights and odors and sounds of this world into a fantasy of "Fairy-Land" or (the subsequent imagery suggests) of an exotic paradise,

> Where Melodies round honey-dropping flowers,
> Footless and wild, like birds of Paradise,
> Nor pause, nor perch, hovering on untam'd wing!

The poet's meditation now shifts (line 34) to recall recurrent occasions in which—not at evening and in the company of the beloved, but alone and while resting from his work at high noon—he lies stretched out on a nearby hillside, watching the dance of sunlight on the sea. In this remembered situation the presently perceived wind-harp remains the vehicle of the metaphoric process of thought, but the poet, when musing in solitude, is preoccupied not with love but with metaphysics. First the sounds of the harp (lines 39–43) become the analogue for the fantasies that, random and various as the breeze, "traverse my indolent and passive brain." Then, in a sudden focus of the random thoughts, the harp modulates into a radical image for the consciousness of all living things, responding with the music of thought to one divine and all-informing breeze:

> And what if all of animated nature
> Be but organic Harps diversely fram'd
> That tremble into thought, as o'er them sweeps
> Plastic and vast, one intellectual breeze,
> At once the Soul of each, and God of all?

The term "plastic" for a formative and organizing principle within nature—derived from Ralph Cudworth and other seventeenth-century Neoplatonists—was widely used in the 1790s, and Coleridge suggested in several other poems written at the time of *The Eolian Harp* that there is in nature an indwelling cause of the organization and consciousness of all individual existents.[6] But he always expressed this concept in a guarded way, and in *The Eolian Harp* he presents it in the mode of a hypothetical question. Even in this form it turns out to be too bold, for even more than in his contemporary poems, it opens up a possibility that filled Coleridge with metaphysical terror: the world-view he called "Pantheism." That is, the passage threatens to absorb a transcendent and personal Creator of the world, without remainder, into an indwelling Soul of Nature, the *Pneuma* or *Spiritus Sacer* or *Anima Mundi* of the Stoics and Neoplatonists, which informs all the material universe and constitutes all modes of consciousness. Furthermore, as in the pagan philosophers who had taken the terms *pneuma, spiritus,* and *anima* in the literal sense of "breeze" or "breath," Coleridge's "intellectual breeze" even suggests a regressive form of the religion of Nature in which the unifying presence is a sacred wind or divine breath.[7] The poet therefore represents his hypothetical speculation as having been spoken aloud, so that Sara—the voice of domestic Christian piety, a dramatized aspect of Coleridge's own divided mind—may dispraise such philosophy as "shapings of the unregenerate mind." The lyric speaker precipitately retracts the analogy and instead acknowledges his faith in a Chrisitan Deity capable of yielding, to a sinful and miserable man, a grace beyond his deserts. The listing of these gifts in the concluding line closes the circle of the poem by repeating, in reverse order, the descriptive details of the beginning: "Peace, and this Cot, and thee, heart-honour'd Maid"—ending thus with the "pensive Sara" addressed in the opening phrase.

3. Except that it dropped "Effusion" from the title, Coleridge's *Poems* of 1797 reproduced the version published in 1796. Coleridge introduced the third major change six years later, in his *Poems* of 1803. Here he deleted lines 21–25—the

comparison of the music of the wind-harp to the sound of twilight elfins[8]—in order to move directly from the relationship of the two human lovers, as imaged in the erotic interplay between breeze and harp, to an encompassing love that relates the poet to all things in a world where even the silent air is potential music. In the original version of this inserted passage:

> Methinks it should have been impossible
> Not to love all things in a World like this,
> Where e'en the Breezes of the simple Air
> Possess the power and Spirit of Melody!

4. The fourth important change completes the poem as we have it now. In his collected poetry of 1817, *Sibylline Leaves*, Coleridge for the first time entitled the poem "The Eolian Harp." He restored the lines on fairy-land and the birds of paradise which he had dropped from the preceding edition, letting them stand between the passage on human love and that on the love for all things. Then, after he had finished correcting the proofs for *Sibylline Leaves*, Coleridge sent the printer a list of Errata in which he included, for insertion immediately after the lines on the birds of paradise, a new quatrain, together with a version of the succeeding passage on the love for all things which he had revised so as to accord with these four new lines. The total insertion, which I reproduce as it was printed in the Errata, constitutes lines 26–33 of the final text:

> O! the one Life, within us and abroad,
> Which meets all Motion and becomes its soul,
> A Light in Sound, a sound-like power in Light,
> Rhythm in all Thought, and Joyance every where—
> Methinks, it should have been impossible
> Not to love all things in a world so fill'd,
> Where the breeze warbles and the mute still Air
> Is Music slumbering on its instrument!

"O! the one Life . . ." The exclamation introduces a moment of vision that every reader feels to be the imaginative climax of the poem. These lines, however, in T. S. Eliot's phrase, communicate before they are understood. In the confidence that they will communicate more subtly and richly after they are understood—and also that to understand them is to understand what is most distinctive in Coleridge's mature thought and imagination—I shall undertake to explicate the passage by seeking answers to four questions: What did Coleridge mean by his allusion to "a light in sound, a sound-like power in light"? How is this allusion related to "the one Life within us and abroad, / Which meets all motion"? In what way does the insight into a light in sound justify the sense of "joyance every where"? And what has this entire complex of a light in sound, the one Life, and universal joyance to do with the relation between the human lovers that precedes it and the culminating love for all things that follows it?

Exploration of the conceptual scheme that underlies this passage involves Coleridge's views about Newton's *Opticks*, Newton's scientific methods and theories, and the post-Newtonian world picture; the new metaphysical system that Coleridge constructed on the basis of his reading in Friedrich Schelling and other German *Naturphilosophen;* concepts that he found in Jacob Boehme and other esoteric thinkers; as well as his interpretation of the biblical accounts of the creation and the Incarnation; so that I must be very selective. But even a cursory survey of the cognitive infrastructure of the imaginative moment expressed in these eight lines will indicate that they implicate a much heavier "burthen of Ideas" than that under which his early bardic poems had sweated and strained. Coleridge lamented repeatedly that metaphysics and "abstruse thought," to which he had turned for refuge from personal disasters, had depressed or destroyed his power of poetry. Unwanted "metaphysical trains of thought," he wrote in a letter to William Sotheby,

> when I wished to write a poem, beat up Game of far other kind—instead of a Covey of poetic Partridges with whirring wings of music . . . up came a metaphysical Bustard, urging it's slow, heavy, laborious, earth-skimming Flight, over dreary & level Wastes.

But less than a week earlier Coleridge had also insisted to the same correspondent that "a great Poet must be, implicitè if not explicitè, a profound Metaphysician. He may not have it in logical coherence. . . . But he must have it by *Tact*."[9] It is because, in the passage of *The Eolian Harp* which is our concern, the burthen of ideas remains largely implicit within the imaginative insight it generates and supports that Coleridge is able to write philosophical poetry with the ease he had earlier sought and here supremely achieved.

I. A LIGHT IN SOUND

What are we to make of the mysterious reference to "a light in sound, a sound-like power in light"? The figures, technically, are oxymorons, and have usually been interpreted as alluding to synesthesia—the phenomenon in which the stimulation of one sense evokes a response involving a different sense. There had during the preceding century been intense interest, among poets and critics as well as philosophers, in such intersensory phenomena, stimulated in part by Newton's analogies in his *Opticks* between the propagation of light and of sound and between the perception of harmony and discord in musical tones and in colors.[10] Coleridge shared this interest in what he called in the *Biographia Literaria* "the *vestigia communia* of the senses, the latency of all in each, and more especially . . . the excitement of vision by sound,"[11] and the line "A light in sound . . ." may include the suggestion of such a vestigial common-sensorium as an instance of the universal "latency of all in each" that leads to the poet's invocation of the one Life. But Coleridge's orbit of reference in this line is much wider than the psychology of sense-perception, for it involves a total metaphysic of the constitution of the material universe, of the nature of life, and of the relation of the mind to the universe it perceives.

The quatrain of *The Eolian Harp* on a light in sound was added to the text in a list of Errata to *Sibylline Leaves* that Coleridge composed no earlier than the spring of 1816, and possibly as late as the spring of 1817.[12] This places the writing of the quatrain squarely in the middle of the remarkable span of four years or so when, in a sudden burst of intellectual activity, Coleridge composed his most important works on philosophy and science, including the *Biographia Literaria*, the *Theory of Life*, his two *Lay Sermons*, his radically revised and enlarged version of *The Friend*, and the series of *Philosophical Lectures* that he delivered between December 1818 and March 1819.[13] All these works contain passages relevant to Coleridge's theories of the relations between light, sound, and life, and I shall later cite some of them. Most immediately pertinent and revealing, however, are a series of philosophical letters that Coleridge wrote between November 1816 and January 1818[14]—that is, during and soon after the time when he composed the Errata—which show that he was almost obsessively preoccupied with the ideas that underlie the passage added to *The Eolian Harp*.

Thus, Coleridge wrote Ludwig Tieck on 4 July 1817, a few weeks before *Sibylline Leaves* was issued, that the positions taken by Newton in his *Opticks* that "*a Ray* of Light" is a "*Thing*," "a physical *synodical Individuum*," and that "the Prism is a mere mechanic Dissector" of "this complex yet divisible Ray," had always appeared to him "monstrous FICTIONS!" Instead he put forward the view—adopted, he said, "probably from Behmen's Aurora, which I had *conjured over* at School"—"that Sound was = Light under the praepotence of Gravitation, and Color = Gravitation under the praepotence of Light."[15] Above all, two letters that Coleridge wrote shortly thereafter to the Swedenborgian, C. A. Tulk, provide decisive clues not only to the line about light and sound but also (as we shall see) to the entire passage we are scrutinizing. In the first letter, written two months after the publication of *Sibylline Leaves*, Coleridge declared that "the two Poles of the material Universe are . . . Light and Gravitation. . . . The Life of Nature consists in the tendency of the Poles to re-unite, and to find themselves in the re-union." Then:

> Color is Gravitation under the power of Light . . . while Sound on the other hand is Light under the power or paramountcy of Gravitation. Hence the analogies of Sound to Light. . . .[16]

"A light in sound, a sound-like power in light"—we find in these letters references to the light, sound, and power alluded to in this line, and to the analogies that the line suggests between sound and light, as well as an indicated relation between these matters and life—"the Life of Nature." But what has all this to do with gravitation, the deficiencies of Newton's theory of light, and the polarity of the material universe, and what are we to make of "praepotence"? At first sight these passages, instead of explaining the mystery of a light in sound, seem to wrap it in an enigma. To explain in turn this enigma, we need to glance at some elements in the world-view that Coleridge was evolving in the period 1815–18.

Coleridge's reference of his views on light and sound to Boehme's *Aurora*, it will appear later, has substantial grounds, but it is misleading nonetheless. Coleridge's immediate precedents for the particular terms and metaphysical constructions in these letters were the writings of the contemporary philosopher Friedrich Schelling and, to a lesser extent, the writings of Schelling's fellow workers in *Naturphilosophie*, especially Henrik Steffens.[17] He had begun to study Schelling intensively in about 1808—his burst of philosophical activity in the 1810s is, in considerable part, a result of the exciting possibilities that Schelling's thought opened out to him. For the sake of brevity I shall attend mainly to Coleridge's own views, with only an occasional glance at the German formulations that he adopted but altered to accord with his prior interests and speculations. Our investigation leads us to the center of Coleridge's philosophy of nature. This is an area of his thought that, until very recently, scholars have either discreetly overlooked or else—assessing it as an attempt to achieve by free fantasy what scientists discover by patient experiment—have rejected as "mere abracadabra," "a bizarre farrago of pretentious nonsense."[18] Such judgments are inevitable if we simply apply to Coleridge's scheme of nature the criteria of the philosophical positivism that Coleridge's scheme was specifically intended to dispossess. If our intent, on the other hand, is not to dismiss but to understand an important development in nineteenth-century intellectual history, then we can do no better than to emulate Coleridge's

own procedure, which John Stuart Mill found to be so intellectually liberating. Mill pointed out that by Bentham (the
great philosophical positivist of his time), men have been led
to ask of an opinion, "Is it true?" By Coleridge, they have
been led to ask, "What is the meaning of it?" and to answer
this question by trying to look at the opinion "from within."

> The long duration of a belief, [Coleridge] thought, is at least
> proof of an adaptation in it to some portion or other of the
> human mind; and if, on digging down to the root, we do not
> find, as is generally the case, some truth, we shall find some
> natural want or requirement of human nature which the doc-
> trine in question is fitted to satisfy.[19]

Let us then take Coleridge's vision of nature seriously and
try to look at it from within, to see what it undertook to
accomplish and what natural want it served to satisfy.

Coleridge's aim was not to replace experimental science
by speculative science, but instead to develop a counter-
metaphysic to the metaphysical foundations of modern science; his philosophy of nature, in short, was not science, nor
anti-science, but metascience. By the reference, in his letter
to Tieck, to Newton's "monstrous Fictions" in the *Opticks,* he
did not mean to oppugn Newton as an experimental physicist, to whose procedures and discoveries he paid spacious
tribute.[20] His objection was to Newton as a man whose prestige as a physicist had given impetus to a metaphysics that, in
Coleridge's view, permeated and vitiated all areas of thought
and culture in the eighteenth century, "the Epoch of the
Understanding and the Sense"[21] in philosophy, psychology,
politics, religion, and the arts. For despite his reluctance to
frame hypotheses, Newton had proposed, in the "Queries"
he added to his *Opticks,* that rays of light are "corpuscular,"
that is, "very small Bodies emitted from shining Substances,"
and that these bodies in motion excite "Waves of Vibrations,
or Tremors" in a hypothetical "aether." This aether, although
very "rare and subtile" is nonetheless a material medium that
pervades, in varying densities, both space and bodies and
serves to explain not only the action at a distance both of
light and gravity, but also the refraction and reflection of

light, as well as the propagation of light and sound from the eye and ear through the nerves "into the place of Sensation" where they are converted into sight and hearing.[22]

This procedure, Coleridge argues, sets up a logical regress, since it undertakes to solve "Phaenomena by Phaenomena that immediately become part of the Problem to be solved."[23] Worse still, Newton in his famed thirty-first Query had put forward the stark image of a universe whose ultimate elements are indivisible particles of matter capable of motion:

> It seems probable to me, that God in the Beginning form'd Matter in solid, massy, hard, impenetrable, moveable Particles, of such Sizes and Figures, and with such other Properties, and in such Proportion to Space, as most conduced to the End for which he form'd them.[24]

And as ultimate reality is thus reduced to masses and motion— for the simple reason that these are the only things that the highly specialized techniques of physical science are capable of managing mathematically—so the Creator of this reality is reconstrued to accord with such a postulated creation. That is, Newton's God is represented as the omnipresent mover of all particles, and also as the infallible seer of the particles in themselves that we are able to see only after they have been translated into the "images" formed by the sense through the intermediation of rays of light. God, Newton says, is "a powerful ever-living Agent, who being in all Places, is . . . able by his Will to move the Bodies within his boundless uniform Sensorium"; he is also the Being

> who in infinite Space, as it were in his Sensory, sees the things themselves intimately . . . wholly by their immediate presence to himself: Of which things the Images only carried through the Organs of Sense into our little Sensoriums, are there seen and beheld by that which in us perceives and thinks.[25]

"Sir Isaac Newton's Deity," Coleridge drily remarked, "seems to be alternately operose and indolent," for he undertakes to do everything, yet delegates so much power to "Vice-regent second causes" as "to make it inconceivable what he can have reserved."[26]

Newton's move, as Coleridge saw it, was an immense extrapolation of a working fiction of physical science—what we now call a "conceptual model"—into a picture of the actual constitution of the universe. The "Mechanic or Corpuscular Scheme," Coleridge said, "in order to submit the various phenomena of moving bodies to geometrical construction," had to abstract "from corporeal substance all its *positive* properties," leaving it only "figure and mobility. And as a *fiction of science,* it would be difficult to overvalue this invention." But Descartes and later thinkers "propounded it as *truth of fact:* and instead of a World *created* and filled with productive forces by the Almighty *Fiat,* left a lifeless Machine whirled about by the dust of its own Grinding."[27]

To Coleridge this view of the ultimate structure of reality was both incredible to human experience of the world and intolerable to human needs. As no more than a drastic subtraction from the rich diversity of sense-phenomena, it remains itself phenomenal, the product of what Coleridge repeatedly described as a "slavery" to the senses, especially to the eye. The "needlepoint pinshead System of the *Atomists*" was a fictional product of that "slavery to the eye" which reduces "the conceivable ... within the bounds of the *picturable,*" and excludes "all modes of existence which the theorist cannot in imagination, at least, *finger* and *peep* at!"[28] Against this world-picture, in the literal sense of "picture" as something that can be visualized, Coleridge again and again brought the charge that it is, precisely speaking, lethal. It has killed the living and habitable world of ordinary experience, as well as the metaphysical world of the pre-Cartesian and pre-Newtonian past, in which the mind of man had recognized an analogon to itself and to its life, purposes, sentiments, values, and needs; a world, therefore, in which man was a participant and could feel thoroughly at home. By the translation of the "scientific calculus" from a profitable fiction into ontology, Coleridge claimed in 1817, "a few brilliant discoveries have been dearly purchased at the loss of all communion with life and the spirit of Nature." And against this "philosophy of death," which leaves only the "relations of unproductive particles to each other," he posed his own philosophy of life, in which "the two component counter-powers actually interpenetrate each other, and generate a higher third, including both the former."[29]

That is, in radical opposition to the picture of a world composed of particles of matter in motion, to whose impact an alien mind is passively receptive, Coleridge sets up what, following Schelling, he calls a "vital," or "dynamic," or "constructive" philosophy. The elements of this philosophy are not moving material particles but inherent energies, or "powers," that polarize into positive and negative "forces" (also called "thesis and antithesis") which operate according to "the universal Law of Polarity or essential Dualism."[30] By this Coleridge means that the generative and sustaining elements of his universe exist only relatively to each other and manifest an irremissive tendency on the one hand to oppose themselves and on the other hand to reunite. These powers and forces are not physical or phenomenal, but metascientific and pre-phenomenal elements (in Coleridge's terms, they are not "real" but "ideal"), hence they cannot be pictured, but only imagined; they do, however, within the phenomenal world which they bring into being, have especially close and revealing analogues that Coleridge calls their "exponents." It is only by their "living and generative interpenetration," or "synthesis," that the polar powers and forces achieve the condition of matter, and so move into the phenomenal realm available to the senses. "In all pure phaenomena," Coleridge says, "we behold only the copula, the balance or indifference of opposite energies," and "matter" is to be considered "a Product— coagulum spiritûs, the pause, by interpenetration, of opposite energies."[31]

We are at length ready to turn back to Coleridge's enigmatic statement, in his letter to C. A. Tulk of September 1817, that "Color is Gravitation under the power of Light . . . while Sound on the other hand is Light under the power or paramountcy of Gravitation." "The two Poles of the material Universe," Coleridge there says, are "Light and Gravitation." Or as he wrote in a manuscript note:

Well then, I say that all Powers may be reduced, in the first instance, into
Light & Gravity.
But each of these beget two other powers. Under Gravity we place Attraction and Repulsion: and under Light the Powers of Contraction and Dilation.[32]

That is, the two elemental counter-powers that generate the cosmos he calls "light" and "gravity." These are not the light we see nor the weight, or gravitational force, we feel; they exist on a different ontological plane as "speculative" or "ideal" powers of which phenomenal light and weight serve as the closest "exponents" in experience. Each of these two powers evolves two counter-forces, constituting a tetrad of forces that Coleridge represents graphically as a north-south line crossed by an east-west line: gravity involves a pull in and its opposite, a push out, while light pulses radially in all directions and at the same time contracts back to its center. The continuous and incremental syntheses of the two counter-powers of gravity and light constitute the material elements and bodies of everything that exists. The innumerable qualitative differences among existing things, hence among the phenomena perceived by the senses, are determined by which of these two elemental powers—at any given level of their synthesis—is "predominant," in a range of ratios that extends from the extreme predominance of gravity, through a mid-point of "indifference" or "neutralization" between the two powers, to the extreme predominance of light. "That a thing *is*," as Coleridge puts it, "is owing to the co-inherence therein of any two powers; but that it is *that* particular thing arises from the proportions in which these powers are co-present, either as predominance or as reciprocal neutralization."[33] (For "predominance," Coleridge elsewhere uses the alternative expressions "praepotence," "dynasty," "under the power of," or "paramountcy.")

The metaphysical enigma has, I trust, become transparent enough so that we can look through it at the initial mystery of *The Eolian Harp*, line 28: "A light in sound, a sound-like power in light." Seated in close communion with his bride and luxuriously open to the light and color and sounds of the outer world, the poet, by a leap of imagination, achieves insight to the common pre-phenomenal powers of which all these phenomena are exponents, and so apprehends the unity within their qualitative diversity—sounds that incorporate the elemental counter-power of light, and light that, appearing as color, incorporates the elemental counter-power of gravity. For as we have seen, the power of gravitation, when predominant over the "co-present" power of light, manifests itself to the senses as sound, and when subordinate to light, manifests itself to the senses as color.

II. THE ONE LIFE

In what Coleridge called his "speculative," as opposed to "empirical," science of nature and life, he "constructs" (in the sense of rendering intelligible by reference to a single genetic principle) the total universe. Driven by their inherent stresses of opposition-in-unity, and manifesting in the struggle diverse degrees of relative "predominance," the powers of light and gravity evolve, by the progressive synthesis of prior syntheses, through the several distinctive orders of organization that Coleridge, following Schelling, calls "potences."[34] At each level of organization, entities are linked by correspondences— according to an equivalence in the predominance of light or gravity—to entities on all other levels. On the first level of potence we get magnetism, electricity, and galvanism (which to Coleridge includes chemical combination), then all the forms of the inorganic world, then the forms of the organic world of plants and animals up to the highest stage of organic life, man; at which point mind, or "consciousness," emerges. This culminating achievment is a radical breakthrough in the developmental process, for consciousness is capable of a reflex act by which—in a continuing manifestation of "the universal Law of Polarity" whereby it counterposes, in order to reconcile, the outer world as "object" to itself as "subject"[35]—it reengenders as knowledge the natural world within which it has itself been engendered, and of which it remains an integral part. Thus man's mind closes the evolutionary circle of polar generation by the powers of light and gravitation, the human and the nonhuman world merging at the focal point of consciousness.

We come to the moment in line 26 of *The Eolian Harp*—"O! the one Life within us and abroad." Coleridge's preoccupation with the one Life as a truth manifested in highest human experience, but alien to the post-Newtonian world-picture, goes back long before 1816 or 1817, when he added this passage to the poem. As early as 1802, for example, he had written to Sotheby that Nature will have her proper interest only to him "who believes & feels, that every Thing has a Life of its own, & that we are all *one Life*." In the Hebrew Psalmists, unlike the mythological poets among the Greeks, you find "genuine Imagination."

> In the Hebrew Poets each Thing has a Life of it's own, & yet they are all one Life. In God they move & live, & *have* their Being—not *had,* as the cold System of Newtonian Theology represents, but *have.*[36]

And in the conversation poems that Coleridge wrote within several years after the 1796 version of *The Eolian Harp*, the climax of each meditation on a landscape had been a moment of insight—the sudden awareness of a single Presence behind and within the phenomena of sense. In all these early poems, however, the visionary moment had been described in terms that had long been traditional. In *The Eolian Harp* of 1796, the poet tentatively put forward a latter-day version of the Stoic World-Soul—"one intellectual breeze"—as the principle that makes all animated nature "tremble into thought." In other conversation poems the poet found "religious meanings in the forms of nature!" or discovered that nature was an orthodox "Temple" built by "God" and that the diversified landscape "seem'd like Omnipresence"; or else the landscape manifested itself to be God's veiled self-revelation,

                              of such hues
        As veil the Almighty Spirit, when yet he makes
        Spirits perceive his presence;

or (in the concept that had persisted from early Christian exegetes through Bishop Berkeley) the objects and aspects of the landscape were recognized to be *verba visibilia* in God's Book of Nature,

> The lovely shapes and sounds intelligible
> Of that eternal language which thy God
> Utters.[37]

Now, some fifteen years later, the metascience of nature that Coleridge had evolved from German *Naturphilosophie* provided him with a full and detailed conceptual structure to support and articulate his earlier intuitions. In this scheme, in which all matter and spirit are generated by the interplay of the same elemental powers, there is no gap between the living and the lifeless, nature and man, or matter and mind, but only a distinction of levels of organization. "What is *not* Life," Coleridge asks, "that really *is?*" For "in the identity of the two counter-powers, Life *sub*sists; in their strife it *con*sists: and in their reconciliation it at once dies and is born again into a new form." This "universal life" of ever-renewing strife and reconciliation pulses through all individual forms and all the orders of being, beginning with "the life of metals"—where in "its utmost *latency* . . . life is one with the elementary powers of mechanism"[38]—up through the progressive levels of "individuation" to the human consciousness, which in its living reciprocity with its specific contrary, nature, is capable of achieving the awareness that there is only one Life within us and abroad.

Hence the statement I quoted earlier from Coleridge's letter to C. A. Tulk that "the Life of Nature" consists in the sustained tendency of the poles of "Light and Gravitation" to separate and re-unite.[39] But this same revealing letter, written within a few months of the final version of *The Eolian Harp,* makes it plain that Coleridge's intuition of "the one Life within us and abroad" has not merely a metascientific basis, but a biblical one as well. It will help to clarify this essential aspect of Coleridge's thought—and of the poem—if we turn back to consider the significance of Coleridge's statement to Tieck, that same year, that he had adopted the idea of the relation of light and gravity to color and sound "probably from Behmen's Aurora, which I had *conjured over* at School."

The Aurora, written in 1611–12, was the first of Jacob Boehme's books; it is incomplete, and even more obscure than Boehme's later expositions of his esoteric but very influential doctrines. Through the fantastic terminology and melodramatic narration, however, we can make out its basic concepts and design. Boehme's undertaking is to elucidate the mystery of the creation of the world and of man, as the initial episode in the history of human and cosmic salvation. He bases his account of the creation on the first chapter of Genesis (which he regards as in fact the story of a second creation, intended to repair the wreck of the angelic world occasioned by the fall of the angel Lucifer) and also upon the commentary on the creation in the Gospel of John (on which Boehme largely relies for his account of the first creation of a perfect world). But Boehme claims that he has been inspired by divine grace infused "in my spirit," and that he is therefore able to decipher the spiritual truths concealed within the esoteric sound-symbolism of the literal biblical narrative.[40] Boehme's symbolic interpretation of the creation (more accurately, of the two creations) turns out, in fact, to be mainly a remarkably elaborated version of the doctrines and terminology he had learned (at this period of his life, at second hand) from the alchemical philosophy of Paracelsus and other Renaissance Hermeticists.

To Boehme, the essential condition for all creativity and progression, both in being and in thinking, is a strenuous tension between contraries, or opposed forces, whose sequential separations and unions give rise to everything that exists. The archetypal struggle in the fallen world is between the contrary forces of good and evil, love and hate, but these are destined to eventuate in the triumph of good and love in the coming redemption. Even the original creation of the angelic world, however, resulted from the energy generated by opponent principles. For God the Father manifests a joyous union of divine powers that Boehme calls, collectively, the "Salliter," or the "Sal-niter." This totality involves seven different *Qualitäten,* which Boehme derives from *Quelle* and *quellen* ("a spring," "to gush forth"), and which are therefore not what we ordinarily call "qualities," but "powers" or "forces" *(Kräfte).* Each one of these elemental powers is a balance of opposing contraries, and each also has its appropriate counter-power. From the divine Salliter, in the successive unions and renewed oppositions of the diverse opponent powers and forces, issues all that constitutes the world, from stones and metals through plants and animals to the body and spirit of man, who as microcosm is the perfect analogue of the world's body and spirit. In Boehme's world there is thus no gap between animate and inanimate, body and mind, conscient and inconscient—all are an emanation of the powers of the one Deity, and throughout all there surges one life, exhibiting itself in the conflict and interpenetration of the same vital forces.

In this great radiation outward from the divine source of all life and being, Boehme puts by far the greatest stress on the role in creation of two elements, sound and light. The reasons for this emphasis are patent. In the Book of Genesis, God's creation is by word, or sound. His first creative sounds are, "Let there be light," which forthwith become light, and His later creative sounds become all forms of life, including man. And in the first chapter of John we find the creative fiat represented as the Word, which is equated with light, and also with life, and finally becomes itself incarnate:

> In the beginning was the Word, and the Word was with God, and the Word was God. . . .
> All things were made by him; and without him was not any thing made that was made.
> In him was life; and the life was the light of men.
> And the light shineth in darkness; and the darkness comprehended it not. . . .
> And the Word was made flesh, and dwelt among us. . . .

Boehme repeatedly echoes these passages from Genesis and John (see, for example, chapters 18 and 26). In his symbolic translation of them into a philosophy of nature, light is represented, not as one of the primal powers, but as something which is generated from the ensemble of the seven powers; as Boehme puts it, light is "perpendicular" to the ontological plane of the powers. This light is equated with the Son, as well as with the sun, the "place" of light in the heavens; while in man, the light constitutes his soul and spirit. Sound, on the other hand, is one of the seven elemental powers within the divine Salliter itself; this power Boehme calls "Mercurius" (that is, Mercury or Hermes Trismegistus, the great magus of the Hermetic philosophers). Boehme identifies this "sound" *(Schall)* with the creative voice and with the harmony of the heavenly music; accordingly, from this "sound, tone, tune or noise . . . ensued *speech*, language, and the *distinction* of everything, as also the ringing melody and *singing* of the holy angels, and therein consisteth the forming or framing of all *colours*, beauty and ornament, as also the heavenly *joyfulness*" *(Aurora,* 10.1). In its manifestation as speech, sound serves as the vehicle for the expression of spirit, hence as the vehicle (in God's creative fiat) by which the third aspect of God, the Holy Spirit, expresses itself. Sound, in Boehme's intricate system of analogies and identities, thus is equated with the Word, or divine Logos itself, and so is integral with light and life and the Son, as an element in the triune nature of God which manifests itself throughout the creation.

Whatever the extent of his claimed knowledge of *The Aurora* during his schooldays, we know that Coleridge closely studied and copiously annotated this and other books by Boehme, in the English "Law edition," from the year 1807 on, just prior to and collaterally with his immersion in Schelling and other *Naturphilosophen* during the second decade of the nineteenth century.[41] Coleridge's thinking was inveterately organic and genetic, always traveling back to the radical of a view— or as he called it, to the "seminal" idea—which has proved historically capable of growing into a total metaphysic.[42] It should be clear even from my brief summation that he found a great deal in Boehme's dualistic vitalism that suited his own mature "dynamic" philosophy; and in the letter to Ludwig Tieck, as well as in his private annotations, Coleridge tended to impose on Boehme's inchoate views the terms and structure of the metascience he had developed on the basis of contemporary German thinkers. It was in line with this persistent tendency (and not in order to hide his debt to Schelling) that Coleridge interpreted Boehme's arcane statements about the primary roles of light and sound in nature to accord with his own doctrines about the elemental counter-powers of gravitation and light and their relative "predominance" in the diverse phenomena of sound and color.[43]

But what in Boehme's writings made the greatest appeal to Coleridge, as against Schelling's early *Naturphilosophie,* was that Boehme had derived his scheme of nature from the biblical accounts of the creation, although Coleridge feared that Boehme had not entirely avoided the "Pantheism" that he found blatantly manifested in Schelling—the assimilation of a transcendent Creator into a religion of Nature.[44] As far back as the letter to Sotheby of 1802, it will be recalled, Coleridge had discovered the sense of "one Life" within all things, specifically, in "the Hebrew poets" of the Old Testament. Now, in a marginal comment on *The Aurora,* he comments on Boehme's treatment of light in the creation and Incarnation:

> That not Heat but Light is the Heart of Nature is one of those truly profound and pregnant Thoughts that ever and anon astonish me in Boehme's writings. . . . The affinity . . . of the Flesh and Blood generally to Light I trust that I shall make clear in my commentaries on the first and sixth chapters of the Gospel of John. Hence in the Logos (distinctive energy) is *Light,* and the *Light* became the *Life* of Man.[45]

The "commentaries" on John to which Coleridge alludes he planned to include in his *Logosophia,* the comprehensive philosophical work on which he labored for decades but never completed. In this "Opus Maximum," the exposition of his own "Dynamic or Constructive Philosophy" was to be "preparatory" to "a detailed Commentary on the Gospel of St. John," in order "to prove that Christianity is true Philosophy"; and this section was in turn to be followed by a treatise on "the Mystics & Pantheists," including Jacob Boehme.[46]

We return to the indispensable letters that Coleridge wrote to C. A. Tulk in 1817 and early 1818. There he begins his

"rude and fragmentary" sketch of "the Science of the Construction of *Nature*" with God, who is the absolute "Identity"
or "*Prothesis*" which precedes any polarity between thesis and
antithesis; Coleridge comments that to adopt the alternative,
the "Lockian, and Newtonian" Creator as "an hypothetical
Watch-maker," is in fact to "live without God in the world."
And he begins his construction of nature—"the Genesis . . .
the *Birth* of Things"—with an interpretation of the opening
sentence of the Book of Genesis, "In the beginning God created the Heaven and the Earth." Coleridge's hermeneutics is
based on his view that the Bible embodies the ideas of "reason" in the mode of "imagination," hence that it is "a science
of realities" expressed in "symbols." His interpretation of the
biblical accounts of the creation, therefore, like Boehme's, is
symbolic, although on quite different grounds.[47]

I will not reconstruct the exegetic maneuvers by which
Coleridge translates "And the Earth was waste and void . . .
and Darkness on the Deep" to signify that what first came
into existence was "gravitation," which is best designated by
"the combination of the Ideas, Darkness & the Deep or Depth."
He continues:

> And God said—Let there be *Light:* and there was *Light.* And
> God divided the *Light* from the *Darkness*—i.e. Light from Grav-
> itation . . . and the two Poles of the material Universe are
> established, viz. Light and Gravitation. . . . The Life of Nature
> consists in the tendency of the Poles to re-unite. . . . God is the
> Sun of the Universe—it's gravitation or Being by his
> Omnipresence, it's Light by his only-begotten Son . . . Deus
> alter et idem!

He also conjoins the account of the creation of light in Genesis with the commentary on the creative Logos in the opening chapter of John:

> God SAID, Let there be Light: and there became LIGHT! In the
> beginning was the Word. All things *became* . . . through the
> Word, the living and vivific Word . . . whose Life is the *Light* of
> men. . . . The Light . . . rose up in the Darkness and in the
> Depth—and in and with it *became* . . . the two Primary Poles of
> Nature, Light and Gravitation.

On these grounds Coleridge proceeds to "construct" the orders of being and of sense-phenomena that make up the universe, including, in the passage which is our central concern, the construction of color as "Gravitation under the power of Light" and of sound as "light under the power or paramountcy of Gravitation."[48]

Coleridge's inserted passage in *The Eolian Harp,* then, is only the visible tip of a massive complex of submerged ideas, scientific and metascientific, Scriptural and theological. We know enough of this substructure to recognize now that the poet's moment of vision is also a theophany, and that the oxymorons in which the moment is expressed signify not only the "law of contradiction," or polarity, on which Coleridge's metascience is based, but also the central Christian mysteries. For in Coleridge's interwoven universe of correspondences and analogues, of exponents and symbols, "a light in sound" is the distant reflection of the light generated by the primal sound, "Let there be light," while "a sound-like power in light" is the distant echo of the creative Word which became flesh and is the Light as well as the Life both of nature and man.

In line 27, this one Life "meets all motion and becomes its soul." In the Newtonian world-picture, motion—as measured by the altering position, through time, of particles of matter in space—had been an elementary postulate. Coleridge, however, by intricate reasoning derives "ideal" (prephenomenal) time and space from his own first premise, or "Prothesis," as the primitive polar opposites whose synthesis constitutes "motion." He conceives motion, that is, as a point moving through space in time, so that it forms, and is represented graphically by, a line; and the bipolar line, in the next synthesis, achieves a third dimension as "depth." Coleridge cryptically summarizes to Tulk the role of these elementary constructs in generating the universe:

Time × Space = Motion. Attraction × Repulsion = Gravity as Depth.—These are ideal relations. The ideal + real, or rather the Ideal = Real, World arises out of chaos (= Indistinction) or begins, with the creation of Light.

He adds, however, that "a Life, a Power, an *Inside,* must have pre-existed" the ideal dimensions of time, space, motion, and depth, of which "the LIFE *appearing*" in the real, or material, world is the result; and that this process of the "interpenetration of opposite energies," of which matter is a product, sustains itself, as process, to constitute the "spirit" in all matter.[49] Otherwise stated: the elemental rhythm of opposing and interpenetrating polarities in which life consists, when it meets all "ideal" motion, brings it into existence as matter, in which the continuing pulsation of the one Life constitutes the spirit or soul; and this vital outer rhythm, he goes on to say in *The Eolian Harp,* has its analogue, in high moments of human consciousness, as a "rhythm in all thought."

III. J O Y A N C E

Now, what of the "joyance every where" in line 29? "Joy" and "joyance" were specialized terms, used by Coleridge as the emotional index to a particular relationship between the conscious self and the outer world. To clarify its significance in *The Eolian Harp,* we need to consider again Coleridge's evolving scale of being, at the point at which the reflexive consciousness emerges in man.

Man, Coleridge says in his letters to Tulk, represents the ultimate product of the two contrary "ends" of the life-process, namely "Individualization, or apparent detachment from Nature = progressive Organization" and "the re-union with Nature as the apex of Individualization."[50] And since, as he says in the contemporary work, the *Theory of Life,* "the form of polarity" applies at this as at every evolutionary stage, "the intensities must be at once opposite and equal," so that the independence of an individual man should ideally be matched by "interdependence" with other men in the social organization, while "as the ideal genius and the originality [i.e., the highest degree of human autonomy], in the same proportion must be the resignation to the real world, the sympathy and the intercommunion with Nature," which exists "in counterpoint to him."[51] But although man is both product and participant in the universal process of life, he is radically different from the rest of nature, in that by achieving consciousness, he also achieves freedom of the will. As Coleridge puts it in the same passage, man "is referred to himself, delivered up to his own charge"; and here things can go drastically wrong. For an excess in the tendency to individuation—especially when fostered by untoward "hardships" and "circumstances"—can force "a man in upon his little unthinking contemptible self," and so cut the individual consciousness off from the sense of its interdependence with other men and of its intercommunion with outer nature.[52]

To be cut off from all relationship to man and nature, to suffer what he called "the evils of separation and finiteness,"[53] was to Coleridge as to other Romantic thinkers and poets the radical affliction of the human condition. This is the state to which the Romantic philosopher Hegel gave the name "alienation," and it is, as Coleridge saw it, the inescapable situation of anyone who accepts the Newtonian world-picture, the dead universe of matter in motion, as existential reality. "Joy," on the other hand, is the term Coleridge specifically appropriated to the state of mind in which all alienation is annulled—it is an equipoise of the contrary mental powers, manifested in an inner life so abundant that it breaks through the barrier of self to yield awareness of the one Life that is shared with other selves and with nature. As Coleridge says about "joy" in his *Philosophical Lectures,* with respect to "genius," which is the term he uses for the creative power of the human mind and imagination:

> All genius exists in a participation of a common spirit. In joy individuality is lost. . . . To have a genius is to live in the universal, to know no self but that which is reflected not only from the faces of all around us, our fellow creatures, but reflected from the flowers, the trees, the beasts, yea from the very surface of the [waters and the] sands of the desert.[54]

To this I shall add a contemporary statement by Coleridge in *The Friend* of 1818. This passage, in its context, ascribes the scientific world-picture to an alienation of mind from nature, and counters it, as the premise of philosophy, with the primal intuition of an integrity of the self and not-self, mind and nature, of which the sign in human consciousness is the condition called "joy":

> The ground-work, therefore, of all true philosophy is the full apprehension of the difference between . . . that intuition of things which arises when we possess ourselves, as one with the whole . . . and that which presents itself when . . . we think of ourselves as separated beings, and place nature in antithesis to the mind, as object to subject, thing to thought, death to life. This is abstract knowledge, or the science of the mere understanding. . . . [The former on the other hand] is an eternal and infinite self-rejoicing, self-loving, with a joy unfathomable, with a love all comprehensive.[55]

IV. L O V E

In this intuition of the community of all life, the movement from "a joy unfathomable" to "a love all comprehensive" parallels the movement in *The Eolian Harp* from "joyance every where" to the universal love described in the next lines, which Coleridge revised and integrated with the added passage on the one Life:

> Rhythm in all thought, and joyance every where—
> Methinks, it should have been impossible
> Not to love all things in a world so filled. . . .

There remains, in conclusion, to show the relation in Coleridge's thinking at this period between all-comprehensive love and the elemental powers of gravity and light, as these manifest themselves in a light in sound.

In this instance, too, the connection is established in one of his letters to C. A. Tulk. There having "constructed," on both metascientific and biblical grounds, "the two Primary Poles of Nature, Light and Gravitation," he goes on to say that these "correlatives and correspondent Opposites, by and in which the Unity is revealed," are

(to borrow your happy and most expressive Symbol) the Male
and female of the World of Time, in whose wooings, and retirings and nuptial conciliations all other marriages . . . are celebrated inclusively.—These truths it is my Object to enforce in
the manner best fitted (alas! how hopeless even the best!) to
the present age.[56]

To indicate what lies behind this astonishing attribution of
sexuality to all phenomenal nature ("the World of Time")
requires another look, from a different vantage point, at Coleridge's metascientific enterprise. The post-Newtonian world-
picture repelled him because it had been deliberately stripped
bare of any correlative to the life of man and any sanction
for human purposes and values. While a young man of thirty
Coleridge had written to Southey that "a metaphysical Solution, that does not instantly *tell* for something in the Heart,
is grievously to be suspected as apocryphal," and in the *Biographia Literaria,* contemporaneously with the last version of
The Eolian Harp, he extolled Boehme, despite the "delusions"
and fantasies he found mixed with his "truths," because he
had contributed "to keep alive the *heart* in the *head;* gave me
. . . [a] presentiment, that all the products of the mere *reflective* faculty partook of DEATH."[57] Coleridge meant that, as
man cannot live by science alone—in his terms, by the evidence of the senses ordered by the "reflective faculty," the
"understanding"—neither can he endure a universe constructed to suit the narrow requirements of Newtonian physics rather than the large requirements of human life. Coleridge
undertook to develop an alternative world-vision that would
suffice to the heart as well as the head, by supplementing
science with imagination—as he put it in terms of his faculty-
philosophy, the phenomena of "the senses," as classed and
ordered by "the understanding," are to be "impregnated" by
"the imagination," and so reconciled and mediated to the
requirements of the supreme and inclusive power of mind,
"the reason."[58]

We can translate Coleridge's terms into the idiom of our
own time. His prime endeavor, like that of his contemporaries, the great German architects of all-inclusive metaphys-

ical "systems," was to assimilate the findings and hypotheses of contemporary science to the inherent demands and forms of the human imagination, in the kind of inclusive vision of man in the world that Northrop Frye calls a "myth of concern."[59] In this undertaking man is put back into nature, from which the sophisticated logic of science had severed him, by applying the primitive imaginative categories of analogy, correspondence, and identity. Through this procedure nature is once more endowed with the inherent energies of life and with humanly intelligible purposes and values, and so constitutes a milieu in which man can fully live and be at home. And since the cultural myth of concern that Coleridge had inherited was the Judeo-Christian one set forth in the Bible, and since Coleridge felt a greater need than contemporary German philosophers to salvage the essentials of its creed of salvation, he undertook explicitly to ground his world-vision on bases common both to the Old and New Testament and to "speculative physics."

No doubt Coleridge would have rejected this description, since it transposes the criterion of his intricately rationalized system from a truth of correspondence to ultimate reality to a truth of correspondence to man's deepest instincts and needs, as these shape the forms of his imagination. But Schelling, I think, might well have accepted it, for Schelling was one of the German philosophers who helped establish the present views, of which Northrop Frye is a distinguished representative, that human needs inevitably compel the creation of a mythology to live by, in civilized no less than in primitive societies. Schelling asserts that in the modern world the mythology of the ancients has been outworn, while "the mythology of Christendom" is unsuitable for valid poetry, so that now "every truly creative individual has to create his own mythology." All these separate creations, however, will prove, in the indeterminate future, to be parts of a single system of myth. The preeminent material for this evolving mythology is contemporary *Naturphilosophie,* such as he has himself developed. It is his conviction, Schelling says, "that in the higher speculative physics is to be sought the possibility of a future mythology and symbolism," which will reconcile the contraries between the pagan and Christian mythologies in one vision of nature; but this achievement, he adds, will be the work not of any one individual, but of "the entire era."[60]

Conspicuous in Schelling's own later *Naturphilosophie* is its tendency to move from abstract concepts to explicitly anthropomorphic and mythical formulations. This tendency is most obvious in the instance of his basic principle of polarity. In his early writings Schelling had based this category on the concepts of bipolarity in recent scientific developments in magnetism and electricity, as well as on Kant's essay of 1786, which undertook a "metaphysical" derivation of the primitive "matter" of Newtonian physics from the elemental "powers" of attraction and repulsion.[61] Coleridge in his turn based his early formulations of the polar-principle on the theory of his scientific friend Humphry Davy that all substances are the product of elementary forces, even before he absorbed the views of Kant and the metaphysical system of Schelling.[62] Coleridge, however, rightly pointed back to a long tradition, from "the Dynamic Theory of the eldest Philosophy" in the pre-Socratic thinkers, through Renaissance Hermeticism, to Jacob Boehme as precedent to Schelling in putting forward "the universal law of polarity."[63] In these earlier thinkers the philosophical representation of an all-originative and sustaining interplay of elemental opposites had not yet completely emerged from its origins in a cosmic myth of universal bisexuality—the myth of male and female divinities or powers, antithetic and warring yet mutually attractive and necessary, which periodically merge in unions that beget the world and all things in it. In its older forms, in other words, universal polarity had been derived from bisexual procreation as its prototype; and it is the sexual dimension of human nature, we may plausibly conjecture, that gives the myth of cosmic bisexuality its persisting hold on imagination even today, in current forms of the "perennial philosophy." After all, as Schelling remarked, human union and procreation is "the single instance in which we are to a certain extent permitted to be witnesses of an original creation."[64]

In his early writings of 1797, Schelling at times referred to the contrary powers of gravity and light as the feminine or

"mother-principle" and the masculine or "procreative principle," which are "represented" or "expressed" in the differentiated sexes of the higher organisms.[65] Increasingly after
that he dramatized his metaphysics of polarity by endowing
it with anthropomorphic features and relationships. He wrote
in 1804, for example, that "made pregnant by light, gravity
gives birth to the diverse forms of things and delivers them
from her fruitful womb to independent life." Driven by the
compulsion to progressive individuation, the powers of gravity and light, at the organic stage of evolution, separate first
into the bisexual organs in a single plant, then into the separate sexes of the animal and human realms. Yet every individual remains the product of both powers, and each
monosexual individual needs its polar opposite in order to
fulfill the contrary compulsion of nature toward identity. "This
is the secret of eternal love . . . in that each is a whole, yet
desires the other and seeks the other." Hence:

> As the being and life of nature rests on the eternal embrace of
> light and gravity, so the unions of the two sexes, their beget-
> ting and propagation of innummerable species, are nothing
> else than the celebration of the eternal love of those two [pow-
> ers] which, when they could have been two, yet wanted to be
> one, and thereby created all of nature.[66]

Such also are the grounds of Coleridge's statement, in his
letter to Tulk, that light and gravitation are "the Male and
female of the World of Time, in whose wooings, and retirings and nuptial conciliations all other marriages . . . are celebrated inclusively." Like the German *Naturphilosophen*,
Coleridge sometimes mythicized his metascience, to humanize his vision of a natural world whose diverse orders of being
are linked by familial correspondences to man and mind, and
whose processes are compelled by inconscient analogues of
love and hate, of oppositions and marriages. Hence those
strange passages in Coleridge's speculative natural history that
seem to a casual reader to be merely fantasies based on free
association. In a manuscript, for example, he declares that,
though all the chemical elements contain the two counter-

powers, "Gravity and Light with Warmth as the Indifference," yet because of the differing "predominance of some one, Carbon most represents Gravity, Oxygen Light, and Hydrogen Warmth." When, in the sequential combinations of these chemical elements, nature achieves the plant, we find in its generative organ, the flower, "the qualitative product of Oxygen = Light in the outness and splendor of Colors, the qualitative product of Hydrogen = Warmth in the inwardness and sweetness of Fragrance"; and this fragrance Coleridge interprets as the accompaniment of "gentle love," of which the flower serves as a material symbol. And when—in the continuing genetic process of the "interpenetration" of the primal opposites, gravity and light—we reach the level of birds, we find that the colors of their plumage correspond to the colors of the flower, but that a new phenomenon, bird-song, or sound, has replaced the odors of flowers and taken over their biological function in ensuring fertilization. In birds, then, Coleridge says, we have "light in the form (under the power) of Gravity in Color, and Gravity sub formâ et ditione Lucis subditione"—that is, "gravity subordinated to the form and dominion of light"—in the bird-song. The "Sounds and sweet yearning varied by quiet provoking challenging sounds" are thus "the surrogates of the Vegetable Odors—and like these, are the celebrations of the Nuptial moments, the hours of Love."[67]

Such passages provide a bridge between the "sound-like power in light" and the love of all things in the inserted section of *The Eolian Harp*. They provide also a broader perspective though which to review the long evolution of that poem between 1795 and 1817, as I described it at the beginning of this essay. In its first short form *The Eolian Harp* had been a love poem which assimilated the relation of the wind and the strings of the harp to the dalliance, the "wooings, and retirings" of the human lovers. It had next been developed into a marriage poem, and also expanded into a metaphysical speculation about "all of animated nature." In its final form it is still a love poem, but a cosmic love poem, in which the love between the poet and his bride becomes the exponent of a universal relationship—the "union of the individual with the Universe" which, Coleridge said, occurs "through love."[68] It is still a marriage poem, too, but one in which the human union becomes, in Coleridge's technical term, an "exponent" of the primal union in which "all other marriages . . . are celebrated inclusively." For in the lines added in 1817 the poet breaks through sensation into vision, in which the phenomenal aspects of the landscape, its colors, music, and odors, are intuited as products and indices of the first manifestations of the creative Word, gravitation and light, in whose multiform unions all nature and life consist; and he goes on to celebrate the world's song of life and joy, which sounds through the wind-harp, in which the silent air is merely music unheard, and of which the subject is the one Life that, in marrying all opposites, also weds the single consciousness to the world without. And however we may judge the meta-scientific and religious beliefs that engendered the moment of vision, they have in this passage been transformed by the imagination from a creed into the poetry of immediate experience, and so compel our participation independently of either belief or disbelief:

> O! the one Life within us and abroad,
> Which meets all motion and becomes its soul,
> A light in sound, a sound-like power in light,
> Rhythm in all thought, and joyance every where—
> Methinks, it should have been impossible
> Not to love all things in a world so fill'd;
> Where the breeze warbles, and the mute still air
> Is music slumbering on her instrument.

Coleridge, we know, printed this passage as an addendum to a poem already set in type. The insertion throws the whole poetic structure into imbalance by locating the climax of the meditation near the beginning. By 1817, however, Coleridge, though capable of poetic moments, was not capable of sustained poetic endeavor; as he said two years later, "Poeta fuimus," but "the Philosopher, tho' pressing with the weight of an Etna, cannot prevent the Poet from occasionally . . . manifesting his existence by smoke traversed by electrical flashes from the Crater."[69] In succeeding printings of *The Eolian Harp* Coleridge simply transferred the added passage into the text without altering its context. But the poet's retraction of his metaphysical speculations in the original conclusion to the poem had never been at ease with its surroundings either in tone or in idiom, and after this high moment of religious as well as metaphysical imagination, the coda is rendered inconsequent as well as anticlimactic.

EIGHT

Coleridge and the Romantic Vision of the World

H<small>IS</small> last name, the poet enjoins us, is to be pronounced as three syllables, with the "o" long. "For it is one of the vilest Belzebubberies of Detraction to pronounce it Colridge, Cŏllĕridge, or even Cōle-ridge. It is & must be to all honest and honorable men, a trisyllabic Amphimacer, $-\smile-$!"[1] And upon his first name Coleridge projected his self-distrust and the contempt he felt for his lack of decisiveness—attitudes which all his life made him heavily reliant on the good opinion of others to buttress his self-esteem. "From my earliest years," he wrote, "I have had a feeling of Dislike & Disgust" for the name Samuel: "such a vile short plumpness, such a dull abortive smartness, in [the] first Syllable . . . the wabble it makes, & staggering between a diss- & a tri-syllable . . . altogether it is perhaps the worst combination, of which vowels & consonants are susceptible."[2]

Samuel Taylor Coleridge—S.T.C., as he preferred to call his ideal image of himself—entered into residence at Jesus College, Cambridge, in October 1791, just as he was turning nineteen. In his *Biographia Literaria* he recalled with nostalgia "the friendly cloysters, and the happy grove of quiet, ever honored Jesus College."[3] In fact, however, the quiet grove had in his student days been the storm center at Cambridge of the excitement and controversy evoked by the early phase of the French Revolution. Coleridge became a follower in religion and a fervent partisan in politics of William Frend, Fellow of Jesus, who was a Unitarian and a radical supporter of the Revolution; in the spring of 1793, Frend was tried before the Vice-Chancellor's court on charges of sedition and defamation of the Church, refused to retract his "errors," and was banished from the University. Nor were the cloisters and the grove unalloyedly happy for Coleridge. After a flurry of inordinate zeal in his studies, he succumbed to the under-graduate temptations of talk instead of work and of mild dissipation in drink and sex. Overwhelmed by debt, a bad conscience, and an unrequited love for Mary Evans, he fled to London and enlisted in the 15th Light Dragoons, retaining a remnant of his identity in the initials of his pseudonym, Silas Tomkyn Comberbache.

Coleridge was doubtless the most maladroit cavalryman in the long history of the Dragoons; not the least of his deficiencies was that he could not stay mounted on a horse, an animal which he profoundly distrusted. He was discovered and ransomed by his family and returned, ignominiously, to his college. He left the university for good during the October term of 1794 without taking a degree, to pursue the abortive scheme of a Utopian Pantisocracy and to enter into his ill-starred marriage to Sara Fricker. It is pleasant to know that Coleridge returned to Cambridge for a happy visit in June 1833, just a year before his death. He reported to Henry Nelson Coleridge, who was both his nephew and his son-in-law:

> My emotions at revisiting the university were at first over-whelming. I could not speak for an hour. . . . I have not passed, of late years at least, three days of such great enjoyment and healthful excitement of mind and body. The bed on which I slept—and slept soundly too—was, as near as I can describe it, a couple of sacks full of potatoes tied together. . . . Truly I lay down at night a man, and arose in the morning a bruise.[4]

My subject, however, is not the comedy and tragedy of the life of Coleridge, that self-defeating, gentle, maddening, beguiling genius, but his vision of the world at the time he reached his philosophical maturity; and for Coleridge's intellectual stance in this middle period the best introduction is his *Biographia Literaria,* which he published in the summer of 1817, when he was forty-four years old.

I want to stress two features of Coleridge's book. The first is the significance of its elected genre. Undertaking a work that was to set forth "my principles in Politics, Religion, and Philosophy," as well as in poetry and criticism,[5] Coleridge cast his statement in the form of a literary autobiography. In this procedure he shared a salient tendency of his age to reshape a variety of earlier literary types into the biographical or autobiographical mode, and thereby to transform fixed intellectual positions into moments in an evolving education, in which each stage is a product of what has gone before and the portent of what is to come. In the 1790s Goethe and other German writers had developed the *Bildungsroman,* the novel about the education of the hero in life; in England the major achievement in this type is Carlyle's *Sartor Resartus.* At the same time many of the major German philosophers, including Lessing, Herder, Schiller, Kant, wrote examples of what they called "universal history"—the account of all human thought and culture, represented as the progressive education of a single protagonist named "Man," "Mankind," or "Humanity." The most extraordinary achievement in this mode is Hegel's *Phenomenology of Spirit,* which narrates the total history of the evolving human consciousness as the adventures and misadventures of a single *dramatis persona* whom he calls "spirit," or "the general individual," as it continuously repossesses its own persistently alienated selves in a progressive educational process, to the point at which the expanding consciousness recognizes its own all-inclusive identity in the final stage of "absolute knowledge"—that is, in the *Wissenschaft* that is Hegel's own systematic philosophy of man and the world. The biographical form is no less prominent in Romantic narrative and lyric poetry. To Wordsworth, for example, it seemed "a reasonable thing" that, before he undertook his great work, *The Recluse,* he should "take a review of his own mind" and "record, in verse, the origin and progress of his own powers." The resulting work Wordsworth referred to as "the poem on the growth of my own mind" and his wife later named *The Prelude;* it turned out to be the masterpiece to which he intended it to serve merely as a "preparatory poem."[6]

The *Biographia Literaria,* then, is in Coleridge's stated intention a Romantic *Bildungsgeschichte,* representing the growth of the poet-philosopher-critic's mind. A second, and neglected, feature of this book is that, like many of the contemporary works to which it is allied, its design is that of a crisis-autobiography. That is, the evolving educational process is broken by a stage of extreme doubt, apathy, and despair, from which the protagonist emerges as a new man, assured of his identity and role in life, who, when he looks about him, sees a new world.

In the tenth chapter of the *Biographia,* Coleridge summarizes his intellectual and spiritual condition when he was in his middle twenties. He had absorbed the English empirical philosophy in the tradition of John Locke and adopted the radical mechanistic views of mind that were held by David Hartley—an earlier Jesus College man, who in his *Observations on Man* (1749) had undertaken to extend the principles of Newtonian physics to perception and all the processes of mind.[7] As Coleridge had said in 1794: "I am a compleat Necessitarian—and understand the subject as well almost as Hartley himself—but I go farther than Hartley and believe the corporeality of *thought*—namely, that it is motion."[8] In religion he had taken over the views of William Frend and Joseph Priestley and become "a zealous Unitarian."[9] He also shared his mentors' enthusiasm for the French Revolution, and the belief of Priestley and other radical Dissenters that the Revolution portended the imminence of the millennium foretold in the Book of Revelation. Coleridge ironically recalls how, while soliciting subscribers to his periodical *The Watchman* in 1796,

> I argued, I described, I promised, I prophesied; and beginning with the captivity of nations I ended with the near approach of the millennium, finishing the whole with some of my own

verses describing that glorious state out of the *Religious Musings.*[10]

The occasion for such prophecy is laconically summarized in Coleridge's prose Argument to *Religious Musings,* a long poem he published that same year: "The present State of Society. The French Revolution. Millennium. Universal Redemption. Conclusion."

Coleridge then describes in the *Biographia* his disillusion with the promise of the French Revolution until, after the French invasion of Switzerland, he became, in a drastic turnabout, a "vehement anti-gallican, and still more intensely an anti-jacobin."[11] He had experienced "the very hey-day of hope," but now "my mind sank into a state of thorough disgust and despondency." Coleridge cites his poem "France, *a Palinodia*" (1798), which expressed his revulsion from his commitment to revolutionary France, and goes on:

> I retired to a cottage in Somersetshire at the foot of Quantock [in 1797], and devoted my thoughts and studies to the foundations of religion and morals. Here I found myself all afloat. Doubts rushed in; broke upon me *"from the fountains of the great deep,"* and fell *"from the windows of heaven."* The fontal truths of natural religion and the books of Revelation alike contributed to the flood; and it was long ere my ark touched on an Ararat, and rested.[12]

Elsewhere in the *Biographia* Coleridge shifts the biblical parallel for his condition at this time from Noah's flood to the Exodus, referring to the religious "mystics" as "always a pillar of fire throughout the night, during my wandering through the wilderness of doubt," enabling him "to skirt, without crossing, the sandy deserts of utter unbelief."[13]

We may note about Coleridge's account of his crisis, first, that, as in other spiritual autobiographies of the age, the precipitating cause is the failure of the inordinate hopes he had invested in the French Revolution. Hegel, for example, in his *Phenomenology of Spirit* represented the Revolution and the Reign of Terror as the ultimate crisis of consciousness in Western man, in which "spirit in the form of absolute freedom" turns upon itself in "the fury of annihilation," in a self-negation which "is meaningless death, the sheer horror of the negative."[14] In Wordsworth's *Prelude* the "disastrous issues" of the times, marking the collapse of his hopes in the Revolution, led finally to "utter loss of hope itself, / And things to hope for," in the stage he describes as the dark night of his soul: "I was benighted heart and mind."[15]

It is clear from the *Biographia*, however, that Coleridge's crisis involved not only politics, but the overall forms of thinking he had derived from the eighteenth century—the empiricism, mechanism, and skepticism in philosophy, together with the Unitarianism in religion which he associated with the rationale that led to the French Revolution and with the radicalism of the English Dissenters who were its zealous supporters. And when, for comfort and sanction, he turned his studies to "the foundations of religion and morals," both his philosophy and theology proved inadequate to the task and merely added to the flood of doubt. In a parallel way Wordsworth tells us in *The Prelude* that, in a desperate effort to reestablish his hope in human possibility, he had turned to the philosophical speculations of William Godwin and other philosophers of the Enlightenment, but that the result was only to complete the disaster. "Sick, wearied out with contrarieties," he says, he

> Yielded up moral questions in despair.
> This was the crisis of that strong disease,
> This the soul's last and lowest ebb.
> (1850 text, XI, 279–307)

Coleridge's crisis, then, was a total one, involving his religion, philosophy, politics, and theory of poetry, and like the spiritual histories of his Romantic contemporaries, his narrative conforms to the plot of that prototype of all spiritual autobiographies, Saint Augustine's *Confessions*, written at the close of the fourth century. Ever since Augustine's circumstantial account of his doubts, anguished self-conflict, and despair—resolved under a fig tree in a garden at Milan, in the experience of "dying unto death and living unto life"[16]—

we have all known how to undergo a spiritual crisis, whether we call it by the religious term "conversion" or by a secular term such as "identity crisis." Augustine's laborious pilgrimage toward the experience of being born into a new life had been not less intellectual than it was religious, and in his *Confessions* the reading of pagan philosophers is hardly less prominent than his poring over the writings of Saint Paul and the rest of the Scriptures. In the *Biographia* Coleridge commented that, before he could achieve his "final reconversion to the whole truth in Christ," a "more thorough revolution in my philosophic principles, and a deeper insight into my own heart, were yet wanting"; and he explicitly compared his conversion, in its double aspect as philosophy and faith, to that of Augustine, according to whose "own confession," Coleridge said, "the books of certain Platonic philosophers . . . commenced the rescue of [his] faith from the same error."[17]

Like other authors of spiritual autobiography, Coleridge wrote his *Biographia Literaria* after he had escaped from the flood of doubt and the wilderness of despair, in the persona of a new creature who sees the world with new eyes; and it will help us to read not only the *Biographia,* but the other writings of Coleridge's middle and later life, if we recognize that, like other converts, religious or philosophical, Coleridge looks upon the intellectual landscape with a radically simplifying bipolar vision. On the one side he puts the thought and products of the eighteenth century, English and French— "the Epoch of the Understanding and the Senses," as he calls it, with its "modes of reasoning grounded on the atomic, Corpuscular and mechanic Philosophy."[18] This was the way of seeing and thinking to which the old Coleridge had in large part succumbed, and on which he now blames not only the disaster of the French Revolution but also the general vitiation of thought, values, and the form of life; it has affected, he says, "the Taste and Character, the whole tone of Manners and Feeling, and above all the Religious (at least the Theological) and the Political tendencies of the public mind."[19] On the other side he puts all the influences which had gone into the formation of the new Coleridge—first, the Bible and

Christian theologians; then Plato and the Neoplatonists, together with Jacob Boehme and the other "mystics" who had helped sustain in him the saving vision; and finally, and decisively, the recent or contemporary German philosophers, especially Kant and Schelling, who provided him with the conceptual grounds for articulating an alternative vision of the universe. And for his new world-view the latter Coleridge speaks as a fervent evangelist, with results, as John Stuart Mill early recognized in his essay on "Coleridge," that did much to alter the intellectual climate in England, and as we now recognize, in America as well.

I. CONVERSION, REVOLUTION, AND VISION IN PHILOSOPHY

More than one historian of philosophy has noted the intense excitement, the extravagant claims, and the breathtaking velocity of the development of German Idealism in the two or three decades after the appearance of Kant's *Critique of Pure Reason* in 1781. The movement has the aspect of an epidemic conversion-experience in philosophy. Its character, Richard Kroner has said, is "explosive"; "there passed through the epoch something of the breath of the eschatological hopes of the era of emergent Christianity; now or never must dawn the day of truth, it is near, we are called to bring it into being." The participants are convinced "that a new evangel has appeared in the world."[20] Sober-minded though he was, Kant remarked that "philosophy too can have its chiliasm . . . which is nothing less than visionary."[21] In his second Preface of 1787 he described his *Critique* as the attempt "to introduce a complete revolution in the procedure of metaphysics," equivalent to the revolution inaugurated by Copernicus, who reversed the assumption "that all the heavenly bodies revolved round the spectator" by assuming "that the spectator revolved, while the stars remained at rest." In place of the philosophical assumption hitherto "that our cognition must conform to the objects," Kant proposed "that the objects must conform to our cognition"—that is, that in all experience the unknowable "things in themselves" are inescapably structured by the mind's own forms of space, time, and the categories.

In the 1790s other German philosophers exploited Kant's metaphor of a philosophical revolution. They shifted the reference, however, from the Copernican revolution in science to the dominant conceptual model of the Romantic age; that is, the violent destruction of existing conditions, the establishment of a totally new order of things, and the explosive enlargement of human expectations represented by the political revolution in France. In 1790, soon after the fall of the Bastille, C. L. Reinhold, writing on Kant's philosophy, described the philosophical era as an unexampled "convulsion of all hitherto known systems, theories, and modes of conception"—a "revolution" paralleling the political revolutions of the age and ascribable to "one and the same cause" in "the spirit of our age," although it manifests itself as "a phenomenon of spirit" and "in the arena of knowledge" rather than of external political struggle.[22] Five years later Fichte said that "the first hints and presentiments" of his philosophical system came to him while he was writing in defense of the French Revolution; his system, in fact, is a revolution that completes Kant's philosophical revolution, in that it frees the mind of man even from the limiting conditions imposed on it by Kant's postulate of unknowable things-in-themselves:

> My system is the first system of freedom; just as [the French] are tearing man loose from his outer chains, so my system tears him loose from the fetters of the *Ding an sich,* from any external influence, and establishes him in his first principle as an autonomous being.[23]

And that same year, 1795, the young Schelling declared that his philosophy, in its turn, aims "not merely at a reform of knowledge, but at a total reversal of its principles; that is to say, it aims at a revolution of knowledge"—a cognitive revolution, the dawning of a "more beautiful day of knowledge" which, by changing man's concept of his mind and powers, will transform the conditions and possibilities of his life in the world.[24]

In his *Phenomenology of Spirit* (1807) Hegel narrates how the spirit—the vanguard of the collective human consciousness—has recovered from the self-destructiveness represented by the convulsions of the French Revolution, to reach the culminating stage of Hegel's own philosophical *Wissenschaft*. In this stage, he says, the spirit's "former being" has been both annulled and transcended, so that "new-born out of knowledge" it is a "new being, a new world and form of the spirit."[25] He describes this latest form of the spirit as "the product of a far-reaching revolution in ever so many forms of culture and education" which will achieve the new heaven and earth sought vainly by the political revolutionists:

> The spirit has broken with what was hitherto the world of its existence and imagination. . . . The spirit that educates itself matures slowly and quietly toward the new form, dissolving one particle of the edifice of its previous world after another. . . . This gradual crumbling . . . is interrupted by the break of day that, like lightning, all at once reveals the edifice of the new world.[26]

It is clear that human consciousness, in breaking through to Hegel's system of knowledge, has been reborn and looks out upon a new world. But this new world is no other than the old world, which has been transformed by a "revolution" in philosophical vision.

Coleridge repeatedly employs metaphors that posit a triple parallel between religious and moral conversion, political revolution, and a radical change in the premises of philosophy. He characterizes the soul's "efforts at self-condemnation and self-reformation" as an attempt at "spiritual Revolution," and classes together "those great Men, who in states or in the mind of man had produced great revolutions."[27] I have already cited his statement that a prerequisite to his "final re-conversion" in religion was "a more thorough revolution in my philosophic principles."[28] He later described his projected *Magnum Opus* as "a revolution of all that has

been called *Philosophy* or Metaphysics in England and France"
since the predominance of "the mechanical system at the
Restoration of our second Charles." In addition, Coleridge
proposed in the *Biographia* that the radical ground of a philosophy consists in a primal way of seeing which he called
"the ascertaining vision" by "the philosophic imagination"—
a vision that is systematically primitive, in the sense that it is
a ground that cannot itself be grounded, except as it confirms its own validity by the consequences in experience when
it is achieved by each philosopher for himself.[29]

In the fourth chapter of the *Biographia*, Coleridge describes
his actual experience of a radical alteration in vision that
shatters habitual categories, and so makes the old world new.
The occasion is his first hearing Wordsworth read a long poem
aloud in 1796, but Coleridge explicitly says that such renovation is also effected by the achievements of "genius" in
"philosophic disquisitions":

> To contemplate the ANCIENT of days and all his works with
> feelings as fresh, as if all had then sprang forth at the first
> creative fiat . . . to combine the child's sense of wonder and
> novelty with the appearances, which every day for perhaps forty
> years had rendered familiar . . . this is the character and priv-
> ilege of genius. . . . And therefore is it the prime merit of genius
> and its most unequivocal mode of manifestation, so to repre-
> sent familiar objects as to awaken in the minds of others . . .
> freshness of sensation.[30]

In a central passage in his periodical *The Friend*, composed
at about the same time as the *Biographia*, Coleridge asserts
that the primitive element of a philosophy, its founding intuition, must be adopted, not by force of evidence, but by an
act of "the will." He then opposes two kinds of philosophical
vision, which yield two diverse worlds. One of these is

> that intuition of things . . . which presents itself when transfer-
> ring reality to . . . the ever-varying framework of the uniform
> life, we think of ourselves as separated beings, and place nature
> in antithesis to the mind, as object to subject, thing to thought,
> death to life. This is abstract knowledge, or the science of the
> mere understanding.

This world-view is that of the preceding century, the epoch of the senses and the understanding from which he had himself escaped. The second and opposed intuition, and its concordant world, is that which he has now achieved. It is, he writes,

> the contemplation of reason, namely, that intuition of things which arises when we possess ourselves, as one with the whole, which is substantial knowledge. . . . [By this] we know that existence is its own predicate, self affirmation. . . . It is an eternal and infinite self-rejoicing, self-loving, with a joy unfathomable, with a love all comprehensive.[31]

I shall sketch the salient features of the conceptual scheme by which Coleridge undertakes to provide a coherent and inclusive structure for this founding philosophical intuition or vision, and then discuss a striking example of the way the scheme informed Coleridge's actual experience of the world. In doing so, I am not merely exploiting a Romantic conceit that the undemonstrable ground for a philosophy is a way of envisioning reality, and that a change of ground is a philosophical conversion which effects a revolution in experience; for we find that philosophers of diverse persuasions have described a radical shift in their premises in similar metaphoric terms of inner transformation, of escape from imprisonment to freedom, and of a revolution in vision that yields a new world.

One instance is the testimony of a recent philosopher associated with Cambridge. In an autobiographical essay, Bertrand Russell describes how the influences of McTaggart and of F. H. Bradley's *Appearance and Reality* "caused me to become a Hegelian." The crucial turn to this world-view occurred in a flash of insight:

> I remember the precise moment, one day in 1894, as I was walking along Trinity Lane, when I saw in a flash (or thought I saw) that the ontological argument is valid. I had gone out to buy a tin of tobacco; on my way back, I suddenly threw it up in the air, and exclaimed as I caught it: "Great Scott, the ontological argument is sound."

During the several years following he planned, he tells us, a series of comprehensive books that "would achieve a Hegelian synthesis in an encyclopaedic work dealing equally with theory and practice." But during 1898 various causes led him to abandon this outlook, and especially the influence of his younger friend G. E. Moore, who "also had had a Hegelian period," but now reverted "to the opposite extreme . . . that *everything* is real that common sense . . . supposes real." As Russell describes his second philosophical conversion and its consequences in experience:

> [Moore] took the lead in rebellion, and I followed, with a sense of emancipation. . . . With a sense of escaping from prison, we allowed ourselves to think that grass is green, that the sun and stars would exist if no one was aware of them, and also that there is a pluralistic timeless world of Platonic ideas. The world, which had been thin and logical, suddenly became rich and varied and solid.[32]

Another Cambridge philosopher, Ludwig Wittgenstein, put forward two distinct philosophies. The first is that of the *Tractatus,* published in 1921. The second, which he developed in a sudden burst of philosophical activity after a ten-year hiatus, is represented by his *Philosophical Investigations,* published in 1953; the book addresses itself specifically to counter what he calls "my old way of thinking" in the *Tractatus.* In the *Investigations,* Wittgenstein says that "philosophy may in no way interfere with the actual use of language," and that philosophy "leaves everything as it is." That may be; but Wittgenstein's writings show that philosophizing has profoundly changed the philosopher himself, who, by developing a new language for doing philosophy, has in his phrase discovered "a new way of looking at things" and thereby has changed everything.[33]

Coleridge began to study Kant at the turn of the nineteenth century when, as he said in the *Biographia,* the writings of that philosopher "took possession of me as with a giant's hand."[34] For a short while Coleridge exhibited a philosophical chiliasm, a sense that he was on the verge of a consummation of all metaphysics hitherto, similar to that of his post-Kantian contemporaries in Germany. In a quick succession of letters early in 1801 Coleridge wrote: "I feel, that I have power within me"; "my heart within me *burns*" to write a book on "the affinities of the Feelings with Words & Ideas" which will "supersede all the Books of Metaphysics hitherto written / and all the Books of Morals too"; "I have not only completely extricated the notions of Time, and Space; but have overthrown the doctrine of Association, as taught by Hartley, and with it . . . the doctrine of Necessity"; and he is about to go on "to solve the process of Life & Consciousness." All this in an "intensity of thought," and of "minute experiments with Light & Figure" which have made him "nervous & feverish," when "Truths so important . . . came to me almost as a Revelation."[35] But this brief afflatus led to no extensive philosophical achievement, and it was followed by the decade that W. J. Bate has called "the dark years," the nadir of Coleridge's life-crisis.

Coleridge's letters and notebooks of the next decade and a half make very painful reading. He is racked by pain, recurrent illness, and nightmares; his marriage shattered, he suffers a hopeless love for Sara Hutchinson; in the medical ignorance of the time, he becomes addicted to opium—that "dirty business of Laudanum," he called it, that "*free-agency-annihilating* poison";[36] he is alienated from Wordsworth; he is guilt-ridden, experiences a paralysis of his intellectual and poetic powers, seems recurrently close to death and longs for it as a release;[37] and at one point wants "to place myself in a private madhouse" since "my Case is a species of madness, only that it is a derangement, an utter impotence of the *Volition*, & not of the Intellectual Faculties."[38]

In the latter part of this dark time (beginning about 1810) Coleridge took up the close study of Friedrich Schelling. To this brilliant young philosopher, Coleridge says in the *Biographia*, he at once felt a special affinity, "a genial coincidence with much that I had toiled out for myself, and a powerful assistance in what I had yet to do."[39] In a sudden burst of activity during a four-year span beginning in 1815, Coleridge composed the bulk of the works on which his intellectual reputation depends: the *Biographia Literaria*, the *Theory of Life*, the two *Lay Sermons*, the "Treatise on Method," the radically revised version of his earlier periodical *The Friend*, two sets of lectures on Shakespeare and other English and European poets and dramatists, a series of lectures on the history of philosophy, as well as a number of important philosophical letters and a mass of manuscript materials which are only now being published in full. The years 1815–19 are for Coleridge as metaphysician and critic what the years 1796–98—the time of *The Ancient Mariner*, *Christabel*, and *Kubla Khan*, as well as his hardly less innovative conversation poems—are for Coleridge as a bard. The range and quality of his achievement in these latter years would for any man be remarkable; for Coleridge, given the circumstances of his life, it must count as a feat of massive spiritual heroism.

In these middle years of Coleridge, it is Schelling who is the dominating philosophical influence—the Schelling who, Coleridge asserted in his *Biographia*, "as the *founder* of the PHILOSOPHY OF NATURE, and as the most successful *improver* of the Dynamic System," completed the "revolution in philosophy" begun by Kant.[40] And it is in Coleridge's special adaptation of this revolution in philosophy—based on Schelling's *Naturphilosophie* and to some extent on the speculations of Schelling's followers, especially Henrik Steffens—that we find the conceptual structure which Coleridge developed to articulate, to support, and to render all-comprehensive his founding vision of the natural world and of man's place in it.

II. THE METASCIENCE OF NATURE

Coleridge's nature-philosophy is a strange and daunting area of his thought.[41] Until recently scholars have either discreetly passed it over or else—assessing it as an attempt to achieve by fantasy what scientists discover by patient experiment—have rejected it (in the terms of Joseph Warren Beach) as "mere abracadabra," "highly fantastic," "a bizarre farrago of pretentious nonsense"; it is, Norman Fruman has charged,

Coleridge's commitment "to the most anti-scientific move-ment of his day."[42] Such judgments are inevitable if we sim-ply apply to Coleridge's scheme of nature the criteria of the philosophical positivism that Coleridge's philosophy was spe-cifically intended to dispossess. If our aim, on the other hand, is to understand an important development in nineteenth-century intellectual history, we need to follow Coleridge's own procedure, which John Stuart Mill identified, and to which he attributed his own liberation from dogmatism. Mill pointed out that by Bentham (the great philosophical positivist of his time), men have been led to ask of an opinion, "Is it true?" By Coleridge, they have instead been led to ask, "What is the meaning of it?" and to answer by looking at the opinion "from within."

> The long duration of a belief, [Coleridge] thought, is at least proof of an adaption in it to some portion or other of the human mind . . . some natural want or requirement of human nature which the doctrine in question is fitted to satisfy.[43]

Let us try to look at Coleridge's nature-philosophy, accord-ing to his own formula, from within, to see what it undertook to do and what natural want it served to satisfy.

The first thing to note is that Coleridge's intention was not to discredit or to replace the findings of experimental sci-ence. Instead he undertook to accommodate valid scientific discoveries within a counter-metaphysic to the metaphysical foundations of contemporary science; his nature-philoso-phy, in short, was not science, nor anti-science, but metasci-ence. In this area Coleridge set up as his chief opponent Isaac Newton, and especially what he called the "monstrous Fic-tions" in Newton's *Opticks*. He did not mean to call into ques-tion Newton as an experiment physicist, whom he called "the immortal Newton," and to whose procedures and discoveries he paid frequent tribute.[44] Coleridge's objection was to New-ton as a speculative thinker whose immense prestige as a physicist had given impetus to a metaphysical world-view, the "Corpuscular and mechanic Philosophy," that had reigned for the preceding century. For despite his reluctance to frame hypotheses, Newton had put forward, in the "Queries" he added to his *Opticks,* the stark image of a machine-universe whose ultimate elements are indivisible particles of matter capable of being set in motion. There Newton wrote:

> It seems probable to me, that God in the Beginning form'd Matter in solid, massy, hard, impenetrable, moveable Particles, of such Sizes and Figures, and with such other Properties, and in such Proportion to Space, as most conduced to the End for which he form'd them.

Newton also proposed a hypothetical "aether," a very "rare and subtile" but nonetheless material medium, that pervades both space and bodies, and serves to explain the phenomena of gravity and light, as well as the conduction of both light and sound from the eye and ear through the nerves into the mental "place of Sensation," where they are converted into the images of sight and hearing.[45]

Worse still, as Coleridge saw it, was that, having reduced ultimate reality to masses and motion, Newton reconstrued the Creator of reality to accord with this picture of his creation. That is, Newton represented God as the omnipresent mover of all particles "within his boundless uniform Sensorium," and also as the seer of the particles as such, "wholly by their immediate presence to himself," which human beings perceive only after they have been altered by the intermediation of the senses. As Newton put it, we are capable of perceiving "the Images only" which, transmitted "through the Organs of Sense . . . are there seen and beheld by that which in us perceives and thinks."[46]

Newton's move, in Coleridge's view, was an immense extrapolation of the working model of physical science—the masses and motion which are the only things that the specialized techniques of the physicist can manage mathematically—into a picture of the actual make-up of the universe. As Coleridge puts the matter, in discussing the grounds of the "Mechanico-corpuscular Philosophy": "In order to submit the various phenomena of moving bodies to geometrical construction, we are under the necessity of abstracting from corporeal substance all its *positive* properties," leaving it only "figure and mobility." "And as a *fiction of science*," he says, "it would be difficult to overvalue this invention." But Descartes and later thinkers "propounded it as *truth of fact:* and instead of a World *created* and filled with productive forces by the Almighty *Fiat,* left a lifeless Machine whirled about by the dust of its own Grinding."[47]

To Coleridge this picture of the elemental structure of reality was both incompatible with human experience and intolerable to human needs. As no more than a drastic subtraction from the rich diversity of sense-phenomena, it remains itself thinly phenomenal, the product of what Coleridge repeatedly described as a "slavery" to the senses, and especially to the eye. And against this world-picture, in the literal sense of "picture" as something that can be visualized, Coleridge again and again brought the charge that it is, precisely speaking, lethal; it "strikes death through all things visible and invisible." It has killed the living, habitable, and companionable world of ordinary experience. It has also killed the metaphysical world of the pre-Cartesian and pre-Newtonian past, in which the mind of man had recognized an outer analogue to itself and to its life, purposes, values, and needs; a world, therefore, of which man was an integral part, with which he was a participant, and in which he could feel thoroughly at home. By translating what he called the "scientific calculus" from a useful working fiction into an ontology, Coleridge claimed in 1817, man has lost "all communion with life and the spirit of Nature," and is left isolated and alien, his mind the passive recipient of the impact of particles which it converts into images of sensation.[48]

Against this "philosophy of death," which posits only the "relations of unproductive particles to each other," Coleridge poses his own philosophy of life, in which, he says, "the two component counter-powers actually interpenetrate each other, and generate a higher third, including both the former."[49] That is, in radical opposition to the post-Newtonian picture of the world Coleridge puts forward what, following Schelling, he calls a "vital," or "dynamic," or "constructive" philosophy of nature. I shall try, very briefly, to outline this system, as Coleridge represented it in his middle years.

The primitives of Coleridge's metascience, from which he constructs the entire cosmos, mental as well as physical, are not material particles and motion, but inherent energies which he calls "powers." There are two primal counter-powers; these polarize into positive, and negative "forces" and interact, as he puts it, according to "the universal Law of Polarity or essential Dualism."[50] By this Coleridge means that the generative and sustaining elements of his universe exist only relatively to each other and manifest a tension-in-unity—that is, an equal and irremissive tendency on the one hand to oppose themselves and on the other hand to reunite in a "synthesis" of "thesis" and "antithesis."

The primitive counter-powers, "the two Poles of the material Universe," Coleridge says, are "Light and Gravitation." These terms, of course, denote the phenomena to which Newton had devoted his great researches in the *Opticks* and the *Principia*. But in Coleridge's system, light and gravitation are not physical or phenomenal matters, but pre-phenomenal concepts; in his terms, they are not "real" but "ideal." That is, the "powers" of light and gravity are not the light we see, nor the weight, or gravitational force, we feel, but have a different and prior conceptual status; hence they cannot be pictured, but only imagined. Of these ideal powers, however, "real" light and gravity are the kind of especially close and revealing analogues that Coleridge calls by a special term, "exponents."

"Under Gravity," Coleridge writes, "we place Attraction and Repulsion: and under Light the Powers of Contraction and Dilation." That is, each of these root-powers manifests two counter-forces: gravity involves a pull in and its opposite, a push out, while light pulses radially in all directions and at the same time contracts back to its center. It is only by their "living and generative interpenetration" that the pre-phenomenal powers and forces achieve the condition of matter, and so move into the phenomenal realm available to the human senses. "Matter," as Coleridge says, is to be considered "a Product . . . the pause, by interpenetration, of opposite energies."[51]

From these two elemental powers and two pairs of contrary forces Coleridge "constructs" (in the sense of rendering intelligible by reference to a single genetic principle) the total universe. Driven by their inherent stresses of opposition-in-unity, and manifesting in the process diverse degrees of "predominance" relative to each other, the powers of light and gravity evolve by a progressive synthesis of prior syntheses. Their evolution can be viewed as a great ascending spiral through the several distinctive orders of organized forms which Coleridge, following Schelling, calls "potences." At each potence, or level of organization, entities are linked by cor-respondences—according to an equivalence in the predomi-nance of elemental light versus gravity in their make-up—to entities on all other levels; Coleridge calls the lower entity that corresponds to an entity on a higher level a "symbol." On the first level of organization we get magnetism, electric-ity, and galvanism (which to Coleridge includes chemical attraction), then comes the level of the inorganic world, then the level of the organic world of plants and animals, up to the highest stage of organic life, man; at which point, the continuing syntheses of opposing powers produce mind or consciousness. This culminating production is a radical breakthrough in the developmental process, for conscious-ness is capable of a reflex act by which—in a continuing play of the law of polarity whereby it counterposes, in order to reconcile, the world, as "object," to itself, as "subject"[52]—con-sciousness re-engenders as knowledge the natural world within which it has itself been engendered, and of which it remains an integral component. Thus man's mind closes the evolu-tionary circle of polar generation, the human and nonhu-man worlds merging at the focal point of consciousness.

What made this world-construction so compelling to Cole-ridge's philosophic sensibility is that it asserts the equal real-ity both of nature and of mind, and also confirms the diversity and distinctiveness of all existing kinds and individuals, with-out postulating any metaphysical jumps or divisions in the scheme of things. All differences in kinds and qualities are saved, in what Coleridge called "distinction without divi-sion," as a "multeity in unity." There is no gap between the living and the lifeless, between nature and man, or between matter and mind, for all these modes of being consist of diverse and intercorrespondent levels of organization of the same two elemental powers and their respective polar forces. And this common component, the primitive pulsation of opposition-in-unity between the counter-powers, Coleridge identifies as the principle of life itself. "What is *not* Life," Coleridge asks, "that really *is?*" For "in the identity of the two counter-powers, Life *subsists;* in their strife it *consists:* and in their reconciliation it at once dies and is born again into a new form." What he calls this "universal life"—or alternatively, "the one Life"—of ever-resolving and ever-renewing opposition and reconciliation pulses through all individual forms and all ascending orders of being, beginning with what he calls "its utmost *latency*" in the inorganic "life of metals," through the progressive spires of "individuation," up to the human body, mind, and consciousness.[53]

It is on this level of consciousness, which culminates and crowns the generative process of nature, that the specifically human troubles begin. For man's consciousness involves "self-consciousness and self-government"—the awareness of self, the power to reflect, the knowledge of alternatives, and the need to make moral choices. Man thus "is referred to himself, delivered up to his own charge." If, as Coleridge puts it, he then turns in "upon his little unthinking contemptible self," man falls into conflict with himself, severs his interdependence with other men, and cuts off his intercommunion with the outer world,[54] in that state in which, Coleridge said, "we think of ourselves as separated beings, and place nature in antithesis to the mind, as . . . death to life." And from this condition we can only be rescued by that redeeming contrary vision which, we recall, Coleridge described as the integrative "intuition of things which arises when we possess ourselves, as one with the whole,"[55] and for which Coleridge's mature philosophic enterprise is a sustained evangel.

III. METASCIENCE AND RELIGION:
COLERIDGE'S MYTH OF CONCERN

In this sketch of Coleridge's metascience I have omitted a conspicuous and pervasive feature. The lack of this feature in Schelling's *Naturphilosophie* dismayed Coleridge and underlay his varying estimates of his predecessor and his recurrent charges that Schelling's system was a form of "Pantheism." By this Coleridge meant that Schelling absorbs a transcendent Creator of nature, without remainder, into the life and processes of nature itself, so that his nature-philosophy is at the same time a nature-religion. "In his Theology," Coleridge exclaimed in a marginal note, Schelling's positions are "in their literal sense scandalous."[56]

Coleridge's own aim, he wrote in *The Friend,* was to remove "the opposition without confounding the distinction between philosophy and faith."[57] His philosophy, accordingly has an explicit theological dimension, in the conviction that his metascience is consonant with his Christian beliefs. He claimed that he had arrived at his derivation of the universe from light and gravitation on the basis of "the First Principle of my Philosophy," and only afterward became aware "of it's exact coincidence with the Mosaic Cosmogony"[58]—that is, with the account of the creation in the Book of Genesis. Coleridge's interpretation of the creation story is grounded on his view that the statements in the Bible are the "living *educts* of the Imagination," which incorporates the ideas of "the Reason in Images of the Sense," and therefore are not to be read literally, but as "a system of symbols."[59] He also regarded the first chapter of the Fourth Gospel—always for Coleridge the key book of the Bible—as an expanded version of the account of the creation in Genesis. In the Book of Genesis, the first creative word is, "Let there be light." In the Gospel, John writes:

> In the beginning was the Word. . . . All things were made by him. . . . In him was life; and the life was the light of men. And the light shineth in darkness. . . . And the Word was made flesh, and dwelt among us. . . .

By a hermeneutic process I won't attempt to analyze here, Coleridge brought this biblical cosmogony into accord with the generative principles of his "speculative physics." For example, he wrote in 1817:

> And God said—Let there be *Light:* and there was *Light.* And God divided the *Light* from the *Darkness*—i.e. Light from Grav-

itation . . . and the two Poles of the material Universe are
established, viz. Light and Gravitation. . . . The Life of Nature
consists in the tendency of the Poles to re-unite. . . . God is the
Sun of the Universe—it's gravitation or Being by his
Omnipresence, it's Light by his only-begotten Son, who is the
Person . . . or *real* Image, of God—Deus alter et idem![60]

And since Coleridge conceived the interrelation of God, the
Son, and the Holy Spirit as itself the founding and paradigmatic instance of a three-in-one of thesis, antithesis, and synthesis, he envisioned the universe as manifesting, in the polar
rhythm of all its living processes, the being of a Christian
God who is, specifically, a Trinitarian God.

It is this theological aspect which, for many readers, dis-
credits Coleridge's metascience, even if they respond imaginatively to the grand architecture of his rationalized vision
of the world. To undertake, in the nineteenth century, to
show the concord between physical science and biblical revelation, and to construct from their merger a unified philosophy of nature, seems a hopeless anachronism. We must
remember, however, that in this enterprise Coleridge was
working in the central tradition of post-classical Western
metaphysics, and that in Coleridge's own lifetime Hegel (of
whom Coleridge, by the way, had read very little) claimed
that his *Wissenschaft*—his all-comprehensive system—
superseded, yet incorporated in conceptual form, the truths
which are adumbrated in what Hegel called the "picture-
thinking," the mythical forms, of the biblical narrative and
the Christian creed.[61] In our endeavor to understand more
fully the "natural want . . . of human nature" which Coleridge's theologico-philosophical system of nature "is fitted to
satisfy," we need to look at his metascientific enterprise from
a new point of vantage.

When he was thirty years old Coleridge had written, "Believe
me, Southey! a metaphysical Solution, that does not instantly
tell for something in the Heart, is grievously to be suspected
as apocryphal"; and all his mature life he insisted that a valid
philosophy must appeal to the "heart" no less than to the
"head," and that "all the products of the mere *reflective* fac-

ulty partook of DEATH."[62] Coleridge meant among other things that, as man cannot live by science alone—in his terms, by the evidence of the senses ordered by the "reflective faculty," the "understanding"—neither can he endure to live in a universe constructed to the narrow requirements of Newtonian physics rather than to the large requirements of human life, with its need to make the world emotionally as well as intellectually manageable. He therefore set out to develop an alternative world-vision that would suffice to the heart as well as the head, by supplementing science with imagination; or, as he put it in terms of his faculty psychology, the sense-phenomena ordered by "the understanding" are to be "impregnated" by "the imagination," and so mediated to the requirements of the supreme and inclusive power of the mind that he called "the reason."[63]

Suppose we translate Coleridge's terms into an idiom of our own time. His prime endeavor was to assimilate the findings of science to the inherent demands and forms of the human imagination, in the kind of structured vision of man in the world that Northrop Frye, in a useful phrase, calls a "myth of concern." Coleridge's myth of concern is a myth of reintegration. That is, he undertakes to put man and his mind back into nature, from which the sophisticated and highly specialized logic of science had severed him, by replacing the causal relations of the post-Newtonian world scheme with the primitive imaginative categories of analogy, correspondence, participation, and identity. These categories define what Coleridge calls the "exponents," "analogons," "indexes," and "symbols" in his cosmic system. As Coleridge wrote, the world of time "presents itself to the understanding . . . as an infinite ascent of Causes, and . . . as an interminable progression of Effects," but when "freed from the phenomena of Time and Space" it "reaveals itself to the pure Reason as the actual immanence of ALL in EACH."[64] Also:

> [It is my philosophical faith that] in Nature Man beholds only . . . the integration of Products, the Differentials of which are in, and constitute, his own mind and soul—and consequently that all true science is contained in the Lore of Symbols & Correspondences.[65]

By this procedure Coleridge reendows a dead and meaning-less universe with the inherent energies and generative pow-ers of life and with humanly intelligible purposes and values, and so makes it a milieu of which man's mind is an integral and reciprocative part, in which he can be at home, and by which he can sanction a workable rule of life. And since the cultural myth of concern that Coleridge had inherited was the Judeo-Christian one based on the Bible, and since Cole-ridge felt a deeper need than the great German system-builders to preserve the essentials of its creed of salvation, he undertook to ground the rational structure of his world-vision on what he regarded as the two distinct but correlative bases of "speculative physics" and Scriptural revelation.

Such a description of Coleridge's nature-philosophy as a myth of concern translates the criterion of his system from a truth of correspondence to ultimate reality to a truth of cor-respondence to man's deep instincts and needs, and so no doubt would have been unacceptable to him. It has, however, at least this affinity with Coleridge's own views: as we know, he regarded the primitive of a metaphysical system, its founding vision, as undemonstrable by rational means, and therefore as a choice—a moral choice—which each individ-ual must make for himself. In Coleridge's opinion, a man is ultimately responsible for the kind of world he sees.

IV. COSMIC ECOLOGY: THE GROWING PLANT

It is one thing to know Coleridge's nature-philosophy as a conceptual scheme and quite another thing to know what nature looks like when viewed through that scheme. I should like, in conclusion, to present to you a passage in which, in an imaginative moment, Coleridge communicates what it is to experience the world in accordance with his informing vision.

This text occurs in an unlikely place. In 1816 Coleridge published a short work, *The Statesman's Manual,* to encourage the study of the Bible as a repository, in symbolic form, of those ideas of reason which are the principles of all political wisdom. To the *Manual* he added, characteristically, five appendices. Appendix C sets out to explain at length the difference between the thin intuition of the world which is filtered through the categories of the understanding, and the full intuition of the world as contemplated by the reason mediated by imagination. While Coleridge sits writing, he looks through his study window at the landscape outside and, just as in his early conversation poems, an aspect of the natural scene springs his imagination free, and so transforms the *visibilia* into vision. Here is Coleridge's text, in part:

I seem to myself to behold in the quiet objects, on which I am gazing, more than an arbitrary illustration, more than a mere *simile*, the work of my own Fancy! I feel an awe, as if there were before my eyes the same Power, as that of the REASON—the same Power in a lower dignity, and therefore a symbol estab-   5 lished in the truth of things. I feel it alike, whether I contemplate a single tree or flower, or meditate on vegetation throughout the world, as one of the great organs of the life of nature. Lo!—with the rising sun it commences its outward life and enters into open communion with all the elements, at once assimilat-   10 ing them to itself and to each other. At the same moment it strikes its roots and unfolds its leaves, absorbs and respires, steams forth its cooling vapour and finer fragrance, and breathes a repairing spirit, at once the food and tone of the atmosphere, into the atmosphere that feeds *it*. Lo!—at the touch of light how   15 it returns an air akin to light, and yet with the same pulse effectuates its own secret growth, still contracting to fix what expanding it had refined. Lo!—how upholding the ceaseless plastic motion of the parts in the profoundest rest of the whole it becomes the visible organismus of the whole *silent* or *elemen-*   20 *tary* life of nature and, therefore, in incorporating the one extreme becomes the symbol of the other; the natural symbol of that higher life of reason, in which the whole series (known to us in our present state of being) is perfected, in which, therefore, all the subordinate gradations recur, and are re-ordained   25 *"in more abundant honor."* We had seen each in its own cast, and we now recognize them all as co-existing in the unity of a higher form, the Crown and Completion of the Earthly, and the

Mediator of a new and heavenly series. Thus finally, the vegetable creation, in the simplicity and uniformity of its *internal*   30
structure symbolizing the unity of nature, while it represents
the omniformity of her delegated functions in its *external* variety and manifoldness, becomes the record and chronicle of her
ministerial acts, and inchases the vast unfolded volume of the
earth with the hieroglyphics of her history.[66]   35

The passage has haunted me since I. A. Richards brought it
to my attention when I was a student at Cambridge several
decades ago. In its projection of a distinctive authorial presence, its rhythms and rhetoric, and its ever-widening orbit
of reference, it gives us, I think, some notion of Coleridge's
conversation—a marvel of the age that attracted crowds of
domestic and foreign visitors and is recorded in more than
a hundred surviving memoirs. John Lockhart describes how
Coleridge cheered and delighted his audience with

> the evident kindliness of his whole spirit and intentions . . . the
> cordial childlike innocence of his smile, the inexpressible
> sweetness of his voice, and the rich musical flow into which his
> mere language ever threw itself.[67]

And James Fenimore Cooper narrates how, at a dinner party,
Coleridge discoursed for an uninterrupted hour about Homer.
Sir Walter Scott sat, like the other auditors, "immovable as a
statue," occasionally muttering, "Eloquent!" "Wonderful!"
"Very extraordinary!"[68] There were a few who were immune
to the enchantment, Carlyle most notably; but Coleridge had
anticipated Carlyle by caricaturing his own talk. My "griev-
ous fault," he confided to his notebook, is that

> my illustrations swallow up my thesis—I feel too intensely the
> omnipresence of all in each . . . [and so] go on from circle to
> circle till I break against the shore of my Hearer's patience, or
> have my Concentricals dashed to nothing by a Snore.[69]

In the passage I have reproduced, notice first that in his
description of the growing plant (lines 9–18) Coleridge

incorporates the findings of experimental botanists, and that the scientific facts are detailed, accurate and up to date. In his *Vegetable Staticks* (1727) Stephen Hales had described the flow of sap, under pressure, from the roots through the plant, and the transpiration of water-vapor through the surface of the leaves. Joseph Priestley in the 1770s published his *Experiments and Observations on Different Kinds of Air*, announcing his discovery that plants restore the purity of "vitiated air" by producing large quantities of the gas he called "dephlogisticated air," thus rendering the atmosphere again fit for human and animal respiration. Not until Jan Ingenhousz published his classic *Experiments upon Vegetables* (1779), however, was it made known that this process does not occur in darkness, but only under "the influence of the light of the sun"; that the operation is performed "only by the leaves and the green stalks" of the plants, which absorb common air, "elaborate" it, and give out the "dephlogisticated air"; and that after absorbing the air, plants "separate from it those substances which are appropriate for their nourishment" and eject those which are "harmful to them" but "wholesome for animals." By the time he wrote *An Essay on the Food of Plants* (1796), Ingenhousz had come to know what he called the "new chemistry" of Lavoisier, and so was able to specify the activity of the green matter in the leaves of plants: under the influence of sunlight, it absorbs carbon dioxide from the atmosphere, decomposes it, exhales the oxygen, and by a process of chemical recomposition, changes the carbon remainder to its own substance and nourishment.[70]

Coleridge composed *The Statesman's Manual* at the time (1815–16) when he was developing his philosophy of nature, and his account of the absorption and transpiration of water, of the chemistry of photosynthesis, and of the process of plant growth is structured throughout by the humanistic categories and relationships predicated by that philosophy. He converts, that is, scientific data into metascientific terms of encounter, communion, kinship, participation, and reciprocity, and he locates the processes of the plant within a universe of correspondences, through which beats the pulse of one shared life. For example:

Lo!—at the touch of light how it returns an air akin to light,
and yet with the same pulse effectuates its own secret growth,
still contracting to fix what expanding it had refined.

The "air akin to light" is oxygen, and Coleridge's phrase is
more than a metaphor, for in his intricate scheme of nature
oxygen is an element that is a phenomenal "exponent"—a
physical correspondent—of the pre-phenomenal power he
calls light. By the "predominance," as Coleridge says elsewhere, of one or the other of the two primal counter-powers,
"Carbon most represents Gravity, Oxygen Light. . . ."[71] The
oxygen that the plant breathes out (lines 13–15 in our passage) is "a repairing spirit" because it revitalizes what Priestley had called the "vitiated air," in that sustained reciprocity
wherein the plant feeds the atmosphere by which it has been
fed. And the "pulse" of the growing plant—the contraction
by which it recomposes and assimilates, and the expansion by
which it decomposes and exhales, the chemical elements of
carbon dioxide—reiterates the polar forces of "Contraction
and Dilation" which, we recall, are the systole and diastole of
the pre-phenomenal power of light that initiate the heartbeat
of all natural and human life.

Coleridge goes on (lines 18–26) to situate the plant in his
spiral scheme of evolving and correspondent nature. The
evolutionary process performs a spiral because, Coleridge
claims, since the generative principle is one that "in every
instant *goes out* of itself, and in the same instant retracts," "the
product" is of necessity a "curve line."[72] Halfway in the evolution between inorganic matter at one end and man at the
other end, the plant occupies a position on the schematic spiral corresponding to that of the chemical elements below it
and of the human reason above it. Thus, in the ceaseless
"plastic" (that is, "formative") recompositions of its chemical
elements within the stillness of its outer form, the growing
plant incorporates, and so is an exponent of, "the whole *silent*
or *elementary* life" of inorganic nature. But the processes by
which a plant grows are in turn incorporated in, and so serve
as a "symbol" of, the mental evolution of what Coleridge else-

where calls the "seminal" ideas at the upper extreme of natural evolution, the human reason.

"Symbol," by the way, is for Coleridge a specialized term that he applies only to objects in the Book of Scripture and the Book of Nature, as he is at pains to point out in *The Statesman's Manual*, in passages which present-day critics unwarily cite as though they applied to any literary use of "symbols," in the broad modern sense. A symbol, Coleridge says in the *Manual*, "always partakes of the Reality which it renders intelligible; and while it enunciates the whole, abides itself as a living part in that Unity, of which it is the representative."[73] In Coleridge's scheme of nature the growing plant is a symbol of reason—"a symbol established in the truth of things" (lines 4–6)—because it is "the same Power, as that of the REASON," but "in a lower dignity." That is, the reason is consubstantial with the plant, since it is a product of the same primitive counter-powers, but on a level of organization in which (lines 22–26) "all the subordinate gradations recur, and are reordained '*in more abundant honor.*' " But to Coleridge's thinking, while human reason is the highest product of natural evolution, it is in its turn a symbol of —therefore participates in, "partakes of the Reality" of—that divine Reason, the Logos, which (in his favorite quotation from John) is the life and the light of men. Hence Coleridge's assertion (lines 27–29) that the human reason, while it is "the Crown and Completion of the Earthly," is also "the Mediator of a new and heavenly series." In other words, man's reason is the middle thing between the natural and the supranatural levels of being.

I shall not carry farther the explication of this text—so terse and lucid, but implicating Coleridge's total philosophy of nature—except for one last remark. ("Lastly!" Coleridge once exclaimed, "O word of comfort!") The passage makes it evident that Coleridge's myth of concern envisions all existing things, from the inorganic through the human, as participants in a single system of cosmic ecology. Man, whatever more he may be, is consubstantial, interdependent, and in communication with the nature of which he is the product. By having achieved self-consciousness, Coleridge says, man "has the whole world in counterpoint to him, but he contains an entire world within himself. Now, for the first time at the apex of the living pyramid, it is Man and Nature, but Man himself is a syllepsis, a compendium of Nature—the Microcosm!" And again, in 1817:

> The whole process is cyclical tho' progressive, and the Man separates from Nature only that Nature may be found again in a higher dignity in the Man.[74]

With whatever differences, this sense of a cosmic ecology of nature, man, and mind is shared by all Romantic visionaries, Christian or non-Christian, from Schelling and Coleridge to D. H. Lawrence and Dylan Thomas. Coleridge's reasoned formulation of such a vision of the world seems to me a reputable metaphysics which has intellectual, emotional, and aesthetic appeal and implies important rules for the conduct of life. It is also eminently pertinent to our own time. Coleridge, we know, claimed that an intuition of the world which is limited to the categories of the utilitarian and merely scientific understanding, by placing "nature in antithesis to the mind," "strikes death" both to the world and to the human spirit. Our developing scientific technology, by its frantic exploitation of nature, has turned Coleridge's metaphoric death into a grimly literal possibility. Scientists have recently taken the lead in trying to persuade us, by an appeal to our understanding, of the imminence of racial suicide. It remains to be seen whether merely understanding the facts is enough, or whether it will take a recovery of something like the Romantic vision—and myth—of nature to give us, in Shelley's great phrase, the power "to imagine what we know," and so suffice to release the emotions, the energies, the invention, and the will to salvage our world while it is still fit to live in.

Coleridge is two hundred years old today, and to commemorate his birth I thought it appropriate to call to mind an area of his wide-ranging thought which has been the least attended to and the least esteemed. A commemoration, however, ought also to leave us with a memory of the man him-self. The Coleridge who developed his philosophy of nature in 1815–19 was in his middle forties and on the verge of his kindly, industrious, marvelously loquacious, but lonely and defeated older age. It is better to remember Coleridge as he himself chose to be remembered, by an episode in an early letter. It is one of a group that he called "Satyrane's Let-ters"—after the satyr's son in *The Faerie Queene* whom Una converted to the true belief—which Coleridge revised and used to fill out the *Biographia Literaria* in 1816. He did so, he tells us, because "I would fain present myself to the Reader," not "under the circumstances of later years," but "as I was in the first dawn of my literary life."[75] In that episode Coleridge presents himself to us dressed all in black and dancing; it was found by the poet Wallace Stevens in its obscure place and quoted by him as a chief exhibit in his essay "The Figure of the Youth as Virile Poet."[76] Here we find the authentic S.T.C.—downrightly eccentric, a bit complacent about his powers, showing forth his frailties, yet savingly self-ironic, talking, talking, and unexpectedly modulating into the music of his prose at its best.

It is a Sunday morning, 16 September 1798. Coleridge is twenty-five years of age; he has very recently composed most of his best poems, including *The Ancient Mariner* and *Frost at Midnight; Lyrical Ballads* is in the press; and he is on a packet taking him to his momentous ten months in Germany. The water roughens, and most of the eighteen voyagers retreat hastily to the cabin. Coleridge is in somewhat better plight, and creeps into a lifeboat for a nap. There he is sought out and summoned to a drinking party by two Danes, one of whom is inordinately vain of his fractured English. "Vat imagination!" he cries to Coleridge, "Vat language! vat vast science! and vat eyes! . . . O my heafen! vy, you're a Got!"

> I went [Coleridge writes], and found some excellent wines and a dessert of grapes with a pineapple. The Danes had chris-tened me Doctor Teology, and dressed as I was all in black, with large shoes and black worsted stockings, I might certainly have passed very well for a Methodist missionary. However I

disclaimed my title. What then may you be? A man of fortune?
No!—A merchant? No! A merchant's traveller? No!—A clerk?
No!—Un Philosophe, perhaps? . . . I was weary of being ques-
tioned, and rather than be nothing . . . I submitted by a bow,
even to the aspersion implied in the word, "un Philosophe."—
The Dane then informed me, that all in the present party were
philosophers likewise. Certes we were not of the stoic school.
For we drank and talked and sung, till we talked and sung all
together; and then we rose and danced on the deck a set of
dances. . . .

NINE

Apocalypse: Theme and Romantic Variations

Near the end of his life D. H. Lawrence wrote an extended interpretation of the Book of Revelation. "From earliest years right into manhood," he said by way of introduction, "like any other nonconformist child I had the Bible poured every day into my helpless consciousness, till there came almost a saturation point." The concluding book of the Bible was the most emphasized and produced the greatest effect:

> By the time I was ten, I am sure I had heard, and read, that book ten times over. . . . Down among the uneducated people, you will still find Revelation rampant. I think it has had, and perhaps still has, more influence, actually, than the Gospels or the great Epistles.[1]

In some aspects Lawrence under-assesses both the prominence and the influence of Revelation in England. The book has attracted the devoted attention, within as well as outside the Established Church, of some of the greatest English scholars, and of the greatest scientists as well; both Newton, for example, and Joseph Priestley wrote more extensively on

the prophecies of Revelation than on the physical sciences.[2]
The influence of Revelation also extends far beyond "uneducated people" who believe in the literal truth of its apocalyptic predictions. For whether we are believers or unbeliev-
ers, uneducated or learned, we, like our Western ancestors
over the last two millennia, continue to live in a pervasively
biblical culture, in which theological formulas are implicated
in our ordinary language and we tend to mistake our inherited categories for the constitution of the world and the universal forms of thought. A century and a half ago Pierre
Proudhon, the radical economic and social theorist, and himself an advocate of "humanitarian atheism," acknowledged
the inescapability of religious concepts and patterns of thinking. He was, he said,

> forced to proceed like the materialist—that is, by observation
> and experience—and to conclude in the language of the believer,
> because there is no other; not knowing whether my formulas,
> theological in spite of me, would be taken literally or figura-
> tively. . . . We are full of Divinity, *Jovis omnia plena;* our mon-
> uments, our traditions, our laws, our ideas, our languages, and
> our sciences, all are infected by this indelible superstition, out-
> side of which we can neither speak nor act, and without which
> we do not even think.[3]

Many of the schemes and ruling concepts of *les sciences
humaines,* as well as the plotting and representation of character in much of our literature, have been shaped by the historical design and theological ideas derived from the Bible
and from biblical exegesis.[4] Especially prominent in this biblical culture has been the imprint, in narrative plot, characters, and imagery, of the Revelation of Saint John the Divine.
In a number of Western philosophers, historians, political
and social theorists, and poets, the thinking and imagination
have been apocalyptic thinking and imagination; sometimes
directly so, at other times by the deliberate enterprise of an
author to translate the biblical myth into abstract concepts
and a non-supernatural design, but increasingly during the
last 150 years by a transposition of the theological model into
secular terms, in a process of which the author himself has
remained largely unaware.

I have been asked to give an overall account of apocalypticism in literary and intellectual history, and to dwell especially on the Romantic period (the several decades after the French Revolution), which has a good claim to be called the most apocalyptic cultural era since the century and a half in Hebrew civilization which preceded and followed the birth of Christ.

I. THE SHAPE AND CONTENT OF HISTORY

Revelation (or in the Greek derivative, Apocalypse) is the concluding book of the biblical canon which presents, in the mode of symbolic visions, a series of events, now beginning, which will culminate in the abrupt end of the present, evil world-order and in its replacement by a regenerate mankind in a new and perfected condition of life. The wisdom of historical hindsight makes it possible to discriminate features of Revelation which have been especially potent in forming Western conceptions of the human past, present, and future.

Most important is the conception of the nature of history itself. Like preceding books in the Bible, but more thoroughly than any of them, Revelation is recursive in its procedure; that is, it represents the present and future by replicating or alluding to passages in earlier biblical texts, especially in Genesis, Exodus, the Old Testament prophets, and the apocalyptic visions in Daniel. The Book of Revelation thus incorporates and confirms an implicit design of the course and prime cause of earthly affairs which was soon made explicit by Christian exegetes—a paradigm of history which is radically distinctive. As against Greek and Roman primitivism and cyclism (the theory of eternal recurrence), the biblical paradigm attributes to earthly history a single and sharply defined plot, with a beginning (the *fiat* of creation), a catastrophe (the fall of man), a crisis (the Incarnation and Resurrection of Christ), and a coming end (the abrupt Second Advent of Christ as King, followed by the replacement of the old world by "a new heaven and a new earth") which will convert the tragedy of human history into a cosmic comedy.

This historical plot, furthermore, has a divine Author, who planned its middle and end before the beginning, created the great stage and agents of history, infallibly controls all its events, and guarantees its ultimate consummation. As the Voice declared to John after his vision of the last things: "I am Alpha and Omega, the beginning and the end, the first and the last" (22:13).

This paradigm has survived the biblical myth in which it was incorporated and has deeply informed Western views of the shape of history and the destiny of mankind and the world, whether in simple or sophisticated, in religious or secular, renderings. History, it is said, "has meaning"; by this is signified that it is not a play of blind contingencies but that it has a plot, and that this plot has a controller who orders it toward its outcome. Increasingly since the eighteenth century, however, the function of controller of history and guarantor of its consummation has been shifted from an external and supervisory Providence to forces which, though immanent within history itself, are no less infallible: an inherent teleology, or dialectical necessity, or set of causal laws which compel the course of events. But the prototype of the Western concept that history has an intelligible and end-determined order, whether fideistic or naturalistic, is the scheme of the course of earthly affairs from genesis to apocalypse which is underwritten by a sacred text.

Within this overall scheme the Book of Revelation envisions the agents and events of the latter and last days in ways which have strongly imprinted Western intellection and imagination; although because of the equivocal composition of Revelation itself, and the flexibility of the interpretive schemes that have been applied to its elucidation, this influence has manifested itself in diverse, and even contrary, forms.

1. The Earthly and Transcendental Kingdom

In Old Testament prophecy and apocalypses, the ultimate peaceable Kingdom under divine dominion is to be a perfected condition of mankind on this earth which will endure forever. So in the dream of Daniel "one like the Son of man," though descended from heaven, is given dominion over the earth that "is an everlasting dominion, which shall not pass away" (Daniel 7:13–14). In Revelation, however, the binding of the dragon and the restoration of earthly felicity under the dominion of Christ and his resurrected Saints will last only a millennium, one thousand years. The dragon will then be loosed again, to be defeated in a final battle at Armageddon, after which will occur a general resurrection and the last judgment. The earthly stage of the cosmic drama, its function in the divine plot completed, will then be replaced by "a new heaven and a new earth," while a "new Jerusalem" will come down "from God out of heaven" to be married to the Lamb in an eternal union.

Believers who are fundamentalists continue to interpret this promise of the felicity of the redeemed as applying only to a supramundane existence in a heavenly Jerusalem, after our bodily life and this temporal world shall have been abolished. Since the Reformation, however, there has been an increasing tendency to assimilate the prophecy of eternal felicity to the enduring state of this world, after it shall have been purged and renovated. John Milton, for one, dismissed the problem of the location of the ultimate human blessedness as insoluble, and of no great consequence. Whether by

> *its final conflagration* . . . is meant the destruction of the substance of the world itself, or only a change in the nature of its constitutent parts, is uncertain, and of no importance to determine. . . . Our glorification will be accompanied by the renovation of heaven and earth, and of all things therein adapted to our service and delight, to be possessed by us in perpetuity.[5]

In the secularized renderings of apocalyptic prophecy during the last two centuries, the felicitous outcome of history is of course held to take place on the stage of the existing earth, with the timelessness of eternity translated into perpetuity— or at least indefinite duration—in this-worldly time.

2. Polarity

Apocalyptic narrative and prophecy is a chiaroscuro history, in which the agencies are the opponent forces of light and of darkness and there is no middle-ground between the totally good and the absolutely evil. On the negative side are ranged Satan, the Beast, and the Great Whore, "Babylon the Great, the Mother of Harlots and Abominations of the Earth," together with the earthly agents of iniquity ("the kings of the earth" and their armies), to whom exegetes soon applied the collective term "Antichrist." Opposed to them are God, Christ, the "new Jerusalem . . . prepared as a bride adorned for her husband," and the company of earthly Saints. The consummation of history will occur, not by mediation between these polar opposites, but only after the extirpation of the forces of evil by the forces of good.

This aspect of the Book of Revelation has fostered a dubious heritage of reductive historical thinking in terms of absolute antitheses without the possibility of nuance, distinction, or mediation. Complex social, political, and moral issues are reduced to the two available categories of good and bad, right and wrong, the righteous and the wicked. Those who are not totally for are totally against; if you are not part of the solution you are part of the problem; and the problem can only be resolved by liquidating the opposition. In the popular mind—especially in countries such as America where there is a long and deep millenarian tradition—Revelation has also fostered a conspiracy-view of history in which all reverses or disasters are attributed to the machinations of Satan or Antichrist, or else of human agencies, whether individuals or classes or races, who are demoniac or (in the secular rendering) are motivated by the negative forces in the historical process. In times of extreme stress such thinking has helped engender a collective paranoia, religious or racial or national, which has manifested itself in crusades, sacred wars, pogroms, witch-hunts and other attempts to achieve, by annihilating the massed forces of evil, a final solution.

On a sophisticated and abstract level, which is not morally pernicious, the apocalyptic paradigm has also contributed toward a mode of thinking in which all process, whether historical, logical, or empirical, is attributed to the dynamic generated by polar opposites. The translation of apocalyptic dualism into a polar logic of process is especially patent in William Blake, who told H. C. Robinson, without inordinate exaggeration, that "all he knew was in the Bible." Blake had no patience for middling positions, for temporizing, and for what he called "Negations," which are "Exceptions & Objections & Unbeliefs" that, lacking a true opposite, are inert. What he sought was a consolidation of opponent-forces into genuine "Contraries," for "without Contraries is no progression"; and "from these contraries spring what the religious call Good and Evil."[6] It is the energy generated by the tension between contraries which impels all development, organization, and creativity. The biblical opposition of absolute contraries, with its destined outcome, was also one among diverse sources of the dialectic of post-Kantian German philosophy, as adumbrated by Fichte, developed by Schelling, and given its final form by Hegel. The driving force of all process—including generic and individual history, logic, and the self-generative, automotive, self-sufficient system of philosophy itself—is the compulsion within any element to pose, or else to pass over into, its opposite, or contrary, or antithesis, which in turn generates its own opponent, in a ceaseless movement toward a consummation which is the annulment, or else the stable equilibrium, of all oppositions.

3. The End in the Beginning

The shape of history implied by Revelation is a circular one which constitutes, as Karl Löwith has put it, "one great detour to reach in the end the beginning."[7] "And he that sat upon the throne said, Behold, I make all things new." But the new is represented as a renewal, and the *Endzeit* as a recovery of the *Urzeit*. The heaven and earth that God in the beginning had created he ends by re-creating; Adam and Eve, who have fallen, are replaced by the Lamb and his redeemed bride; the paradise which has been lost recurs in an equivalent state which includes the Edenic properties of the "river of water of life" and the "tree of life"; and men and women shall in the end regain their original innocence and its attendant felicity, for "there shall be no more curse," hence "no more death, neither sorrow, nor crying, [nor] any more pain."

In a number of Church Fathers the biblical pattern of a

paradise-to-be-regained was assimilated to the Neoplatonic paradigm of an emanation from, division, and return to the Absolute One, and gave rise to the persistent concept that the temporal process—both in the history of mankind and in the life of each individual—is a circular movement from a unitary felicity, through self-division, sin, exile, and suffering, back to the initial felicity. This circular course was often figured according to the biblical (and Plotinian) metaphor of the *peregrinatio vitae*, and to it was adapted Christ's parable of the Prodigal Son, who leaves home, journeys "into a far country" where he wastes "his substance with riotous living," and, penitent, returns home to a rejoicing father (Luke 15:11–32).

In a consequential variant of this figure of history as a great-circle route back to the origin, the blessedness at the end is conceived not simply to equal, but to exceed the innocence and happiness at the beginning. To Milton, for example, a Puritan exponent of the strenuous moral life, the fall of man was a fortunate fall, not only because it gave us Christ, but because the ultimate paradise will have been earned, whereas the initial paradise was merely inherited. Thus when Christ shall receive his faithful into bliss, the earth

> Shall all be Paradise, far happier place
> Than this of *Eden*, and far happier days.
> (*Paradise Lost*, XII, 461–65)

A century or so later philosophers and poets translated this myth of man's circuitous course from Eden to a far happier paradise into the distinctive Romantic figure of development—whether in history, the individual life, intellection, or the realm of morality, culture, and art—as a spiral: all process departs from an undifferentiated unity into sequential self-divisions, to close in an organized unity which has a much higher status than the original unity because it incorporates all the intervening divisions and oppositions. As Hugo von Hofmannsthal later epitomized the Romantic concept: "Every development moves in a spiral line, leaves nothing behind, reverts to the same point on a higher turning."

The recurrent plot of Blake's prophetic poems, as he describes it at the opening of *The Four Zoas,* concerns "a Perfect Unity . . . of Eden," figured as a single Universal Man, followed by "His fall into Division & his Resurrection to Unity." This course of events, as Blake describes it elsewhere, is a spiral progress from simple innocence up and back to an "organized innocence"; or in an alternative description, it is mankind's loss of Eden and his struggle to achieve, by "mental fight," the New Jerusalem, which is not simply the garden of the origin but the great city of civilization, intellection, and the arts. No less explicitly Friedrich Schelling adverts to the language of the Book of Revelation as the ground for his spiral view of intellectual and historical process. "I posit God as the first and the last, as Alpha and Omega, but as Alpha he is not what he is as Omega." For at the beginning he is merely *"Deus implicitus,"* and only "as Omega is he *Deus explicitus.*"[8] Translated into conceptual terms, this theological representation yields Schelling's philosophic method. "Philosophy," he declares, "opens with the Absolute and with the absence of all oppositions," and its "ultimate destination" is "to bring about a higher, truly all-encompassing unity"—the "perfect inclusion of all-in-one" that is "the one truly absolute knowledge, which is also . . . a knowledge of the Absolute." And this process, Schelling adds, "applies just as much to the sciences as to art."[9]

We recognize a similar provenience and pattern in Hegel's dialectic. As he says at the conclusion of his shorter *Logic:* "We have now returned to the notion of the Idea with which we began," but "the return to the beginning is also an advance."[10] And so in the self-compelled movement of spirit in all its manifestations, whether in history, logic, metaphysics, science, or art, the consummation, or "Absolute," having overcome yet preserved all intervening self-alienations, is that "Truth" which includes in an organized form not less than everything. As Hegel puts it—in an explicit parallel of his conceptual scheme to the "life of God and divine cognition"—the True is "not an *original* or *immediate* unity as such," for which "otherness and alienation, and the overcoming of alienation are not serious matters." Instead it is a circuitous progression—

> the process of its own becoming, the circle that presupposes the end as its goal, having its end also as its beginning; and only by being worked out to its end, is it actual.[11]

II. TWO WAYS TO THE MILLENNIUM

The plot of biblical history is sharply discontinuous. Each of its crucial events is abrupt, cataclysmic, and inaugurates a drastic change: the creation, the fall, the Incarnation and Resurrection, and the advent of what Rufus Jones has called "the fierce comfort of an apocalyptic relief expedition from the sky"[12] to establish the millennium. Revelation represents all present-day rulers and institutions as radically evil, and promises that these will be annihilated and replaced by the millennial kingdom. After the triumph of Christianity this millennial component posed an obvious threat to the Church and the established social order—a threat the more obvious because the seat of the Western Church was the very Rome which in Revelation had been figured as unholy Babylon, the Great Whore. Repeated attempts were made in the early Christian centuries to delete this threat by eliminating Revelation from the biblical canon. Much more effectively and enduringly, however, Saint Augustine succeeded in saving yet denaturing Revelation by proposing the allegorical interpretation that the millennium signifies the present, but invisible, spiritual kingdom that has in fact been inaugurated at the Resurrection of Christ. Although Augustine's view became authoritatitve for the Church, belief in a literal millennium remained alive in the Middle Ages, and was widely revived after the Reformation.

As a consequence, Christianity has through the centuries harbored a strong historical prospectivism—the certainty that, though mankind is radically corrupt and inhabits a vale of tears, the best is inevitably about to be, in this life and this world. This millennial expectation has helped engender Western convictions about the future of mankind which have no close parallels in civilizations that developed outside the Judeo-Christian orbit.

1. Millennialism, Meliorism, and the Idea of Progress

One such conviction is that the human race is gradually progressing toward a much better, or even perfect, condition in the material, intellectual, moral, and social realms. As early as the twelfth century the Cistercian monk Joachim of Floris reinterpreted Revelation in accordance with a Trinitarian conception of history, dividing the course of events into three great eras: the initial age of the Old Testament Father, the present age of the Son, and the coming age of the Holy Spirit when, by the joint agencies of God and men, all the world will achieve a state of perfect spiritual liberty. Joachim thus transformed the single-fall, single-redemption shape of biblical history into a sequence of three upward quantum leaps and levelings-off, ending in an earthly perfection. After Joachim's death some of his followers, especially the Spiritual Franciscans, converted his prophecy of a Third Age into a militant program of radical political, as well as moral and religious, reform which has had a recurrent influence on revolutionary thinking, particularly in Catholic countries.

The modern form of the idea of progress, however, has been mainly a product of Protestant Christianity. Recent researches have shown that this idea was not, as it was once represented by historians, simply an optimistic extrapolation into the future of the conspicuous advances in Europe, during and after the Renaissance, in science, technology, geographical exploration, and the arts. Instead, these advances in the sciences and the practical arts were assimilated into the inherited theological scheme of historical prospectivism, but in a way that drastically altered both the shape and dynamics of the scheme. For beginning with the Renaissance, mankind seemed to have developed the human means to achieve the promised state of felicity gradually and peacefully instead of by an abrupt and destructive intervention; and in the course of centuries, progress was increasingly conceived to be attainable by purely human agency, and to be guaranteed by the operation of purely natural causes, without the need for an apocalyptic relief expedition from the sky.

Francis Bacon, for example, was one of the earliest proponents of the idea of historical progress, as a destined consequence of the use of experimental science to increase man's control over the material conditions of his well-being. He presents this view, however, within the express context of the Christian pattern of providential history, and with persistent allusion to apocalyptic prophecy. He thus reads the assertion in Daniel concerning "the last ages," that "many shall run to and fro, and knowledge shall be increased," to signify that geographical exploration "and the advancement of the sciences, are destined by fate, that is, by Divine Providence, to meet in the same age."[13] In Bacon's interpretation of the first and last things, man's fall, in its moral aspect, was a fall from innocence, but in its cognitive aspect it was a divorce of mind from nature, hence of man's original dominion over the creation. Experimental science, however, promises to restore the "commerce between the mind of man and the nature of things . . . to its perfect and original condition." The end of human progress on earth will thus be a return to the condition of Eden, which Bacon equates with the heavenly Kingdom of the latter days: "The entrance into the kingdom of man, founded on the sciences," is "not much other than the entrance into the kingdom of heaven, whereinto none may enter except as a little child." And he celebrates the anticipated consummation in the great apocalyptic figure of a marriage, although not between Christ and the renovated Jerusalem, but between

> the mind and the universe, the divine goodness assisting, out of which marriage let us hope (and be this the prayer of the bridal song) there may spring . . . a line and race of inventions that may in some degree subdue and overcome the necessities and miseries of humanity.[14]

Even in the heyday of the idea of progress in the nineteenth century, when the sanction of its inevitability was asserted to be the inherent laws of social development, many proponents of social reforms to expedite a perfected society continued to use the language of biblical prophecy. In some part, of course, the biblical allusions were merely metaphors for secular convictions, designed to make new concepts and programs intelligible and acceptable to a traditionalist public and to endow new ideas with the potency of an existing religious faith. The biblical language, however, manifests an unbroken continuity with the origin of the concept of inevitable progress in millennial prophecy. As Coleridge said of classical myths, which he called the "fair humanities of old religion,"

> They live no longer in the faith of reason!
> But still the heart doth need a language, still
> Doth the old instinct bring back the old names.[15]

The socialist and industrial reformer Robert Owen, for example, even though he repudiated all religious creeds, repeatedly expressed his conviction about the peaceful evolution to a "New Moral World" in terms of the new heaven and new earth prophesied in Isaiah and Revelation. On his trip to America in 1824–25 Owen declared, in an address about his social schemes to the President and Congress, that "the time is now come, when the principle of good is about to . . . reign triumphant over the principle of evil. . . . Old things shall pass away and all shall become new." Later he declared to the population of the Owenite community New Harmony, Indiana:

> The day of your deliverance is come, and let us join heart and hand in extending that deliverance . . . until it shall pass to all people, even unto the uttermost parts of the earth. Then will be the full time of that universal sabbath, or reign of happiness, which is about to commence here, and which I trust you who are ready to put on the wedding garment will long live to enjoy.

Followers of Owen hailed him as the Messiah who, in the fullness of time, had now appeared; and just before his death

Owen himself soberly declared that, in "a calm retrospect of my life . . . there appears to me to have been a succession of extraordinary or out-of-the-usual-way events . . . to compel me to proceed onward to complete a mission, of which I have been an impelled agent."[16]

2. *Millenarianism and Revolution*

Another historical concept which, in its original development, was unique to Western culture, is both more primitive than the idea of gradual progress (in that it is much closer to the apocalyptic prototype) and more sophisticated (in that it has in the last century and a half been sanctioned by a complex structure of economic and social theory). This is the concept that both the institutional and moral evils of the present world will, by an inner necessity, be abolished once for all by a sudden, violent, and all-inclusive political and social revolution.

The millenarian feature of Revelation, Ernest Tuveson has remarked, provides a scenario for revolution. And recurrently in Protestant Europe the Book of Revelation, together with the apocalypse in Daniel, has inspired revolutionary uprisings against the institutional powers of evil. In the sixteenth century the Anabaptists in northern Europe, under such leaders as Thomas Müntzer and John of Leyden, "The Messiah of the Last Days," initiated violent movements against the established powers in order to prepare the way for the divine Kingdom. In the English civil wars of the next century, radical sects such as the Fifth Monarchy Men and the Diggers were possessed by the fervent belief that the conflict was the inauguration of the Second Coming and millennium—a belief that for an interval was shared by Oliver Cromwell and John Milton. In the latter eighteenth century the American Revolution evoked millenarian excitement among some adherents, while the early period of the French Revolution was widely interpreted as the glorious prelude to the universal felicity prophesied in Apocalypse—in Catholic France only by a few fringe groups, but in Protestant England and Germany by many of the major intellectuals of the 1790s.

The event of the French Revolution and its European after-waves precipitated the development, in the course of the nineteenth century, of the theory of absolute revolution, which is best known in the version of Marx and Engels.[17] In its distinctive features, an absolute revolution is conceived to be: (1) inevitable, because compelled by iron laws, or by a dialectical teleology, operative within the historical process itself; (2) abrupt and relatively imminent; (3) effected through the radical and irreconcilable opposition between institutions, races, or economic classes, in which one side (fated to prevail) embodies the historical right and good and its opponent (fated to be defeated and annihilated) embodies historical wrong and evil; (4) led by a militant élite, who recognize, cooperate with, and so expedite the irresistible process of history; (5) violent, because destined to be achieved by a fierce but purifying destruction of the forces of historical evil; (6) absolute, in that instead of gradual improvement or reform, there will be a rapid transformation of the very foundations of society and its institutions so as to effect a state of peace, community, justice, and the optimal conditions for human well-being; (7) universal—though it is to be initiated at a critical time and place, the revolution will, by irresistible contagion, spread to encompass all the inhabited world; and (8) ultimate and irrevocable, in that the transformation of society will also transform those attributes of human nature which have brought us to our present plight, restore man to his original humanity, and thus ensure the perpetuation of the new era.[18]

The certainty that the future will culminate in such a radical transformation, it is usually claimed, is based on valid induction from the historical past. But in its salient features we recognize in the theory of absolute revolution the stark outline of the apocalyptic prophecy, guaranteed by omnipotence, that history, after an imminent and violent victory of a messianic leader and his forces of good over the consolidated forces of evil, will eventuate in an abrupt and total alteration of the conditions of mankind into a state which is figured as a redeemed city that will recuperate the felicity of the aboriginal garden.

III. THE APOCALYPSE WITHIN

The Apocalypse, as Milton remarked, rises "to a Prophetick pitch in types, and Allegories." The symbolic and typological mode in which it is set forth has made Revelation a very flexible text for historical application. The antitype of the Beast, or of Antichrist, in accordance with the time, place, and persuasion of the interpreter, has been variously identified as the Jews, the Ottomans, the Pope, France, Charles I, Cromwell, priestcraft, the alliance against revolutionary France, the landholding aristocracy, capitalists, the American slaveholder, and Hitler; even in a single interpreter, the antitype has sometimes shifted drastically, in consonance with a shift in the interpreter's outlook and preoccupations. This flexibility has also served to make predictions based on Revelation invulnerable to disconfirmation. In the demotic type of prediction—in which the group, having computed the precise date, dispose of their worldly goods, don white robes, and ascend a hill to await the relief expedition from the sky—the failure of the event to happen on schedule usually results, not in a rejection of the prediction, but in a recalculation of the prophetic arithmetic. In the derivative, secular mode of prediction, the failure of a political revolution to effect the predicted transformation in the nature and well-being of mankind leads to the postponement of the change to a secular second advent after an ever-extending period of the dictatorship of the proletariat, or to its reformulation as the emergent product of an indefinitely continuing revolution. In both instances, religious and secular, the capacity of the predictive scheme to survive all counter-evidence rests on faith in an infallible but equivocal charter which allows broad play to the force of human desire.

The freedom of interpretive maneuver was greatly increased by the early application to Revelation of an allegorical mode of reading, either as an overlay or as a total displacement of its "literal"—that is, historical—reference, and especially by the interpretation of its "carnal sense" as encoding an inner "spiritual sense." The tendency to internalize apocalypse by a spiritual reading began in the Gospels themselves: "For, behold, the kingdom of God is within you" (Luke 17:21). Saint Paul, the first exemplar of the distinctively Christian experience of conversion, enlarged the analogy to include an equivalent, in the spirit of the individual convert, of a second creation, of a new heaven and new earth, and of the marriage between the Lamb and the New Jerusalem: "Therefore if any man be in Christ, he is a new creature: old things are passed away; behold, all things are become new" (II Corinthians 5:17); "Wherefore, my brethren, ye also are become dead to the law . . . that ye should be married to another . . . who is raised from the dead" (Romans 7:4). In his *Confessions* Augustine, who rejected the literal reading of the millennial promise, effected instead the full transfer of apocalyptic prophecy from the outer world to the theater of the individual spirit, where one experiences the pre-enactment, in this life, of the historical events of the latter days. Building, as he himself indicates, on the established pattern of Christian conversion from Paul to Athanasius' recent *Life of St. Anthony*, Augustine describes in detail the sustained and anguished conflict between his "two wills" (the inner equivalent of the forces of Christ and Antichrist), culminating in a spiritual Armageddon in the garden at Milan, the final triumph of the good will, and the abrupt interposition of grace to effect the annihilation of the old creature and the birth of the new: "dying unto death and living unto life" (*Confessions*, VIII, xi).

By completing the process of psycho-historical parallelism, Augustine established the distinctive Christian paradigm of the interior life as one of polar self-division, internecine self-conflict, crisis, abrupt rebirth, and the consequent renovation of the way we experience the world; at the same time, by his detailed narration of these events in the course of his own life, he established the enduring literary genre of the spiritual autobiography. We recognize the mode, for example, on the moral level of its multiple significations, in Dante's account of his toilsome spiritual journey through hell and purgatory to the vision of paradise—a personal, inner experience which is proleptic of what will happen, historically, to all those who shall be redeemed *all'ultima giustizia* to dwell in that "true kingdom" which is "our city," where at the appointed time Dante too shall attend the wedding feast as a member of the Spouse (*Paradiso,* XXX). In *The Faerie Queene* Spenser converted the chivalric quest-romance of the Middle Ages into his "continued Allegory, or darke conceit," of which the chief prototype was the Book of Revelation. In its reference to the historical future, the narrative signifies the events preparatory to the Second Advent of Christ, His ultimate victory over the dragon, and the apocalyptic marriage which will inaugurate the restoration of Eden; at the same time, spiritually it signifies the quest for redemption, the fights against the agents and deceptions of evil, the triumph, and the spiritual marriage which is enacted in this present life within the soul of each wayfaring Christian, including Spenser himself. Augustine's *Confessions* has also engendered numerous spiritual autobiographies in prose; most of these writings are Protestant, and many represent a working-class pilgrim who makes his laborious interior way past the pitfalls of Satan toward the celestial city and the apocalyptic marriage of the Lamb. John Bunyan, who wrote a proletarian form of the Augustinian autobiography, *Grace Abounding,* also wrote in *Pilgrim's Progress* the immortal allegory of the proletarian spiritual journey—a pedestrian equivalent to the quest for an inner apocalypse by Spenser's courtly knight on horseback.

In the central tradition of Christian, and especially of Protestant, exegesis, the spiritual sense is justified as an overreading of the basic sense of Scripture, which is literal and historical. Some radical inner-light Protestants, however, proposed a mode of interpretation which regarded the spiritual meaning not as supplementing, but as totally displacing the literal sense. Gerrard Winstanley, leader of the sect of Diggers—that is, Christian communists—during the Puritan Revolution in England, proclaimed that any reading of the Bible which substitutes "bare letters, words and histories for spirit" is the work of the "great Dragon," for "all that which you call the history . . . is all to be seen and felt within you." Not only the places, events, and doctrines, but all the human and supernatural protagonists in the Bible, including Jehovah and Jesus, are nothing more than figurative vehicles for the powers and processes of individual minds in mundane experience. Anyone who worships an external God "in the heavens" in fact worships the Devil; also, not "Jesus Christ at a distance from thee . . . but a Christ within is thy Saviour. . . . *And besides him there is no Saviour."* By the same token the events of the last days in Revelation signify solely a personal and internal experience: "Now the second *Adam* Christ, hath taken the Kingdom my body, and rules in it; *He makes it a new heaven, and a new earth, wherein dwells Righteousness";* "And this is to be made a new creature." The new heaven and new earth, it thus turns out, instead of being a transcendent habitat that "shal not be known and seen, til the body is laid in the dust," is simply our present world, perceived in a new way by our redeemed and glorified senses:

> I tel you, this great mystery is begun to appear, and it must be seen by the material eyes of the flesh: And those five senses that is in man, shall partake of his glory.[19]

A century and a half later Blake told H. C. Robinson that "all he knew was in the Bible," but added the crucial proviso that "he understands by the Bible the spiritual sense." Blake's "spiritual sense" is very like Winstanley's, in that it invalidates the literal sense as a fiction propagated by "Priesthood" and internalizes both the divine and human agents and events of the biblical narrative. "All deities reside in the human breast"; all powers to effect drastic change in the perceived world are mental powers; and heaven, hell, and paradise are states of mind:

> I know of no other . . . Gospel than the liberty both of body & mind to exercise the Divine Arts of Imagination. . . . What is the Joy of Heaven but Improvement in the things of the Spirit? What are the Pains of Hell but Ignorance, Bodily Lust, Idleness & devastation of the things of the Spirit? . . . to Labour in Knowledge is to Build up Jerusalem.

Blake identifies Christ the Redeemer with the human imagination, and therefore conceives the apocalyptic new earth to be this world, when it is perceived imaginatively—that is, through our redeemed and liberated senses. "The ancient tradition that the world will be consumed in fire is true," but in the spiritual sense that "this will come to pass by an improvement of sensual enjoyment"; for "if the doors of perception were cleansed every thing would appear to man as it is, infinite." It is in this radical sense that "the Eye altering, alters all."[20]

Blake probably derived his version of biblical hermeneutics from left-wing dissenting sects in late-eighteenth-century England. To spiritualize biblical history and prophecy, however, was a common poetic procedure among Blake's young contemporaries. Wordsworth, for example, proclaimed that the theme of his poetic autobiography concerned divine powers and actions, internalized as processes of his own mind:

> Of genius, power,
> Creation, and divinity itself,
> I have been speaking, for my theme has been
> What passed within me. . . .
> This is in truth heroic argument,
> And genuine prowess.
> (*The Prelude*, 1805 text, III, 171–83)

And in the verse "Prospectus" to his overall poetic enterprise, which resonates with echoes of Revelation, Wordsworth announced that his poetic journey must ascend beyond "the heaven of heavens" past "Jehovah, with his thunder, and the choir / Of shouting Angels," and must also sink deeper than the lowest hell; all this, however, without leaving the confines of

> the mind of Man,
> My haunt, and the main region of my Song.

The conclusion of his "high argument" is the recovery of a lost paradise, but a paradise which is the very world of all of us, to be achieved by a consummation figured as an apocalyptic marriage between the prime Romantic opposites of subject and object, spirit and its alienated other—or in the English terms, between mind and nature: "Paradise, and groves / Elysian, Fortunate Fields,"

> why should they be
> A history only of departed things,
> Or a mere fiction of what never was?
> For the discerning intellect of Man
> When wedded to this goodly universe
> In love and holy passion, shall find these
> A simple produce of the common day.
> . . . This is our high argument.[21]

IV. AMERICAN MILLENNIALISM

Writers in diverse times and places have claimed that their nation is the typological "New Israel," divinely chosen to play the leading role in initiating the earthly Kingdom. The nation possessed of the most thoroughly and enduringly millennial ideology, however, is America, in a tradition that began even before it was settled by Europeans. Columbus himself suggested that the New World he had discovered was to be the locale of the new earth prophesied in Revelation. This belief was brought to America by the early Franciscan missionaries (heirs to the preachings of Joachim of Floris), and entrenched by the fervent iteration of America's millennial destiny by the Puritan settlers of New England. "For your full assurance," Edward Johnson reminded his fellow New Englanders in 1653, "know this is the place where the Lord will create a new Heaven and a new earth . . . new Churches and a new Commonwealth together." A century later Jonathan Edwards viewed the Great Awakening as the initial stage in fulfilling the New World's apocalyptic destiny, interpreted in the spiritual sense: "This new world is probably now discovered . . . that God might in it begin a new world in a spiritual respect, when he creates the *new heavens* and *new earth*."[22] In our time the Great Seal of the United States, as reproduced on the one-dollar bill, echoes the persistent expectation in its motto, derived from Virgil's prophecy of a new age of gold: *Novus Ordo Seclorum.*

Belief in the providential role of the New World helped form the concept of the American's identity as a new Adam, freed from the corruptions of the Old World. In its secularized form this view fostered the stress, especially prominent among the Transcendentalists, on the American as one who is uniquely able to re-achieve the innocent vision of a child, and so to experience the unspoiled American world as a pristine Eden. The militant application of millennial prophecy emerged in the American Revolution, in the Civil War (which produced the greatest of all hymns on the imminent Second Advent, "Mine eyes have seen the glory of the coming of the Lord"), and again in the First World War. In an alternative form the indurate myth of a millennial America resulted in the imperialist doctrines of the American Mission and of Manifest Destiny. We recognize in William Gilpin's proclamation of 1846 the ancient faith in America as the divine agency and initial theater of the world-wide consummation of history:

> The untransacted destiny of the American people is to subdue the continent . . . to regenerate superannuated nations . . . to carry the career of mankind to its culminating point . . . to absolve the curse that weighs down humanity, and to shed blessings round the world![23]

This awesome mission, however, entailed corresponding responsibilities and dire penalties for failure, as native prophets have persistently warned in American jeremiads that have preempted the imagery of the *dies irae;* it has also fostered a paranoid tendency to blame historical setbacks on diverse baleful conspirators, determined to frustrate the divine intention. And the investment of inordinate hope in the American promise has effected, in times of disillusion, an equal but opposite reaction of unqualified despair. Herman Melville in 1850 had shared the ardent belief that "we Americans are the peculiar, chosen people—the Israel of our time. . . . God has predestined, mankind expects great things from our race." In this "New World," the "political Messiah . . . has come in *us.*" A quarter-century later Melville voiced the depressive other-side of America's manic millennialism. Beyond all the saddest thought of old Europe, he lamented in *Clarel,*

> Might be the New World's sudden brought . . .
> To feel the arrest of hope's advance,
> And squandered last inheritance;
> And cry—"To Terminus build fanes!
> Columbus ended earth's romance:
> No New World to mankind remains!"[24]

V. ROMANTIC APOCALYPTICISM: POLITICAL, COGNITIVE, IMAGINATIVE

In its founding and continuing ideology, America is the most millennial of nations, but the period of English and German Romanticism, in its preoccupation with the philosophic, social, or poetic seer who demonstrates the way to a secular redemption, is the most apocalyptic of cultural eras.[25] In England, with its inheritance of Puritan millenarianism during the civil wars, and in Germany, with its even older chiliastic tradition and the emphasis on eschatological renewal in Pietist theology, the outbreak of the French Revolution revived the ancient hope. In both countries a chorus of preachers, poets, and young intellectuals endowed the Revolution with the myth of apocalypse, in the excited expectation that this local event heralded a renovated world for a regenerate mankind. As Robert Southey said, in retrospect from his conservative middle age, few persons who have not lived through the bright initial period of the French Revolution "can conceive or comprehend . . . what a visionary world" it seemed to open: "Old things seemed passing away, and nothing was dreamt of but the regeneration of the human race."[26] "Bliss was it in that dawn to be alive," Wordsworth recalled of those years, in *The Prelude,* with

France standing on the top of golden hours,
And human nature seeming born again.
(X, 692; VI, 353–54)

Hegel, Schelling, and Hölderlin, while fellow students at Tübingen Seminary, all shared this perfervid millenarian enthusiasm. Looking back, like Southey and Wordsworth, from the standpoint of his later conservatism, Hegel described the effect of this "world-historical" event of his youth in theological terms similar to theirs:

> It was a glorious dawn. All thinking beings shared in the jubilation of the epoch. . . . An enthusiasm of the spirit thrilled through the world, as though the time were now come of the actual reconciliation of God with the world.[27]

Through the mid-1790s the poets Blake, Wordsworth, Coleridge, and Southey, like Hölderlin in Germany, responded to the great events of the time by writing visionary epics, verse narratives, or Pindaric odes which, with a lavish use of apocalyptic symbols, depicted the dark and violent past and present of mankind, then hailed the outbreak of the French Revolution as the critical event which would usher in a new world combining the features of the biblical paradise and the pagan age of gold. The conclusion of Coleridge's prose Argument for his extended poetic vision, *Religious Musings*, written in 1794, tersely summarizes this prophetic reading of current events: "The present State of Society. The French Revolution. Millennium. Universal Redemption. Conclusion."

At the French excesses that began with the Reign of Terror, English and German commentators abandoned hope in the imminence of a literal millennium. But as in earlier ages, the paradigm demonstrated its capacity to survive disconfirmation by the course of events. The scientist and Unitarian preacher Joseph Priestley, despite some wavering, insisted near the end of his life in 1804 that the mistake was merely in computing the Second Coming, and that the "greatest of all events is not less certain for being delayed beyond our expectations."[28] Much more representative, however, was the view of Coleridge, who wrote to Wordsworth in 1799 that there had been a "complete failure of the French Revolution," but exhorted his friend to write a poem designed to banish the despair of those who, in consequence of that failure, "have thrown up all hopes for the amelioration of mankind."[29] As late as the second decade of the nineteenth century Shelley wrote that the French Revolution continued to be "the master theme of the epoch in which we live," and that this theme was a central element in what he, like many English and German contemporaries, called "the spirit of the age" with its great "new birth" in poetry and philosophy. But as Shelley also recognized, this theme was that of a failed revolution, the resulting collapse of millenarian expectation, and the need to salvage hopes for the amelioration of mankind.[30] Writing in 1815 Thomas Noon Talfourd observed—and his opinion has many contemporary parallels—that this crisis, which was intellectual and moral no less than political, interpenetrated and inspired the great new literature of the age. In the early days of the Revolution, "all was hope and joy and rapture; the corruption and iniquity of ages seemed to vanish like a dream; the unclouded heavens seemed once more to ring with the exulting chorus of peace on earth and goodwill to men." But suddenly these "sublime expectations were swept away" by "the terrible changes of this august spectacle." And one effect "of this moral hurricane . . . this rending of the general heart," was "to raise and darken the imagination," hence to help "form that great age of poetry which is flourishing around us."[31]

"The Revolution," Talfourd added, "completed the regeneration of our poetry." This remark applies to Germany as well as England, and to post-Kantian philosophy as well as literature. In both countries, and in both the cognitive and the imaginative realms, the apocalyptic design survived, but was given a spiritual interpretation—a new kind of spiritual interpretation, adapted to the social and intellectual conditions of the times. In what Wordsworth in 1805 called "this melancholy waste of hopes o'erthrown . . . this time / Of dereliction and dismay" (*The Prelude*, II, 447–57), he and other vanguard writers undertook to reconstitute the grounds of hope, in a way that would be not only pertinent to post-Revolutionary despair but acceptable to post-Enlightenment thinking. For an apocalypse by revelation or an apocalypse by revolution, they substituted an apocalypse of consciousness: the mind of man possesses the power, by an interior revolution, to transform his intellect and imagination, and by so doing to perceive the everyday world as a new earth in which he will be thoroughly at home.

1. Philosophic Chiliasm and Poetic Chiliasm

Romantic philosophers and poets were steeped in the Bible and in biblical exegesis. Schiller assiduously read theology in his early youth, and Fichte, Schelling, and Hegel, as well as the poet Hölderlin, had all been university students of theology. Wordsworth and Coleridge narrowly escaped becoming preachers; for Novalis, no less than for Blake, the Bible was what Blake called "the great code of art"; and Shelley, although an uncompromising agnostic, studied the Bible constantly and listed it as "last, yet first" among fifteen books adequate to constitute a good library.[32]

The new philosophy, like the new poetry of the Romantic era, achieved innovation by reverting to, but re-translating, the biblical paradigm of paradise, the fall, the redemption, and paradise-to-be-regained. Herder, Kant, Schiller, Fichte, Schelling, and Hegel (following the precedent of Lessing's *The Education of the Human Race,* 1780) all undertook, as they expressly asserted, to translate the conceptual truth incorporated in biblical myth into the secular mode that the Germans call *Universalgeschichte.* In this historical genre, the vanguard of human consciousness, represented as a single character called "Mankind," falls from the paradisal unity of a purely instinctual life into the "evil" of having to make moral choices, as well as other kinds of self-division and conflicts which, by their internal energy, compel him along the journey back toward the unity and felicity of his origin. To such a rational transposition of the biblical millennium by himself and other writers, Kant applied the term *der philosophische Chiliasmus.* "One sees," he also remarked, "that philosophy

too can have its chiliasm . . . which is nothing less than visionary."[33] In the 1790s the frustrated promise of the French
Revolution became for philosophers (including the elderly
Kant)[34] a crucial event in this progressive educational journey of Mankind. In addition it was increasingly stressed that
man's fall from instinctual self-unity into dispersion and self-
conflict was a *felix culpa,* because the way back is also a way
up, from a simplex unity to the complex integrity of a superior Mankind inhabiting a paradise happier far than the distant and undivided original. In parallel with this
Universalgeschichte was the Romantic *Bildungsgeschichte,* nar-
rating, in the vehicle of a life-journey, the educational growth
of a single mind; among its instances are Hölderlin's *Hyperion*
(1797–99), Wordsworth's *Prelude* (1805), and Carlyle's *Sartor
Resartus* (1833–34). This latter genre, constituting a theodicy
of the individual life, was a secular revision of the Christian
spiritual autobiography. In the Romantic mode the frag-
mented consciousness reaches a crisis, or spiritual breakdown, immediately followed by a breakthrough to a higher
integrity, from which vantage the individual finally is able to
discern the implicit teleology that governs, and justifies, his
painful educational journey—that is, the achievement of his
mature identity and the recognition of his predestined vocation as public spokesman in his time of troubles.

What is less obvious—though the fact was expressly asserted
by the philosophers themselves, and reiteratively implied by
the design, imagery, and allusions in their writings—is that
the great post-Kantian philosophical systems, no less than the
"universal history" these thinkers expounded, were secularized versions of the Christian paradigm of the creation, fall,
and apocalyptic consummation of history. What Novalis said
of Fichte's philosophy, that it is "perhaps nothing else than
applied Christianity,"[35] can be even more emphatically claimed
for the speculative systems of Fichte's younger contemporaries, Schelling and Hegel. As Hegel repeatedly said, while
philosophy "must not allow herself to be overawed by religion," it cannot neglect, but must translate into its own non-
supernatural terms, "the tales and allegories of religion."[36]

In Hegel's *Phenomenology of Spirit* the emergence of "the

Revealed Religion," with what he calls its "picture-thinking" in "the form of objectivity," is the penultimate stage of the spirit's process of self-education toward a consummation in philosophical *Wissenschaft*. In his narration of this process Hegel systematically translates the crucial occurrences and concepts of biblical history into the conceptual mode of genuine philosophy, which transcends, while preserving its truth-content, the mythical representations of revealed Christianity.[37] Carlyle's German philosopher, Professor Teufelsdröckh, speaks for his major contemporaries when he asserts that "the Mythus of the Christian Religion looks not in the eighteenth century as it did in the eighth," then sets himself the task "to embody the divine Spirit of that Religion in a new Mythus, in a new vehicle and vesture."[38]

The overall plot and critical events of biblical history, conceptualized, thus reappear as the constitutive paradigm in the systems of Romantic philosophy, however diverse the details in each system. These philosophies, unlike most traditional systems, are not static structures of truth, but are constantly on the move, and their movement is end-oriented. In the beginning is the creation, at the timeless "moment" when the unitary Absolute, or universal Ego, or Spirit sets itself off as object from itself as subject. "Thus," in Hegel's version, "the merely eternal or abstract Spirit becomes an 'other' to itself, or enters into existence. Accordingly"—in the language, that is, of picture-thinking—"it *creates* a world." This primal self-division inaugurates a process of ever-renewing others, or oppositions, or antitheses which impel a movement, through a crisis, toward that last, far-off, divine event toward which both speculative thinking and the universe inevitably move. In the *Phenomenology* the Armageddon, or *crise de conscience*, of the self-alienated spirit manifests itself, historically, in the French Revolution and the Reign of Terror. And the goal-event of the process, which Hegel calls "Absolute Knowledge" or the self-reunited "Spirit that knows itself as Spirit," is presented, in Hegel's persistent use of double-entendres, as the cognitive translation both of the human restoration of its original mode of existence and of the new heaven and new earth prophesied in the picture-thinking of

Revelation. As Hegel puts it in the concluding page of the *Phenomenology:* "This transformed existence—the former one, but now reborn of the Spirit's knowledge—is the new existence, a new world and a new shape of Spirit."[39]

Hegel's *das neue Dasein* which is *eine neue Welt*—the "goal" and "fulfillment," as he calls it, both of consciousness and history that will justify their agonized evolution—has its equivalent in his fellow philosophers. In Schiller's *Aesthetic Education of Man* (1795), the equivalent is the "aesthetic state"; this state replaces what Schiller describes as the "vain hope" invested in political revolution by "a complete revolution" of consciousness which will yield—although, for the time being, only in the realm of "aesthetic semblance"—a condition of genuine liberty, fraternity, and equality.[40] In Fichte's version of 1806, this ultimate state is the life of "Blessedness" which Fichte substitutes for his earlier millenarian hope in the French Revolution; this "Doctrine of Blessedness," he now asserts, "can be nothing else than a Doctrine of Knowledge," by means of which we will achieve "the new world which rises before us" and "the new life which begins within us."[41] To Schelling, writing in 1804, the consummation of philosophy will be a "golden age, of an eternal peace"; this is to be reached, however, not by "external activity" but by a cognitive turn-around, back to the lost "inner identity with the Absolute" which "will be the true revolution [*Revolution*], the idea of which is utterly different from that which has been called by that name."[42]

Kant's "philosophical chiliasm" has its literary parallel in the imaginative chiliasm espoused by Romantic writers in verse and prose. In *The Prelude* Wordsworth narrates the spiritual crisis consequent on the failure of his revolutionary millenarianism, followed by his recovery and a recognition of his mature identity which is also the discovery of his poetic vocation. Attendant upon this discovery is his vision of the world transformed by imagination, which it is his poetic mission to make public:

> And I remember well
> That in life's every-day appearances
> I seemed about this period to have sight

> Of a new world—a world, too, that was fit
> To be transmitted and made visible
> To other eyes—

a new world which is to be achieved, not by political activity, but by an "ennobling interchange / Of action from within and from without" (XII, 368–771). A similar new world, brought about by a spiritual revolution which yields an apocalypse of imagination, is the end-state in many other Romantic writings, whether in the form of autobiography, epic, prose romance, or drama. These include Blake's prophetic poems, Shelley's *Prometheus Unbound* and other visionary works, Carlyle's *Sartor Resartus,* Hölderlin's *Hyperion,* as well as Novalis' *Heinrich von Ofterdingen* and the literary genre he called the *Märchen,* with its fusion of classical, scientific, occult, and especially eschatological elements. What Novalis says in his cryptic notes on the *Märchen* is relevant to the vatic literary works of his age. "It is at the end the primal world, the golden age." But this end is to be achieved by "Man" himself as "the Messiah of nature," and the event is told in the form of a "New Testament—and new nature—as New Jerusalem."[43] In *Sartor Resartus* Carlyle echoes Novalis on man as "the Messias of Nature," and his Teufelsdröckh says that, after his agonized mental crisis, he "awoke to a new Heaven and a new Earth"; this, however, was the old earth, seen anew because "my mind's eyes were now unsealed." And he exhorts the reader that if his "eyesight" were to become "unsealed," he would also see "that this fair Universe, were it in the meanest province thereof, is in very deed the star-domed City of God." In the early 1830s Carlyle thus summarized the endeavor of the preceding generation to achieve a New Jerusalem not by changing the world, but by changing the way we see the world, through an exchange of what he calls the "Imaginative" faculty for the "Understanding" and the merely physical eye.[44]

2. The Seer and the Bard

Throughout the altering interpretations and applications of the apocalyptic theme, a persistent element is the interpreter's representation of himself as a philosopher-seer or poet-prophet—in the British version, a "Bard"—in the lineage of the biblical prophets of apocalypse. At the height of his millenarian expectations in 1641, Milton had celebrated the coming of "the Eternal and shortly-expected King" to proclaim "thy universal and milde Monarchy through Heaven and Earth." At that time "some one" (patently Milton himself)

> may perhaps bee heard offering at high *strains* in new and lofty *Measures* to sing and celebrate thy . . . *marvelous Judgments* in this Land throughout all ages.[45]

Two centuries later, in *The Ages of the World* (1811), Schelling announced the approaching culmination of philosophy in a renewal of the primordial union between mind and nature which will effect a paradisal world: "There will be one world, and the peace of the golden age will make itself known for the first time in the harmonious union of all sciences." Like Milton, Schelling (who had himself once undertaken an epic poem) heralds the seer who will chant this ultimate state of consciousness:

> Perhaps he will yet come who is to sing the greatest heroic poem, comprehending in spirit what was, what is, what will be, the kind of poem attributed to the seers of yore.[46]

Hegel in his *Phenomenology of Spirit* (1807) had already assumed the office of a seer who, as the qualified spokesman for, as well as participant in, the Spirit is able to recapitulate its long evolution in human consciousness and history; in the final paragraph he represents the consummation of the Spirit's development in "Absolute Knowing" as an event that takes place in the consciousness of Hegel himself, in the very act of writing that conclusion. Schelling's seer who comprehends "what was, what is, what will be" coincides exactly with Blake's prophetic persona as "the Bard! / Who Present, Past & Future, sees." This role is assumed also by Novalis, as well as by Carlyle, who is the transitional figure between the Romantic seer and the Victorian prophet.[47] In the original introduction to the "Prospectus" for his high poetic argument, Wordsworth claims that he has been granted "an internal brightness" that "is shared by none," which both qualifies and compels him, "divinely taught," to speak "of what in man is human and divine." He proceeds to announce the paradise which will be regained by the wedding of mind to nature, and his office as the poet-prophet who

> long before the blissful hour arrives,
> Would chant in lonely peace the spousal verse
> Of this great consummation.[48]

Hölderlin had also assumed the stance of elected prophet in his odes of the early 1790s which proclaimed that "zur Vollendung geht die Menschheit ein,"[49] and again, late in the 1790s, in the visionary passages of his prose *Hyperion*.

More than two decades later Shelley announced, in the final chorus of *Hellas* (1821),

> The world's great age begins anew
> The golden years return.

In a note appended to this chorus Shelley reveals that, in the course of his poetic life, he has become a touch ironic about assuming the role of "bard," and much less assured about the validity of bardic prophecy. But with that combination of empirical skepticism and indefeasible idealism characteristic of his poetic maturity, Shelley pleads as his exemplars Isaiah, the Old Testament prophet of an enduring earthly millennium, and Virgil, whose "messianic" fourth eclogue, interpreted as an approximation to revealed truth, had over the Christian centuries motivated the conflation of the return of the pagan golden age with the recovery of paradise prophesied in Revelation:

> . . . to anticipate however darkly a period of regeneration and happiness is a . . . hazardous exercise of the faculty which bards possess or feign. It will remind the reader . . . of Isaiah and

Virgil, whose ardent spirits overleaping the actual reign of evil which we endure and bewail, already saw the possible and perhaps approaching state of society in which the *"lion shall lie down with the lamb,"* and "omnis feret omnia tellus." Let these great names be my authority and my excuse.

Notes

ONE / *Wordsworth and Coleridge on Diction and Figures*

From *English Institute Essays, 1952*, ed. Alan S. Downer (New York: Columbia University Press, 1954), pp. 171–201. Reprinted by permission of the publisher.

1. James Beattie, *Essays: On Poetry and Music As They Affect the Mind*, 3rd ed. (London, 1779), pp. 7, 27, 66.
2. Ibid., p. 234.
3. Ibid., p. 265; Johnson, "Milton," in his *Lives of the English Poets*, ed. G. B. Hill (Oxford, 1905), I, 170.
4. Johnson, "Cowley," in *Lives of the English Poets*, I, 58; Blair, *Lectures on Rhetoric and Belles Lettres*, 10th ed. (London, 1806), I, 332; Kames, *Elements of Criticism* (Boston, 1796), II, 236; Johnson, "Pope," in *Lives of the English Poets*, III, 229.
5. Beattie, pp. 193–94, 245.
6. Note to *The Thorn*, added to the *Lyrical Ballads* of 1800.
7. Preface to *Lyrical Ballads*, in *The Prose Words of William Wordsworth*, ed. W. J. B. Owen and Jane W. Smyser (Oxford, 1974), I, 137, 142. This passage was added in the edition of 1802.
8. Ibid., I, 160; II, 70, 73.
9. Ibid., I, 160.
10. Ibid., I, 137.
11. Ibid., II, 84.
12. See, for example, Ben Jonson, *Timber, or Discoveries*, in *Critical Essays of the Seventeenth Century*, ed. J. E. Spingarn (Oxford, 1908–1909), I, 36–39; John Smith, *Mysterie of Rhetorique Unveil'd* (London, 1665), pp. 5–7; George Campbell, *The Philosophy of Rhetoric* (1776), new ed. (New York, 1846), p. 238.

13. *Ueber die neuere deutsche Literatur,* in *Herders sämmtliche Werke,* ed. Bernhard Suphan (Berlin, 1877–1913), I, 394–97.
14. A. C. Bradley, "Poetry for Poetry's Sake" (1901), in *Oxford Lectures on Poetry* (London, 1909), p. 17. Flaubert, for example, said: "C'est comme le corps et l'âme; la forme et l'idée, pour moi, c'est tout un" (*Correspondance,* Paris, 1926–33, IV, 243).
15. Beattie, pp. 248–49 n.
16. Ibid., pp. 212, 217 n., 233, and cf. p. 193; *Prose Works of William Wordsworth,* I, 133.
17. Beattie, pp. 247, 249 n.
18. *Prose Works of William Wordsworth,* I, 163–64.
19. Johnson, "Pope," in *Lives of the English Poets,* III, 255; *Prose Works of William Wordsworth,* II, 83. In his later years, when giving advice to the would-be poet, Wordsworth placed greater stress on what he had never entirely left out of account: the indispensability of forethought and practice to a process which, in the act of composition itself, is a spontaneous overflow of feeling. He wrote to William Rowan Hamilton in 1831 that "the composition of verse is infinitely more an art than Men are prepared to believe," and that Milton's assertion "of 'pouring easy his unpremeditated verse' . . . is not *true* to the letter, and tends to mislead" (*The Letters of William and Dorothy Wordsworth: The Later Years,* Pt. II, ed. Ernest de Selincourt, 2nd ed., rev. Alan G. Hill, Oxford, 1979, p. 454).
20. *Biographia Literaria,* ed. J. Shawcross (Oxford, 1907), II, 28–29.
21. *Collected Letters of Samuel Taylor Coleridge,* ed. E. L. Griggs (Oxford, 1956–71), II, 830; see also p. 812.
22. See, for example, *Biographia Literaria,* I, 169–70; *Anima Poetae* (Boston and New York, 1895), pp. 142–43.
23. E.g., *Biographia Literaria,* II, 10, 14, 69–73, 97–98, 109, 115.
24. Ibid., II, 56; see also *Collected Letters,* II, 812, and *Shakespearean Criticism,* ed. T. M. Raysor (Cambridge, Mass.,1930), II, 102–103.
25. *Biographia Literaria,* II, 50.
26. Ibid., I, 180, 185, 202; II, 12. An antecedent of Coleridge's distinction between "poem" and "poetry" may have been the ancient distinction between *poema* and *poesis*—between the poem and the poetic art. Behind his exposition of the role of imagination in producing "poetry," of course, was the concept of the "creative imagination" as this had developed in the preceding century from Addison and Vico through Friedrich Schelling.
27. *Biographia Literaria,* II, 68; *Shakespearean Criticism,* I, 212–13; see also *Biographia Literaria,* II, 16–18. Contrast Beattie's use of Lear's speech on the heath to demonstrate that tropes and figures "are often more *natural,* and more *imitative,* than proper words," on the ground that prosopopoeia is among "the most passionate of all the figures" (Beattie, pp. 245–46).
28. *Biographia Literaria,* I, 62, II, 129.
29. Johnson, "Denham," in *Lives of the English Poets,* I, 77.
30. *Collected Letters,* II, 864–66.
31. In *The Verbal Icon* (Lexington, Ky., 1954), pp. 106–107.
32. *Shakespearean Criticism,* I, 212; see also *Biographia Literaria,* II, 16.

33. *Biographia Literaria*, I, 58–62.
34. Ibid., II, 79, 84, 124–25.

T W O / *The Correspondent Breeze: A Romantic Metaphor*

From *English Romantic Poets: Modern Essays in Criticism*, ed. M. H. Abrams (New York: Oxford University Press, 1960), pp. 37–54. An earlier version of the essay was published in the *Kenyon Review*, 19 (1957), 113–30.

1. "Essay on the Poetical Works of Mr. Wordsworth," in *The Works of Sir Henry Taylor* (London, 1878), V, 1–4.
2. Coleridge, *Biographia Literaria*, ed. J. Shawcross (Oxford, 1907), I, 5.
3. *A Defence of Poetry*, in *Shelley's Prose*, ed. D. L. Clark (Albuquerque, 1954), p. 277.
4. Letters of 18 October and 1 November 1800, *Collected Letters of Samuel Taylor Coleridge*, ed. E. L. Griggs (Oxford, 1956–71), I, 638, 643. Genius, Coleridge wrote in one of his notebooks in 1807, may "lie hid as beneath embers, till some sudden & awakening Gust of regenerating Grace . . . rekindles & reveals it anew" (*The Notebooks of Samuel Taylor Coleridge*, ed. Kathleen Coburn, London, 1957–   , II, entry 3136).
5. 14 January 1803, *Collected Letters*, II, 916. On 20 October of that year Coleridge wrote in a notebook: "Storm all night—the wind scourging & lashing the rain . . . I half-dozing, list'ning to the same, not without solicitations of the poetic Feeling" (*Notebooks*, I, entry 1577).
6. 29 November 1805, *The Letters of William and Dorothy Wordsworth: The Early Years*, ed. Ernest de Selincourt, 2nd ed., rev. Chester L. Shaver (Oxford, 1967), p. 650.
7. In his "Prospectus" to *The Recluse*, Wordsworth wrote:

> To these emotions, whenceso'er they come,
> Whether from breath of outward circumstance,
> Or from the soul—an impulse to herself—
> I would give utterance in numerous verse.

(*The Poetical Works of William Wordsworth*, ed. Ernest de Selincourt and Helen Darbishire, Oxford, 1940–49, V, 3)

8. I have inserted a passage from MS W into the standard version from *Sibylline Leaves;* see *The Complete Poetical Works of Samuel Taylor Coleridge*, ed. E. H. Coleridge (Oxford, 1912), I, 403–407.
9. *Autobiographic Sketches*, chap. 1: "The Affliction of Childhood."
10. *Alastor*, lines 41–46. In *A Defence of Poetry:* "The mind in creation is as a fading coal which some invisible influence, like an inconstant wind, awakens to transitory brightness" (*Shelley's Prose*, p. 294).
11. Cf. Dante, *Paradiso*, II, 7 ff.:

> L'acqua ch'io prendo già mai non si corse;
> Minerva spira, e conducemi Apollo.

Shelley's passage has a weak counterpart in the conclusion to Tennyson's *Locksley Hall*, where the abrupt turn from despair to hope, accompanied by the welling of "ancient founts of inspiration," materializes in a sudden outer storm:

> Let it fall on Locksley Hall, with rain or hail, or fire or snow;
> For the mighty wind arises, roaring seaward, and I go.

Valéry's *Cimetière Marin* concludes with a similar turn:

> Le vent se léve. Il faut tenter de vivre.

12. *The Civil War*, V.82–101. In a draft of *Epipsychidion* Shelley described "a Power" in mortal hearts,

> A Pythian exhalation, which inspires
> Love, only love—a wind which o'er the wires
> Of the soul's giant harp . . .

(*The Complete Poetical Works of Percy Bysshe Shelley*, ed. Thomas Hutchinson, London, 1934, p. 429)

13. *The Prelude* (1805 text), I, 428–31; and MS text quoted in *The Prelude, 1799, 1805, 1850*, ed. Jonathan Wordsworth, M. H. Abrams, and Stephen Gill (New York, 1979), p. 489.
14. Cassian, *The Institutes of the Coenobia*, Books IX and X. See also Sister Mary Madeleva, *Pearl: A Study in Spiritual Dryness* (New York, 1925).
15. *Collected Letters*, II, 713–14; cf. letter of 12 March 1799, describing his imagination as "flat and powerless," and his inner state "as if the *organs* of Life had been dried up; as if only simple BEING remained, blind and stagnant!" (ibid., I, 470–71).
16. For the winds in these gardens see Dante, *Purgatorio*, XXVIII, 7–21, 103–14; Augustine, *Confessions*, VIII, xi–xii, Song of Solomon 4:12–16.
17. *The Prelude*, ed. Ernest de Selincourt, 2nd ed., rev. Helen Darbishire (Oxford, 1959), p. 4 n.
18. Blake, letter to Thomas Butts, 22 November 1802, *The Complete Writings of William Blake*, ed. Geoffrey Keynes (London, 1957), p. 818; Coleridge, *Biographia Literaria*, I, 74, and *Coleridge on Logic and Learning*, ed. Alice D. Snyder (New Haven, 1929), p. 126; Wordsworth, *The Prelude* (1850 text), XII, 93–131.
19. See also Northrop Frye's comment on Blake's "the wind of Beulah that unroots the rocks and hills" as an analogue of both inspiration and destruction, in "Notes for a Commentary on *Milton*," in *The Divine Vision*, ed. Vivian de S. Pinto (London, 1957), p. 125.

T H R E E / *English Romanticism: The Spirit of the Age*

From *Romanticism Reconsidered: Selected Papers from the English Institute*, ed. Northrop Frye (New York: Columbia University Press, 1963), pp. 26–72. Reprinted by permission of the publisher.

1. *Lectures on the English Poets* (1818), in *The Complete Works of William Hazlitt*, ed. P. P. Howe (London, 1930–34), V, 161.
2. *The Spirit of the Age*, ibid., XI, 86–87.
3. John Stuart Mill, *The Spirit of the Age*, ed. Frederick A. von Hayek (Chicago, 1942), pp. 1–2, 67. In 1812 Thomas Belsham spoke of "the spirit of the times," the "mania of the French Revolution," which "pervaded all ranks of society" (*Memoirs of the Late Reverend Theophilus Lindsey*, 2nd ed., London, 1820, p. 216). See also "Letter on the Spirit of the Age," *Blackwood's Magazine*, 28 (1830), 900–920.
4. *Shelley's Prose*, ed. D. L. Clark (Albuquerque, 1954), pp. 239–40; the passage was later used, almost verbatim, as the conclusion of *A Defence of Poetry*. See also the Preface to *Prometheus Unbound*, ibid., pp. 327–28, and the letter to Charles Ollier, 15 October 1819 (*The Letters of Percy Bysshe Shelley*, ed. F. L. Jones, Oxford, 1964, II, 127). Shelley called the French Revolution "the master theme of the epoch in which we live" (ibid., I, 504).
5. Review of Walter Scott's edition of *The Works of Jonathan Swift*, in *Contributions to the Edinburgh Review* (London, 1844), I, 158–67.
6. "William Wordsworth," in *The Collected Writings of Thomas De Quincey*, ed. David Masson (Edinburgh, 1889–90), II, 273–74.
7. *Romanticism: Points of View*, ed. Robert F. Gleckner and Gerald E. Enscoe (Englewood Cliffs, N.J., 1962).
8. "William Wordsworth," in *Collected Writings*, II, 274.
9. *The Correspondence of Robert Southey with Caroline Bowles*, ed. Edward Dowden (Dublin, 1881), p. 52.
10. M. Ray Adams, *Studies in the Literary Backgrounds of English Radicalism* (Lancaster, Pa., 1947), p. 7.
11. Romilly in Alfred Cobban, ed., *The Debate on the French Revolution, 1789–1800* (London, 1950), p. 354; Fox as cited by Edward Dowden, *The French Revolution and English Literature* (New York, 1897), p. 9. "Era of happiness in the history of the world!" John Thelwall described the Revolution; "Dawn of a real golden age" (Charles Cestre, *John Thelwall*, London, 1906, p. 171).
12. C. F. C. de Volney, *The Ruins*, 5th ed. (London, 1807), pp. 92, 98–113.
13. Marquis de Condorcet, *Outlines of an Historical View of the Progress of the Human Mind* (London, 1795), pp. 261–62, 370–72.
14. William Godwin, *Enquiry Concerning Political Justice*, ed. F. E. L. Priestley (Toronto, 1946); see, for example, II, 463–64, 528–29; III, 180–81.
15. *Complete Works*, VII, 99. Some of this minor revolutionary literature is reviewed in Adams, *Literary Backgrounds of English Radicalism*, and Allene Gregory, *The French Revolution and the English Novel* (New York, 1915).
16. *The Road to Ruin* (London, 1792).
17. *The Origin and Stability of the French Revolution: A Sermon Preached at St. Paul's Chapel, Norwich, July 14, 1791*, p. 5, quoted by Mark Schorer, *William Blake: The Politics of Vision* (New York, 1946), p. 205. For apocalyptic thinking among the Illuminists in France, see A. Viatte, *Les Sources occultes du Romantisme* (Paris, 1928), chap. 6.
18. C. Kegan Paul, *William Godwin: His Friends and Contemporaries* (London, 1876), I, 69.

19. Richard Price, *Observations on the Importance of the American Revolution* (London, 1785), pp. 6–7, 21; *A Discourse on the Love of Our Country* (4 November 1789), in S. MacCoby, ed., *The English Radical Tradition, 1763–1914* (London, 1952), p. 54. The dissenter Nash wrote in reply to Burke's *Reflections:* "As I am a believer in Revelation, I, of course, live in the hope of better things; a millennium . . . a new heaven and a new earth in which dwelleth righteousness . . . a state of equal liberty and equal justice for all men" (*A Letter to the Right Hon. Edmund Burke from a Dissenting Country Attorney*, Birmingham, 1790, quoted by Anthony Lincoln, *Some Political and Social Ideas of English Dissent, 1763–1800*, Cambridge, 1938, p. 3).

20. Elhanan Winchester, *The Three Woe Trumpets*, 1st American ed. (Boston, 1794), pp. 37–38, 71. Winchester also published in 1793 *The Process and Empire of Christ: An Heroic Poem* in blank verse, in which Books VIII–XII deal with the Second Advent, the Millennium, and the apocalyptic "New Creation; or, The Renovation of the Heavens and Earth after the Conflagration."

21. *Letters to the Right Honourable Edmund Burke*, 2nd ed. (Birmingham, 1791), pp. 143–50; *The Present State of Europe Compared with Antient Prophecies*, 4th ed. (London, 1794), pp. 18 ff., 30–32. See also Priestley's *Sermon Preached . . . in Hackney, April 19th, 1793*, and *Observations on the Increase of Infidelity* (1796).

22. *The Excursion*, III, 716–65; see also II, 210–23. On the relation of the Solitary to Joseph Fawcett see Adams, *Literary Backgrounds of English Radicalism*, chap. 7.

23. *The Complete Writings of William Blake*, ed. Geoffrey Keynes (London, 1957), p. 799.

24. *Fearful Symmetry* (Princeton, 1947), pp. 167 ff.; "Towards Defining an Age of Sensibility," in *Eighteenth-Century English Literature: Modern Essays in Criticism*, ed. James L. Clifford (New York, 1959), pp. 311–18.

25. *An Essay on the Genius and Writings of Pope* (1756) (London, 1806), II, 402.

26. See M. H. Abrams, *The Mirror and the Lamp* (New York, 1953), pp. 274–76 and nn.

27. Leigh Hunt, *The Feast of the Poets* (London, 1814), p. 90; John Keats, sonnet *Addressed to the Same* (B. R. Haydon), line 1; *Shelley's Prose*, pp. 239–40.

28. *Blake: Prophet Against Empire* (Princeton, 1954), pp. 246 ff.; and see Frye, *Fearful Symmetry*, p. 262.

29. *Europe: A Prophecy*, Plates 9, 12–15. See also *America: A Prophecy* (1793), Plates 6, 8, 16; *The Song of Los* (1795), Plates 3, 7.

30. *Vala, or the Four Zoas*, I, 5, 21; IX, 827, 845.

31. *Proposals for an Association of Philanthropists* (1812), in *Shelley's Prose*, p. 67. Concerning the early formative influences on Shelley's thought, see K. N. Cameron, *The Young Shelley* (London, 1951). Mary Shelley testified that "in English, the Bible was [Shelley's] constant study," that the sublime poetry of the Old Testament "filled him with delight," and that over an extended period in 1816 and 1817 Shelley read both the Bible and *Paradise Lost* aloud to her (*The Complete Poetical Works of Percy Bysshe Shelley*, ed. Thomas Hutchinson, London, 1934, pp. 551, 156, 536). See

also Bennett Weaver, *Toward the Understanding of Shelley* (Ann Arbor, 1932).

32. F. M. Todd, *Politics and the Poet: A Study of Wordsworth* (London, 1957), p. 11. Both of Wordsworth's long poems turn on an extended treatment of the French Revolution—in *The Prelude* as the crisis of his own life as exemplary poet, and in *The Excursion* as the crisis of his generation. See also Carl R. Woodring, *Politics in the Poetry of Coleridge* (Madison, 1961); William Haller, *The Early Life of Robert Southey* (New York, 1917); and Cameron, *The Young Shelley*.

33. E.g., Blake's letter to Thomas Butts, 25 April 1803; Shelley, *A Philosophical View of Reform*, in *Shelley's Prose*, p. 240.

34. MS A, III, 82–93, in William Wordsworth, *The Prelude*, ed. Ernest de Selincourt, 2nd ed., rev. Helen Darbishire (Oxford, 1959), p. 75; Coleridge, *To William Wordsworth*, lines 3, 45, 48.

35. On Milton's millennialism see H. J. C. Grierson, *Milton and Wordsworth* (Cambridge, 1937), pp. 32–36.

36. Quoted by Edward Dowden, *Southey* (New York, 1880), p. 189.

37. Preface to *Joan of Arc* (1837), in *The Poetical Works of Robert Southey* (Boston, 1860), I, 11–12. The next year (1794), with even greater revolutionary élan, Southey dashed off in three mornings the Jacobin *Wat Tyler: A Drama* (ibid., II, 28).

38. *Joan of Arc: An Epic Poem* (Bristol, 1796), Book I, lines 497–99; Book IX, lines 825–27, 837–72. In the MS version of 1793, the references to the French Revolution are explicit; see Book XI, lines 633–749, in Benjamin W. Early, "Southey's *Joan of Arc*: The Unpublished Manuscript, the First Edition, and a Study of the Later Revisions" (Ph.D. thesis, Duke University, 1951). Southey wrote in 1830 that "forty years ago I could partake the hopes of those who expected that political revolutions were to bring about a political millennium" (*Correspondence . . . with Caroline Bowles*, p. 200). By 1797, however, he seems to have been prepared to give back to Christ the task of realizing the dreams of Plato and Milton for total "happiness on earth":

> Blessed hopes! awhile
> From man withheld, even to the latter days,
> When CHRIST shall come and all things be fulfill'd.
> (*Inscription IV. For the Apartment in Chepstow Castle*, in *Poems*, 1797)

39. *The Destiny of Nations*, lines 464, 326–38, 421–58. See Woodring, *Politics in the Poetry of Coleridge*, pp. 169–73.

40. To Joseph Cottle, April 1797, *Collected Letters of Samuel Taylor Coleridge*, ed. E. L. Griggs (Oxford, 1956–71), I, 320–21.

41. Ibid., pp. 197, 205.

42. Ibid., pp. 147, 162 and n.

43. *The Complete Poetical Works of Samuel Taylor Coleridge*, ed. E. H. Coleridge (Oxford, 1912), I, 108–23 and nn. David Hartley had included his interpretation of millennial prophecy in his *Observations on Man*, Part II, Sections IV and V. In lines 126–58 of *Religious Musings* Coleridge, like Blake in his later prophecies, interpreted the fall of man as a splintering of social fraternity into anarchic individuality, and his redemption at the Second Coming as a rejunction of separate selves

into a single "Self, that no alien knows!" Cf. the opening of Blake's *The Four Zoas*, I, 9–23.

44. *Descriptive Sketches* (1793 version), lines 774–91; Blake, *The Four Zoas*, IX, 844–45; see also Blake, *America*, VIII, 15. For Wordsworth's opinion of the apocalyptic passage in Coleridge's *Religious Musings* see *Collected Letters of Samuel Taylor Coleridge*, I, 215–16. As late as 1808 the Spanish insurrection against Napoleon revived Wordsworth's millennial hopes: "We trust that Regeneration is at hand; these are works of recovered innocence and wisdom ... redeunt Saturnia regna" (*The Convention of Cintra*, in *The Prose Works of William Wordsworth*, ed. W. J. B. Owen and Jane W. Smyser, Oxford, 1974, I, 297; see also pp. 227–28).

45. *Queen Mab*, IV, 88–89; VIII, 107 ff.; IX, 1–4.

46. Friedrich Hölderlin, *Sämtliche Werke*, ed. Friedrich Beissner (Stuttgart, 1946–), I, Pt. I, pp. 139–42. See Geneviève Bianquis, "Hölderlin et la révolution française," *Études Germaniques*, 7 (1952), 105–16; and Maurice Delorme, *Hölderlin et la révolution française* (Monaco, 1959). The relevance of Hölderlin was pointed out to me by my colleague Paul de Man.

47. *To William Wordsworth*, lines 34–38. Cf., for example, *The Prelude* (1805 text), II, 448–66, X, 355–81, 690–728; *The Excursion*, II, 210–23; *The Convention of Cintra*, in *Prose Works of William Wordsworth*, I, 227–28, 319, 339; Shelley, Preface to *The Revolt of Islam*, in *Poetical Works*, pp. 33–34; Hazlitt, *Complete Works*, IV, 119–20, XVII, 196–98, 316, and his *Life of Thomas Holcroft*, ed. Elbridge Colby (London, 1925), II, 92–93.

48. It is an interesting coincidence that Blake's "I want! I want!" (which is illustrated by a man climbing a ladder reaching to the moon) was his retort to a political cartoon by Gillray which caricatured the inordinacy of revolutionary hope by depicting a short ladder pointing futilely toward the moon. See Erdman, *Blake: Prophet Against Empire*, pp. 186–88. The parable, in its political application, was a familiar one; thus Edmund Burke had said (1780): "If we cry, like children, for the moon, like children we must cry on" (*The Works of the Right Honorable Edmund Burke*, London, 1899, II, 357).

49. *The Prelude* (1850 text), VI, 322–640. On the glory of infinite promise aroused by the Revolution see also ibid., XI, 105–23. Wordsworth's later revision of the passage of apocalyptic hope in the *Descriptive Sketches* of 1793 parallels the emblematic significance of the Alpine crossing:

> Lo, from the flames a great and glorious birth;
> As if a new-made heaven were hailing a new earth!
> —All cannot be: the promise is too fair
> For creatures doomed to breathe terrestrial air.

(*The Poetical Works of William Wordsworth*, ed. Ernest de Selincourt and Helen Darbishire, Oxford, 1940–49, I, 89)

50. *Poetical Works*, V, 3–5.

51. *The Spirit of the Age*, in *Complete Works*, XI, 87. Cf. "On the Living Poets," ibid., V, 161–64. Christopher Wordsworth, though his loyalties were the polar opposites of Hazlitt's, also accounted for the theory of *Lyrical Ballads* in political terms: "The clue to his *poetical* theory, in some of its

questionable details, may be found in his *political* principles; these had been democratical, and still, though in some degree modified, they were of a republican character" (*Memoirs of William Wordsworth*, Boston, 1851, I, 127).

52. *Complete Works*, XI, 89, V, 162–63. On the novelty of Wordsworth's poems see also ibid., V, 156, and XVII, 117.

53. *The Prelude* (1850 text), XIII, 11–312.

54. *Complete Works*, XI, 87–89.

55. *The Ruined Cottage*, in *Poetical Works*, V, 379 ff., lines 53–59, 145–66, 264–75; and p. 411, note to line 341 of the revised version in *The Excursion*, Book I.

56. Robert Lowth, *Lectures on the Sacred Poetry of the Hebrews* (1953) (London, 1847), pp. 79–84 and passim. On earlier theological discussions of the Christian paradox of *humilitas-sublimitas*, see Erich Auerbach, *Mimesis* (Princeton, 1953), pp. 72–73, 151–55, "Sermo Humilis," *Romanische Forschungen*, 64 (1952), 304–64, and "St. Francis of Assisi in Dante's *Commedia*," in *Scenes from the Drama of European Literature* (New York, 1959), pp. 79–98; see also Joseph Mazzeo, "St. Augustine's Rhetoric of Silence," *Journal of the History of Ideas*, 23 (1962), 183 ff.

57. *The Prelude* (1850 text), VIII, 256–76, 492–94. Cf. Phillippians 2:7–9: Christ took on "the form of a servant" and "humbled himself" even unto "the death of the cross. Wherefore God also hath highly exalted him. . . ." See also Matthew 23:11–12 and I Corinthians 1:27–28. On the history of the theological concept of "condescensio," with special reference to the eighteenth century, see Karlfried Gründer, *Figur und Geschichte* (Freiburg / Munich, 1958). Bishop Lowth discusses God's condescension, with respect to the form and figures of the Song of Solomon, in his thirty-first lecture.

58. "Essay, Supplementary to the Preface," in *Prose Works of William Wordsworth*, III, 65–83. Cf. the letter to Joseph Kirkham Miller, 17 December 1831 (*The Letters of William and Dorothy Wordsworth: The Later Years*, Pt. II, ed. Ernest de Selincourt, 2nd ed., rev. Alan G. Hill, Oxford, 1979, pp. 464–65). De Quincey agreed with Wordsworth (and Hazlitt) that the *Lyrical Ballads* were without literary precedent: "I found in these poems . . . an absolute revelation of untrodden worlds . . ." (*Collected Writings*, II, 139).

59. In a letter to Lady Beaumont, 21 May 1807, on the same subject as the "Essay, Supplementary," in *The Letters of William and Dorothy Wordsworth: The Middle Years*, Pt. I, ed. Ernest de Selincourt, 2nd ed., rev. Mary Moorman (Oxford, 1969), p. 150.

60. *The Prelude* (1850 text), XIII, 352–78.

61. *Home at Grasmere* (1800), in *Poetical Works*, V, 334 ff., lines 625–34, 664–750; "Prospectus," lines 25–71.

62. To John Thelwall, 13 May 1796, *Collected Letters*, I, 216.

F O U R / *Structure and Style in the Greater Romantic Lyric*

From *From Sensibility to Romanticism: Essays Presented to Frederick A. Pottle*, ed. Frederick W. Hilles and Harold Bloom (New York: Oxford

University Press, 1965), pp. 527–60. Reprinted by permission of the publisher.

1. *The Prelude* (1850 text), XII, 222–23. Even Keats, though he sometimes longed for a life of sensations rather than of thought, objected to the poems of John Clare that too often "the Description overlaid and stifled that which ought to be the prevailing Idea" (letter to John Clare from John Taylor, 27 September 1820, quoted by Edmund Blunden, *Keats's Publisher*, London, 1936, p. 80).

2. *Descriptive Sketches* (1793) drew from a contemporary reviewer the cry: "More descriptive poetry! Have we not yet enough? . . . Yes; more, and yet more: so it is decreed" (*Monthly Review*, 2nd ser., 12 [1793], cited by Robert A. Aubin, *Topographical Poetry in XVIII-Century England*, New York, 1936, p. 255; see also pp. 217–19).

3. Perhaps that is the reason for Coleridge's later judgment that *The Eolian Harp* was "the most perfect poem I ever wrote" (quoted by James D. Campbell, ed., *The Poetical Works of Samuel Taylor Coleridge*, London, 1893, p. 578). The first version of the poem and a MS version of 1797 (Coleridge then entitled it "Effusion") are reproduced in *The Complete Poetical Works*, ed. E. H. Coleridge (Oxford, 1912), II, 1021–23. For accounts of the revisions of the poem, see J. H. W. Milley, "Some Notes on Coleridge's 'Eolian Harp,'" *Modern Philology*, 36 (1938–39), 359–75, and M. H. Abrams, "Coleridge's 'A Light in Sound': Science, Metascience, and Poetic Imagination," pp. 158–91 in the present volume.

4. *Collected Letters of Samuel Taylor Coleridge*, ed. E. L. Griggs (Oxford, 1956–71), IV, 545.

5. Keats used a different figure for the poetic return. In a letter of December 1818–January 1819 he transcribed *Fancy* and *Bards of passion and of mirth*, in which the last lines are variants of the opening lines, and said, "These are specimens of a sort of rondeau which I think I shall become partial to" (*The Letters of John Keats*, ed. H. E. Rollins, Cambridge, Mass., 1958, II, 21–26). In the next few months he exemplified the rondeau form in *The Eve of St. Agnes* and *La Belle Dame sans Merci*, as well as in the descriptive-meditative lyric *Ode to a Nightingale*.

6. So titled in the Dowden MS in the Morgan Library; see Carl R. Woodring, *Politics in the Poetry of Coleridge* (Madison, 1961), p. 255, n. 16.

7. *Lives of the English Poets*, ed. G. B. Hill (Oxford, 1905), I, 77.

8. *The Subtler Language* (Baltimore, 1959), chap. 3.

9. *The Works of Sir Thomas Browne*, ed. Geoffrey Keynes (London, 1928–31), I, 17.

10. The opening eight lines of *Cooper's Hill*, despite some approximation to neoclassic neatness and dispatch, are much closer to Donne's couplets, in the cramped syntax of their run-on lines, which deploy a tortuous analogical argument to demonstrate a paradox that inverts and explodes a mythological cliché:

> Sure there are Poets which did never dream
> Upon *Parnassus*, nor did taste the stream
> Of *Helicon*, we therefore may suppose
> Those made no Poets, but the Poets those.

And as Courts make not Kings, but Kings the Court,
So where the Muses and their train resort,
Parnassus stands; if I can be to thee
A Poet, thou Parnassus are to me.

Compare the opening of Andrew Marvell's *Upon the Hill and Grove at Billborow* (probably written in the early 1650s) for the jolting movement, the doughty hyperbole, and witty shock tactics of the thoroughly metaphysical management of a local hill-poem.

11. See Earl R. Wasserman, "Nature Moralized: The Divine Analogy in the Eighteenth Century," *ELH*, 20 (1953), 39–76. For commentators on the local poem, the chief structural problem was how to establish easy, just, yet varied connections between its two components, the *visibilia* and the *moralia*. Joseph Warton's observation is typical, that "it is one of the greatest and most pleasing arts of descriptive poetry, to introduce moral sentences and instructions in an oblique and indirect manner" (*An Essay on the Genius and Writings of Pope* [1756], London, 1806, I, 29).

12. Preface to *Lyrical Ballads*, in *The Prose Works of William Wordsworth*, ed. W. J. B. Owen and Jane W. Smyser (Oxford, 1974), I, 133.

13. *Biographia Literaria*, ed. J. Shawcross (Oxford, 1907), I, 13.

14. Ibid., pp. 8–16.

15. *The Poetical Works of William Lisle Bowles*, ed. George Gilfillan (Edinburgh, 1855), I, 1.

16. *Recollections of the Table-Talk of Samuel Rogers* (New York, 1856), p. 258 n. For Bowles's effect on Southey see William Haller, *The Early Life of Robert Southey* (New York, 1917), pp. 73–76. As late as 1806–20, in *The River Duddon*, Wordsworth adopted Bowles's design of a tour represented in a sequence of local-meditative sonnets.

17. Coleridge, Introduction to the "Sheet of Sonnets" (1796), in *Complete Poetical Works*, II, 1139. As early as November of 1797, however, Coleridge as "Nehemiah Higginbottom" parodied "the spirit of *doleful egotism*" in the sonnet. See *Biographia Literaria*, I, 17, and David Erdman, "Coleridge as Nehemiah Higginbottom," *Modern Language Notes*, 73 (1958), 569–80.

18. *Biographia Literaria*, I, 10.

19. Ibid., pp. 2–3, and 203–204 n. Coleridge's claim that he had recognized the defects of the "swell and glitter" of his elevated style, even as he employed it, is borne out by his Preface to the *Poems* of 1797, in *Complete Poetical Works*, II, 1145.

20. See "English Romanticism: The Spirit of the Age," pp. 44–75 in the present volume.

21. *Complete Poetical Works*, II, 1113–14; see also p. 1145.

22. 11 December 1794, *Collected Letters*, I, 133–37.

23. *Biographia Literaria*, I, 10, 15–16.

24. Ibid., p. 16.

25. See, for example, Humphry House, *Coleridge* (London, 1953), chap. 3; George Whalley, "Coleridge's Debt to Charles Lamb," in *Essays and Studies* (1958), pp. 68–85; and Max F. Schulz, *The Poetic Voices of Coleridge* (Detroit, 1963), chap. 5. A comment of Lamb to Coleridge in December 1796 substantiates Coleridge's own statements about the relative

importance for him of Bowles and Cowper: "Burns was the god of my idolatry, as Bowles of yours. I am jealous of your fraternising with Bowles, when I think you relish him more than Burns or my old favourite, Cowper" (*The Works of Charles and Mary Lamb*, ed. E. V. Lucas, London, 1903–1905, VI, 73).

26. Introduction to the "Sheet of Sonnets" (1796), in *Complete Poetical Works*, II, 1139.

27. *Biographia Literaria*, I, 1.

28. *Collected Letters*, I, 354, 349. See also ibid., IV, 574–75, and *The Note-books of Samuel Taylor Coleridge*, ed. Kathleen Coburn (London, 1957–   ), II, entry 2151.

29. *The Friend* (London, 1818), III, 261–62.

30. *The Ruined Cottage*, addendum to MS B, in *The Poetical Works of William Wordsworth*, ed. Ernest de Selincourt and Helen Darbishire (Oxford, 1940–49), V, 402.

31. *Hints Towards the Formation of a More Comprehensive Theory of Life*, ed. Seth B. Watson (London, 1848), p. 63.

32. Friedrich Schelling, *Sämmtliche Werke*, ed. K. F. A. Schelling (Stuttgart and Augsburg, 1856–61), Pt. I, Vol. VII, pp. 81–82.

33. *Religious Musings*, lines 126–58.

34. To Wordsworth, 30 May 1815, *Collected Letters*, IV, 574–75.

35. *Biographia Literaria*, I, 174–85.

36. Ibid., I, 202; II, 12. See *The Friend*, III, 263–64, on the "one principle which alone reconciles the man with himself, with other [men] and with the world."

37. In *Biographia Literaria*, II, 253–55. Though "On Poesy or Art" takes its departure from Schelling's "On the Relation of the Plastic Arts to Nature," the quoted statements are Coleridge's own.

38. 10 September 1802, *Collected Letters*, II, 864.

39. *Hints Towards the . . . Theory of Life*, p. 63.

40. In *Biographia Literaria*, II, 258.

41. "The Structure of Romantic Nature Imagery," in *The Verbal Icon* (Lexington, Ky., 1954), pp. 106, 111.

42. Coleridge, *Collected Letters*, IV, 974–75, and *Notebooks*, II, entry 2546; Wordsworth, *Poetical Works*, IV, 463; *Shelley's Prose*, ed. D. L. Clark (Albuquerque, 1954), p. 174; Byron, *Childe Harold*, III, lxxii, lxxv; Keats, *Letters*, I, 387.

43. *Introduction to the Devout Life*, trans. John K. Ryan (Garden City, N.Y., 1955), p. 88.

44. See "The Correspondent Breeze: A Romantic Metaphor," pp. 25–43 in the present volume.

45. Coleridge's comments on Herbert are gathered in *Coleridge on the Seventeenth Century*, ed. Roberta F. Brinkley (Durham, N.C., 1955), pp. 533–40.

46. Coleridge wrote his later poem of aridity in a spring landscape, *Work Without Hope* (1825), expressly "in the manner of G. HERBERT" (*Complete Poetical Works*, II, 1110–11).

47. *Introduction to the Devout Life*, pp. 256–57; on "spiritual desolation," see also Saint Ignatius of Loyola, *Spiritual Exercises*, ed. Orby Shipley (London, 1870), pp. 139–40.

48. *Collected Letters,* I, 470; II, 713–14; see also I, 643.
49. In the *Meditations and Contemplations,* 7th ed. (London, 1750), II, xv–xvii, Hervey describes his aim to "exhibit a Prospect of still *Life,* and grand *Operation*" in order "to *open* the *Door* of Meditation," and show how we may "*gather up* the unstable, fluctuating *Train* of Fancy; and collect her fickle Powers into a consistent, regular, and useful Habit of Thinking."
50. See Louis L. Martz, *The Poetry of Meditation* (New Haven, 1954), pp. 27–28.
51. *Frost at Midnight,* lines 58–62; cf. *This Lime-Tree Bower,* lines 39–43, and *Fears in Solitude,* lines 22–24. In Coleridge's *Hymn before Sunrise* (1802), unlike his greater lyrics, the meditation moves from the creatures to the Creator by a hereditary symbolism as old as Psalm 19: "The heavens declare the glory of God; and the firmament sheweth his handywork."
52. Dr. Johnson listed Denham among the metaphysical poets, then added, in the great commonplace of neoclassical literary history, that he "and Waller sought another way to fame, by improving the harmony of our numbers" ("Cowley," in *Lives of the English Poets,* I, 22).

F I V E / *Coleridge, Baudelaire, and Modernist Poetics*

From *Immanente Ästhetik, ästhetische Reflexion: Lyrik als Paradigma der Moderne,* ed. W. Iser (Munich: Wilhelm Fink Verlag, 1966), pp. 113–38. Reprinted by permission of the publisher. The essay was originally a colloquium paper at Cologne in 1964; for subsequent comment and debate at the colloquium see *Immanente Ästhetik,* pp. 419–28.

1. F. R. Leavis, "Coleridge in Criticism," *Scrutiny,* 9 (1940), 69.
2. S. E. Hyman, *The Armed Vision* (New York, 1948), p. 11.
3. Edmund Wilson, *Axel's Castle* (New York, 1936), pp. 1–2.
4. Frank Kermode, *Romantic Image* (London, 1957), Preface and pp. 5 ff.
5. Richard Foster, *The New Romantics* (Bloomington, Ind., 1962), pp. 21, 29.
6. M. H. Abrams, *The Mirror and the Lamp* (New York, 1953), p. vii.
7. Graham Hough, *Reflections on a Literary Revolution* (Washington, D.C., 1960), p. 112.
8. To Baggesen, April 1795, in J. G. Fichte, *Briefwechsel,* ed. Hans Schulz (Leipzig, 1925), I, 449–50.
9. "William Wordsworth," in *The Collected Writings of Thomas De Quincey,* ed. David Masson (Edinburgh, 1889–90), II, 273–74.
10. On the relations of the French Revolution to the Romantic imagination, see "English Romanticism: The Spirit of the Age," pp. 44–75 in the present volume.
11. T. S. Eliot, "Yeats," in *On Poetry and Poets* (London, 1957), p. 252. See

also René Taupin, *L'Influence du symbolisme français sur la poésie améri-caine* (Paris, 1929).

12. T. S. Eliot, "Baudelaire," in *Selected Essays, 1917–1932* (London, 1932), pp. 367, 371–72.

13. See, for example, Marcel Raymond, *From Baudelaire to Surrealism* (New York, 1950), and Hugo Friedrich, *Die Struktur der modernen Lyrik von Baudelaire bis zur Gegenwart* (Hamburg, 1956), esp. pp. 25 ff., 107 ff.

14. *Correspondance*, in *Œuvres complètes de Charles Baudelaire*, ed. F.-F. Gautier and Y.-G. Le Dantec (Paris, 1918–37), VII, 130; *Œuvres complètes de Baudelaire*, ed. Y.-G. Le Dantec (Paris, 1961), pp. 689, 1213.

15. Ibid., pp. 11, 254–55, 705.

16. Ibid., p. 637.

17. Ibid., pp. 1036–38, 1044.

18. Ibid., p. 705.

19. Ibid., pp. 1040–41. See also Margaret Gilman, *Baudelaire the Critic* (New York, 1943), pp. 128–33.

20. "On Poesy or Art," in *Biographia Literaria*, ed. J. Shawcross (Oxford, 1907), II, 257, 259.

21. Cf., for example, *Coleridge's Miscellaneous Criticism*, ed. T. M. Raysor (Cambridge, Mass., 1936), p. 43: As nature "works from within by evo-lution and assimilation according to a law," so Shakespeare "too worked in the spirit of nature, by evolving the germ within by the imaginative power according to an idea."

22. "On Poesy or Art," in *Biographia Literaria*, II, 258–59, 262.

23. *Coleridge's Shakespearean Criticism*, ed. T. M. Raysor (Cambridge, Mass., 1930), I, 224.

24. "On Poesy or Art," in *Biographia Literaria*, II, 262–63.

25. *Biographia Literaria*, I, 202.

26. Ibid., II, 12.

27. Cf. Taupin, *L'Influence du symbolisme français*, Pt. II.

28. A. G. Lehmann, *The Symbolist Aesthetic in France* (Oxford, 1950), p. 271.

29. *The Literary Essays of Ezra Pound*, ed. T. S. Eliot (London, 1954), p. 9.

30. T. E. Hulme, *Speculations*, ed. Herbert Read (London, 1936), pp. 134–35.

31. *Œuvres complètes* (1961), p. 1295.

32. C. Day Lewis, *The Poetic Image* (New York, 1948), pp. 17–18.

33. "Crise de vers," in *Œuvres complètes de Stéphane Mallarmé*, ed. Henri Mondor and G. Jean-Aubry (Paris, 1945), pp. 366–67.

34. *Miscellaneous Criticism*, p. 89.

35. *Biographia Literaria*, I, 202.

36. *Hints Towards the Formation of a More Comprehensive Theory of Life*, ed. Seth B. Watson (London, 1848), p. 63.

37. *Œuvres complètes* (1961), p. 1266.

38. "The Poetic Principle," in *The Complete Works of Edgar Allan Poe* (New York, 1902), XIV, 274.

39. "The Colloquy of Monos and Una," ibid., IV, 203.

40. "The Black Cat," ibid., V, 146; "The Imp of the Perverse," ibid., VI, 145–47.

41. *Correspondance*, in *Œuvres complètes* (1918–37), VII, 130–31.

42. Joseph de Maistre, *Les Soirées de Saint-Pétersbourg* (Paris, 1960), p. 53.

43. "Notes nouvelles sur Edgar Poe," in *Œuvres complètes* (1918–37), X, 15–17.
44. *Correspondance*, ibid., VII, 131.
45. *Œuvres complètes* (1961), pp. 1037, 739–40; "Notes nouvelles sur Edgar Poe," in *Œuvres complètes* (1918–37), X, 19.
46. *Œuvres complètes* (1961), p. 1067.
47. Ibid., pp. 1277, 1296.
48. In the early statement of his position in *Trois idées politiques*, for example, Maurras used as epigraph Poe's attack against democracy in "The Colloquy of Monos and Una," on the grounds of the universal laws of gradation on earth and in heaven; see Maurras, *Œuvres capitales* (Paris, 1954), II, 69.
49. Hulme, pp. 114–17, 254–55.
50. "Baudelaire," in *Selected Essays*, p. 378.
51. *After Strange Gods* (New York, 1934), pp. 22, 33.
52. Ibid., pp. 12, 45, 61–62.
53. Hulme, p. 256.
54. *Collected Letters of Samuel Taylor Coleridge*, ed. E. L. Griggs (Oxford, 1956–71), I, 395–96.
55. *The Table Talk*, ed. H. N. Coleridge (London, 1917), p. 84 (1 May 1830).
56. *Aids to Reflection* (London, 1913), pp. 172–200.
57. 30 May 1815, *Collected Letters*, IV, 575. Cf., for example, Hölderlin's Preface of 1795 to his novel, *Hyperion*, in *Sämtliche Werke*, ed. Friedrich Beissner (Stuttgart, 1946–   ), III, 194–95.
58. *The Statesman's Manual*, in *Lay Sermons*, ed. R. J. White (London, 1972), p. 71. Cf. Schiller's description, in the opening paragraphs of *Über naive und sentimentalische Dichtung*, of the human response to the simple beauty and self-unity of the natural objects in a landscape: "Sie sind, was wir waren; sie sind, was wir wieder werden sollen."
59. "On Poesy or Art," in *Biographia Literaria*, II, 253–55.
60. *Biographia Literaria*, II, 12.
61. Ibid., II, 50.
62. Ibid., II, 19; *Coleridge's Shakespearean Criticism*, I, 224. A passage from Hölderlin demonstrates clearly how, in Romantic organicism, life provides the paradigm for art, so that the product of human artistry is viewed as a higher-order natural organism. The poetic masterpiece is a systematic whole, "das aus lebendiger Seele des Dichters und der lebendigen Welt um ihn hervor und durch seine Kunst zu einer eigenen Organisation, zu einer Natur in der Natur sich bildete" (to Goethe, July 1799, in Hölderlin, *Sämtliche Werke*, VI, pt. I, p. 350).
63. *Œuvres complètes* (1961), pp. 1182–83.
64. Ibid., p. 1183.
65. Ibid., p. 1077.
66. *Correspondance*, in *Œuvres complètes* (1918–37), VII, 111.
67. *Œuvres complètes* (1961), pp. 1184, 254.
68. Ibid., pp. 303–304.
69. Ibid., p. 97.
70. Ibid., p. 1175.
71. Ibid., p. 1184.
72. Hulme, pp. 9, 53 ff., 92.

73. Yeats, *Sailing to Byzantium* and *Byzantium*.
74. *The Statesman's Manual*, in *Lay Sermons*, p. 72.
75. *The Prelude* (1805 text), XIII, 431 ff.
76. Paul Valéry, "A Foreword," in *The Art of Poetry*, trans. Denise Folliot (New York, 1958), p. 40.
77. *Œuvres complètes* (1961), pp. 787–88.
78. "Notes nouvelles sur Edgar Poe," in *Œuvres complètes* (1918–37), X, 29–30.
79. "The Poetic Principle," in *Complete Works*, XIV, 272.
80. *Philebus* 60.
81. *Eudemian Ethics* VII.1244b.
82. *Enneads* V.2.1.
83. *Œuvres complètes* (1961), pp. 303–304. Or as Flaubert said: "Tout ce qui est de la vie me répugne; tout ce qui m'y entraîne et m'y plonge m'épouvante." "La vie est une chose tellement hideuse que le seul moyen de la supporter, c'est de l'éviter. Et on l'évite en vivant dans l'Art . . ." (letters of 20 December 1846 and 18 May 1857, Flaubert, *Correspondance*, Paris, 1926–33, I, 429, and IV, 182).
84. *Œuvres complètes* (1961), pp. 1177–80.
85. Ibid., pp. 1294, 1296. Baudelaire also images the poet as "l'enfant déshérité," exiled and contemned, who recapitulates, like the saintly martyrs, the sufferings and passion of Christ; see "Bénédiction," ibid., pp. 7–9.
86. *A Portrait of the Artist as a Young Man*, in *The Portable James Joyce*, ed. Harry Levin (New York, 1947), pp. 478, 481–82, 518–19.
87. *Les Fenêtres*, in *Œuvres complètes de Stéphane Mallarmé*, p. 33.
88. "Notes nouvelles sur Edgar Poe," in *Œuvres complètes* (1918–37), X, 25, 31, 35.
89. "Richard Wagner," in *Œuvres complètes de Stéphane Mallarmé*, p. 546.
90. "Magie," ibid., p. 400.
91. "Crise de vers," ibid., p. 368.
92. Ibid., pp. 366–67. Mallarmé wrote to Verhaeren, 22 January 1888, that "the poet disappears (this is absolutely the discovery of our time)" (in Mallarmé, *Propos sur la poésie*, ed. Henri Mondor, Monaco, 1953, p. 158).
93. "Quant au livre," in *Œuvres complètes de Stéphane Mallarmé*, p. 372.
94. "Crise de vers," ibid., p. 368.
95. To Viélé Griffin, 8 August 1891, in Mallarmé, *Propos sur la poésie*, p. 174. Mallarmé had earlier said: "Je n'ai créé mon œuvre que par *élimination*, et toute vérité acquise ne naissait que de la perte d'une impression qui, ayant étincelé, s'était consumée et me permettait . . . d'avancer plus profondément dans la sensation des Ténèbres Absolues. La Destruction fut ma Béatrice" (to Eugène Lefébure, 17 May 1867, ibid., p. 91).
96. "La Musique et les lettres," in *Œuvres complètes de Stéphane Mallarmé*, p. 647.
97. To François Coppée, 5 December 1866, in *Propos sur la poésie*, p. 85.
98. To Henri Cazalis, 14 May 1867, ibid., p. 89.
99. A. O. Lovejoy, *The Great Chain of Being* (Cambridge, Mass., 1936), p. 30.

100. To Henri Cazalis, March 1866, in *Propos sur la poésie*, pp. 65–66.
101. To Henri Cazalis, July 1866, ibid., p. 77.
102. To Villiers de l'Isle-Adam, 24 September 1866, ibid., pp. 82–83.
103. To François Coppée, 20 April 1868, ibid., p. 97.
104. To Henri Cazalis, 14 May 1867, ibid., p. 88.
105. "Le Mystère dans les lettres," in *Œuvres complètes de Stéphane Mallarmé*, p. 385; "Crise de vers," ibid., p. 367.
106. Paul Valéry, "Avant-propos," in *Variété* (Paris, 1924), pp. 103–105.
107. "On Poesy or Art," in *Biographia Literaria*, II, 254, 259.
108. To Robert Southey, 29 July 1802, *Collected Letters*, II, 830. In the same letter Coleridge describes Wordsworth's section (added in 1802) on "the Dignity & nature of the office & character of a Poet" as "very grand, & of a sort of Verulamian Power & Majesty."
109. Preface to *Lyrical Ballads*, in *The Prose Works of William Wordsworth*, ed. W. J. B. Owen and Jane W. Smyser (Oxford, 1974), I, 141.
110. Ibid., pp. 138–42.
111. Ibid., p. 138.
112. *The Friend* (London, 1818), III, 261–62.
113. *The Eolian Harp*, line 26; see also the three lines that follow.
114. Shelley, *A Defence of Poetry*, in *Shelley's Prose*, ed. D. L. Clark (Albuquerque, 1954), pp. 292, 294.
115. Kermode, pp. 6–10, 89–91.

S I X / *Two Roads to Wordsworth*

From *Wordsworth: A Collection of Critical Essays*, ed. M. H. Abrams (Englewood Cliffs, N.J.: Prentice-Hall, Inc., 1972), pp. 1–11. Reprinted by permission of the publisher. The essay was an introduction to a volume of Wordsworth criticism containing selections by Bradley, Darbishire, Danby, Brooks, and a dozen others (see the notes below).

1. Arnold, "Wordsworth" (1879), in *Essays in Criticism: Second Series* (London, 1891), pp. 153, 159.
2. *Memorial Verses* (1850), lines 43, 57; *Stanzas in Memory of the Author of "Obermann"* (1859), lines 54, 79.
3. A. C. Bradley, "Wordsworth," in *Oxford Lectures on Poetry* (London, 1909), pp. 99–145, esp. pp. 124–25 and 130–34 (and see also pp. 140–41 n.).
4. Helen Darbishire, *The Poet Wordsworth* (Oxford, 1950), pp. 26, 161, 172.
5. John F. Danby, *The Simple Wordsworth* (London, 1960), pp. 35–38, 48–57.
6. Cleanth Brooks, "Wordsworth and the Paradox of the Imagination," in *The Well Wrought Urn* (New York, 1947), pp. 114–38.
7. Jonathan Wordsworth, *The Music of Humanity: A Critical Study of Wordsworth's "Ruined Cottage"* (London, 1969), pp. 91–96, 142–53.

8. Stephen M. Parrish, " 'The Thorn': Wordsworth's Dramatic Monologue," *ELH*, 24 (1957), 153–63; revised in Parrish's *The Art of the "Lyrical Ballads"* (Cambridge, Mass., 1973), pp. 98–109.

9. Neil H. Hertz, "Wordsworth and the Tears of Adam," *Studies in Romanticism*, 7 (1967), 15–33.

10. Paul de Man, "Intentional Structure of the Romantic Image," in *Romanticism and Consciousness,* ed. Harold Bloom (New York, 1970), pp. 65–77 (originally in French in *Revue internationale de philosophie,* 14 [1960], 68–84).

11. Geoffrey H. Hartman, *Wordsworth's Poetry, 1787–1814* (New Haven, 1964), pp. x, 17–18, 39, 61, 63, 101, 124, 184, 211, 226–27, 233, 338.

12. David Perkins, *The Quest for Permanence* (Cambridge, Mass., 1959), pp. 24, 30, 40, 45, 47, 48, 50, 55, 89–90.

13. David Ferry, *The Limits of Mortality* (Middletown, Conn., 1959), pp. ix, 32–33, 51–53, 160, 173.

14. Lionel Trilling, "Wordsworth and the Iron Time," in *Wordsworth: Centenary Studies,* ed. G. T. Dunklin (Princeton, 1951), pp. 131–52; revised in Trilling's *The Opposing Self* (New York, 1955), pp. 118–50.

15. Jonathan Wordsworth, p. 153.

16. Harold Bloom, *The Visionary Company,* rev. ed. (Ithaca, 1971), pp. 144–45, 124–28, 198.

17. M. H. Abrams, *Natural Supernaturalism* (New York, 1971), esp. pp. 73–80, 278–92.

S E V E N / *Coleridge's "A Light in Sound": Science, Metascience, and Poetic Imagination*

From *Proceedings of the American Philosophical Society,* 116 (1972), 458–76. Reprinted by permission of the American Philosophical Society. The essay was originally read at a symposium on Wordsworth, Scott, and Coleridge, 21 April 1972.

1. Quoted by James D. Campbell, ed., *The Poetical Works of Samuel Taylor Coleridge* (London, 1893), p. 578.

2. Dedication to *Ode on the Departing Year* (1796), in *The Complete Poetical Works of Samuel Taylor Coleridge,* ed. E. H. Coleridge (Oxford, 1912), II, 1114.

3. Coleridge, *Biographia Literaria,* ed. J. Shawcross (Oxford, 1907), I, 3; 11 December 1794, letter to Robert Southey, *Collected Letters of Samuel Taylor Coleridge,* ed. E. L. Griggs (Oxford, 1956–71), I, 137.

4. This version is printed from the MS at Rugby School in *Complete Poetical Works,* II, 1021. The editor also prints a transcript of a MS draft of *The Eolian Harp* written in 1797 (II, 1021–23).

5. This poem was written in the period of love and happiness between Coleridge's at first reluctant courtship and his stormy family life. As he wrote to his close friend Thomas Poole on 7 October 1795, in a passage

closely related to details of the poem: "'On Sunday morning I was *married* . . . united to the woman, whom I love best of all created Beings.— We are settled—nay—quite domesticated at Clevedon—Our comfortable Cot!—! . . . The prospect around us is perhaps more *various* than any in the kingdom—Mine Eye gluttonizes.—The Sea—the distant Islands!—the opposite Coasts!—I shall assuredly write Rhymes—let the nine Muses prevent it, if they can" (*Collected Letters*, I, 160; see also p. 164).

6. H. W. Piper, *The Active Universe* (London, 1962), pp. 43–46. For related passages of verse written by Coleridge in the mid-1790s, see *Religious Musings*, lines 402–408; *The Destiny of Nations*, lines 36–49, and the earlier draft of this work in *Complete Poetical Works*, II, 1025.

7. See "The Correspondent Breeze: A Romantic Metaphor," pp. 25–43 in the present volume. A detailed account of Coleridge's long struggle with Pantheism is Thomas McFarland, *Coleridge and the Pantheist Tradition* (Oxford, 1969).

8. Coleridge had made an unsuccessful attempt to get his printer to delete the passage on fairy-land and the birds of paradise from the preceding version in the *Poems* of 1797; see George Whalley, "Coleridge and Southey in Bristol, 1795," *Review of English Studies*, new ser., 1 (1950), 332 n.

9. To William Sotheby, 19 and 13 July 1802, *Collected Letters*, II, 814, 810. Coleridge wrote to Wordsworth on 3 July 1803: "You were a great Poet by inspirations, & in the Moments of revelation, but . . . a thinking feeling Philosopher habitually . . ." (ibid., p. 957).

10. Erika von Erhardt-Siebold, "Harmony of the Senses in English, German, and French Romanticism," *PMLA*, 47 (1932), 577–92; Marjorie Nicolson, *Newton Demands the Muse* (Princeton, 1946), chap. 4. For the association of synesthetic experience with the music of the Eolian harp, see Glenn O'Malley, "Shelley's 'Air-Prism,' " *Modern Philology*, 55 (1958), 181–82.

11. *Biographia Literaria*, II, 103. See also Coleridge's letter of 16 March 1801, in which he expressed his intention "to evolve all the five senses, that is, to deduce them from *one sense*" (*Collected Letters*, II, 706).

12. On 10 February 1816 Coleridge returned to his publisher, John Gutch of Bristol, the signatures of the proof sheets of *Sibylline Leaves* that included *The Eolian Harp* (*Collected Letters*, IV, 621, nn. 2 and 3). On 6 June 1816 he wrote to Gutch that he would need to send him "a very long List" of Errata; and on 14 June he wrote a note to the printer, on the revised proof sheets of the final signature of *Sibylline Leaves*, that "I shall send a List of the Errata" (ibid., p. 645 and n. 2). Then on 22 May 1817 he wrote in a letter to Thomas Curtis—the London printer for Gale and Fenner, to whom Coleridge had transferred the publishing of *Sibylline Leaves* and the *Biographia Literaria*—that "the Day after tomorrow" he would visit him "& bring with me all that remains for me to do with regard to the Literary Life & the Sibylline Leaves— Errata &c." (ibid., p. 734). E. L. Griggs has written to me that the Errata are printed on the type of paper used by the London rather than the Bristol printer. It is possible, then, that the Errata (including the additional passage for *The Eolian Harp*) were not composed until May 1817.

13. See Griggs, Introduction, *Collected Letters*, V, lvi. Griggs's index to the *Letters* makes it possible to determine the dates during which Coleridge was working on each of these items.

14. To James Gillman, 10 November 1816; to Ludwig Tieck, 4 July 1817; to Lord Liverpool, 28 July 1817; to C. A. Tulk, September 1817 and, again, 12 January 1818.

15. *Collected Letters*, IV, 750–51.

16. To Tulk, September 1817, ibid., pp. 771, 773. (*Sibylline Leaves* had been issued by 22 July 1817; see ibid., p. 754, n. 1.) In the second letter to Tulk, 12 January 1818, Coleridge said again: "Sound is to Light what Color is to Gravity—viz. Sound = Light under the predominance of Gravity: Color = Gravity under the predominance or, as it were, the Dynasty of Light" (ibid., p. 807).

17. For a balanced estimate of the complex relations of Coleridge's thought of this period both to Boehme and to Schelling, see Richard Haven, *Patterns of Consciousness: An Essay on Coleridge* (Amherst, Mass., 1969), pp. 89–96, 134–42. On the relations of Coleridge's philosophy to Schelling, the fullest treatment is G. N. G. Orsini, *Coleridge and German Idealism* (Carbondale, Ill., 1969), chaps. 8 and 9.

18. Joseph Warren Beach, "Coleridge's Borrowings from the German," *ELH*, 9 (1942), 38 n., 50.

19. *Mill on Bentham and Coleridge*, ed. F. R. Leavis (London, 1950), pp. 99–100. For Coleridge's own statements on this subject see *Collected Letters*, I, 398; *Biographia Literaria*, I, 161–62, 169–70; and *The Table Talk*, ed. H. N. Coleridge (London, 1917), p. 157 (12 September 1831).

20. For Coleridge's lifelong interest in experimental science, together with a collection of his representative judgments on Newton—who as physicist was "the immortal Newton" whose "ethereal intuition" revealed "the constructive principle of the material Universe"—see *Coleridge on the Seventeenth Century*, ed. Roberta F. Brinkley (Durham, N.C., 1955), pp. 393–408; also *The Statesman's Manual*, in *Lay Sermons*, ed. R. J. White (London, 1972), pp. 51, 85. As early as 23 March 1801, when he began to study Newton's *Opticks*, Coleridge wrote that he was "exceedingly delighted with the beauty & neatness of his experiments, & with the accuracy of his *immediate* Deductions from them," but that his opinions and theories "founded on these Deductions" were so superficial as "to be deemed false" (*Collected Letters*, II, 709).

21. Written by Coleridge on the flyleaf of a copy of *The Friend* (1818), and transcribed in *The Friend*, ed. Barbara E. Rooke (London, 1969), I, 203 n. See also *Collected Letters*, IV, 759, 956.

22. Newton, *Opticks* (4th ed.), ed. I. Bernard Cohen et al. (New York, 1952), Query 29, p. 370, and Queries 17–23, pp. 347–53.

23. To C. A. Tulk, 12 January 1818, *Collected Letters*, IV, 809. Cf. *The Friend*, ed. Rooke, I, 500: "The solution of Phaenomena can never be derived from Phaenomena."

24. *Opticks*, Query 31, p. 400.

25. *Opticks*, Query 31, p. 403; Query 28, p. 370. See also Newton's "General Scholium" to the *Principia*.

26. Note to Southey's *Joan of Arc*, in *Complete Poetical Works*, II, 1113.

27. Coleridge, "Conclusion," in *Aids to Reflection* (London, 1913), pp. 268–

69; see also his *Philosophical Lectures,* ed. Kathleen Coburn (New York, 1949), pp. 356 ff. On Schelling's analysis of the atomistic and mechanical theory as "empirical fictions," or a "picture speech [*Bildersprache*] which is valid only inside its determinate bounds," see his *Ideen zu einer Philosophie der Natur* (1797), in *Sämmtliche Werke,* ed. K. F. A. Schelling (Stuttgart and Augsburg, 1856–61), Pt. I, Vol. II, pp. 70, 99–100.

28. *The Notebooks of Samuel Taylor Coleridge,* ed. Kathleen Coburn (London, 1957–), II, entry 3159; *Biographia Literaria,* I, 189; *Hints Towards the Formation of a More Comprehensive Theory of Life,* ed. Seth B. Watson (London, 1848), pp. 45, 58. See also the letter to Lord Liverpool, 28 July 1817, *Collected Letters,* IV, 758–59.

29. To Lord Liverpool, *Collected Letters,* IV, 760–61; *The Statesman's Manual,* in *Lay Sermons,* p. 87; see also p. 96.

30. *The Friend,* ed. Rooke, I, 94 and n.; and see *Collected Letters,* VI, 601.

31. *The Statesman's Manual,* in *Lay Sermons,* pp. 89–90; to Lord Liverpool, *Collected Letters,* IV, 760; to C. A. Tulk, ibid., p. 775. On details of Coleridge's metascience in this period see the pioneering study by Craig W. Miller, "Coleridge's Concept of Nature," *Journal of the History of Ideas,* 25 (1964), 77–96. A lucid and comprehensive treatment of the role of these ideas in the various areas of Coleridge's mature thinking is Owen Barfield, *What Coleridge Thought* (Middletown, Conn., 1971).

32. From a MS quoted by Barfield, p. 141. Compare this to the related, but in many details different, scheme in Schelling, *Von der Weltseele* (1798), in *Sämmtliche Werke,* Pt. I, Vol. II, pp. 357 ff.: "On the Relation of the Real and Ideal in Nature, or Development of the First Axioms of the Philosophy of Nature, on the Principles of Gravity and of Light"; also, *Darstellung meines Systems der Philosophie* (1801), ibid., Vol. IV, pp. 146 ff. On Schelling's distinction between phenomenal and non-phenomenal light and gravity, see ibid., Vol. III, pp. 133–36, and Vol. IV, pp. 43–47. In *Collected Letters,* VI, 900, Coleridge stresses "the blunder of taking *Light,* not as a Power, but as a phaenomenon."

33. *Hints Towards the . . . Theory of Life,* p. 69; cf. p. 58. See also letter to James Gillman, *Collected Letters,* IV, 690, and letter to C. A. Tulk, ibid., p. 808. For Schelling on the role of preponderance [*Übergewicht*] between polar forces, see *Sämmtliche Werke,* Pt. I, Vol. III, pp. 314 ff.; Vol. VII, pp. 178, 244, 452; and on the intuition of the unity of all things in their common elements of gravity and light, see Vol. II, pp. 342–43.

34. See *Biographia Literaria,* I, 189, and the comment on "potence" by Orsini, p. 234.

35. *Biographia Literaria,* I, 173–88, 196–98; for the description of human perception as a "repetition" of "the eternal act of creation," see ibid., p. 202.

36. *Collected Letters,* II, 864–66; the biblical echo is from Acts 17:28. See also *Collected Letters,* I, 349–50, 397–98; II, 893, 916.

37. The quotations are from *Fears in Solitude,* line 24; *Reflections on Having Left a Place of Retirement,* lines 38–39; *This Lime-Tree Bower,* lines 41–43; *Frost at Midnight,* lines 59–61.

38. *Hints Towards the . . . Theory of Life,* pp. 38, 40, 42, 51–52, 70. Cf. Schelling, *Von der Weltseele,* in *Sämmtliche Werke,* Pt. I, Vol. II, p. 374: "The source of life in the universal or great Nature is therefore the copula

between gravitation and the light-essence [*Lichtwesen*]; except that this source from which all things flow is concealed in universal Nature and is not itself visible."

39. *Collected Letters*, IV, 771; and see the letter to Gillman, 10 November 1816, ibid., p. 690. On 25 October 1815 Coleridge wrote that the artist must maintain "communion with Nature"—"not the dead Shapes, the outward *Letter*—but the Life of Nature revealing itself in the Phaenomenon, or rather attempting to reveal itself . . ." (ibid., p. 607).

40. *The Aurora*, trans. John Sparrow, ed. C. J. B. and D. S. H. (London, 1914), 18.5 and 25.49. There is a detailed commentary on *Aurora* in Alexandre Koyré, *La Philosophie de Jacob Boehme* (Paris, 1929), pp. 69–168.

41. See Haven, *Patterns of Consciousness*, p. 89, and on Coleridge's relations to Boehme as well as Schelling, pp. 89–96, 134–35, 138–42.

42. Thus Coleridge persistently traced his, as well as Schelling's, views back through Boehme and Giordano Bruno to the pre-Socratic philosopher Heraclitus: Coleridge's own dynamic philosophy, he said, was no more than "Heraclitus *redivivus*" (to Tulk, *Collected Letters*, IV, 775; see also ibid., p. 760, and *The Friend*, ed. Rooke, I, 94 n.).

43. For specific passages in Boehme's *Aurora* that exhibit some similarity to Coleridge's views on light, sound, and color, see Duane B. Schneider, "Coleridge's Light-Sound Theory," *Notes and Queries*, May 1963, pp. 182–83; and J. B. Beer, "Coleridge and Boehme's *Aurora*," ibid., pp. 183–87. In his reply (ibid., May 1966, pp. 176–78), Richard Haven cites among other materials Coleridge's annotation (written c. 1817) on *The Aurora*, 4.27: "27 is admirable—the Messenger or Mercury of the Salitter is indeed Sound, which is but Light under the paramouncy of Gravitation. It is the Mass-Light." Haven comments, justly, that this concept is presented by Coleridge not as Boehme's own idea, but "as an assumed principle in terms of which Boehme's obscure statements may be rendered intelligible and sensible," and that it is based on a "system of natural philosophy, obviously heavily indebted to the work of Schelling and Steffens."

44. See, for example, *Biographia Literaria*, I, 98–99; and McFarland, *Coleridge and the Pantheist Tradition*, esp. Excursus XIX, "Coleridge and Boehme." After the turn of the nineteenth century, Schelling himself increasingly built Boehme's concepts into his own philosophy, but without emulating Boehme's persistent attempt to maintain an identity between the first principle of his philosophy of nature, the personal God of the Bible, and the triune God of Christian doctrine.

45. As transcribed by Alice D. Snyder, "Coleridge on Boehme," *PMLA*, 45 (1930), 618.

46. Letters of 27 September and 7 October 1815, in *Collected Letters*, IV, 589–90, 591–92. Cf. *The Statesman's Manual*, in *Lay Sermons*, p. 19: "What is *expressed* in the inspired writings, is *implied* in all absolute science."

47. *Collected Letters*, IV, 767–69. For Coleridge's exposition of the Scriptures as a "system of symbols," products of the faculty of "Imagination," which incorporates the ideas of reason "in Images of the Sense," see *The Statesman's Manual*, in *Lay Sermons*, pp. 29–31; and see p. 79, where he states: "True natural philosophy is comprized in the study of

the science and language of *symbols*," and a symbol is not a "figure of speech or form of fancy, but an actual and essential part of that, the whole of which it represents."

48. *Collected Letters*, IV, 770–73, 805–806.
49. Ibid., pp. 771, 774–75. See also *Hints Towards the . . . Theory of Life*, pp. 50–56; and Miller, "Coleridge's Concept of Nature," pp. 87–91.
50. *Collected Letters*, IV, 807. And from the coral to the man of genius, who represents "the maximum of Individuation . . . the whole process is cyclical tho' progressive, and the Man separates from Nature only that Nature may be found again in a higher dignity in the Man" (to Tulk, ibid., p. 769).
51. *Hints Towards the . . . Theory of Life*, pp. 85–86.
52. Ibid., p. 86; *Philosophical Lectures*, p. 179.
53. A marginal annotation to Boehme, as transcribed by Haven, *Patterns of Consciousness*, p. 127. On the central role of alienation and integration in Romantic philosophy and literature, see M. H. Abrams, *Natural Supernaturalism* (New York, 1971), chaps. 4–5.
54. *Philosophical Lectures*, p. 179. The relevance of this passage to the music described in *The Eolian Harp* is strengthened by Coleridge's statement near the end of the preceding lecture (p. 168) that music "produces infinite Joy. . . . It is in all its forms still Joy."
55. *The Friend*, ed. Rooke, I, 520–21.
56. *Collected Letters*, IV, 806.
57. 7 August 1803, *Collected Letters*, II, 961; *Biographia Literaria*, I, 95–98.
58. *The Statesman's Manual*, in *Lay Sermons*, pp. 69–70; see also p. 29.
59. See Northrop Frye, "The Critical Path," in *In Search of Literary Theory*, ed. Morton W. Bloomfield (Ithaca, 1972).
60. Schelling, *Philosophie der Kunst*, in *Sämmtliche Werke*, Pt. I, Vol. V, pp. 442–49. Friedrich Schlegel had earlier pronounced the need for a "new mythology" to serve as the ground for modern poetry, and anticipated the emergence of such a mythology from a synthesis between current philosophical idealism and the discoveries of contemporary natural science (*Gespräch über die Poesie* [1800], in *Kunstanschauung der Frühromantik*, ed. Andreas Müller, Leipzig, 1931, pp. 184–90).
61. *Metaphysische Anfangsgründe der Naturwissenschaft*, in *Immanuel Kants Werke*, ed. Ernst Cassirer, IV (Berlin, 1913), 400–446. Both Schelling and Coleridge refer repeatedly to this essay. Goethe's science, in his *Metamorphosis of Plants* (1790) and *The Theory of Colors* (1810), was candidly based on the concept of the quasi-sexual generative power of contraries throughout the realm of nature. See Ronald D. Gray, *Goethe the Alchemist* (Cambridge, 1952), chap. 10.
62. On Humphry Davy's early theories, and Coleridge's use of them before he began an intensive study of Schelling, see Haven, *Patterns of Consciousness*, pp. 134–41.
63. *The Friend*, ed. Rooke, I, 94 n.; to Lord Liverpool, *Collected Letters*, IV, 760. Coleridge goes on (p. 761) to decry the modern view that "nothing grows, all is made," as against "the ancients," with their basic view of "the natura rerum—i.e. the birth of things," their search after "the *acts* of the world," and their central use of "the symbol of begetting."
64. Schelling, *The Ages of the World*, ed. and trans. Frederick de Wolfe Bol-

man, Jr. (New York, 1942), p. 212; on the following pages Schelling translates into philosophical categories the phenomena of sexual attraction, union, and generation.

65. Schelling, *Ideen zu einer Philosophie der Natur* (1797), in *Sämmtliche Werke*, Pt. I, Vol. II, pp. 109–10; see also Vol. II, pp. 375–76, 532–34; Vol. III, pp. 324–25, n. 4; Vol. IV, pp. 204–205; Vol. VII, pp. 174, 217, 453.

66. Schelling, *System der gesammten Philosophie* (1804), ibid., Vol. VI, pp. 266, 407–409. This work was unknown to Coleridge, since it was first published from the manuscript remains in the *Sämmtliche Werke* in 1860.

67. Transcribed from MS in *Inquiring Spirit*, ed. Kathleen Coburn (London, 1951), pp. 223–25.

68. *Notebooks*, II, entry 3159: "Coadunatio Individui cum Universo per Amorem." In the same passage Coleridge describes his experience in viewing a landscape as capable of annihilating "in a deep moment all possibility of the needlepoint pinshead System of the *Atomists* by one submissive Gaze!"

69. To Thomas Allsop, 13 December 1819, *Collected Letters*, IV, 979.

E I G H T / *Coleridge and the Romantic Vision of the World*

From *Coleridge's Variety: Bicentenary Studies*, ed. John Beer (London: Macmillan; Pittsburgh: University of Pittsburgh Press, 1974), pp. 101–33, 248–49. Reprinted by permission of John Beer. The essay was originally read as a bicentenary lecture at Jesus College, Cambridge, 21 October 1972.

1. *Collected Letters of Samuel Taylor Coleridge*, ed. E. L. Griggs (Oxford, 1956–71), III, 518 n.

2. Ibid., II, 1126.

3. *Biographia Literaria*, ed. J. Shawcross (Oxford, 1907), I, 114.

4. *Collected Letters*, VI, 953 n.

5. *Biographia Literaria*, I, 1. As early as 1803 Coleridge had jotted in his notebook: "Seem to have made up my mind to write my metaphysical works, as *my Life*, & *in* my Life—intermixed with all the other events / or history of the mind & fortunes of S. T. Coleridge" (*The Notebooks of Samuel Taylor Coleridge*, ed. Kathleen Coburn, London, 1957–   , I, entry 1515).

6. *The Poetical Works of William Wordsworth*, ed. Ernest de Selincourt and Helen Darbishire (Oxford, 1940–49), V, 1–2; *The Prelude*, ed. de Selincourt, 2nd ed., rev. Darbishire (Oxford, 1959), p. xxxvii.

7. On Hartley's adaptation of Newton's theories into his own views of the mechanistic bases of sensation and of the association of ideas, see Henry Guerlac, "An Augustan Monument: The Opticks of Isaac Newton," in *The Varied Pattern: Studies in the 18th Century*, ed. Peter Hughes and David Williams (Toronto, 1971), pp. 145–46, 160–61.

8. 11 December 1794, *Collected Letters*, I, 137. Cf. *Biographia Literaria*, I,

121: "So profound was my admiration at this time of Hartley's Essay on Man, that I gave his name to my first-born" (in 1796).

9. Ibid., pp. 114, 136.
10. Ibid., p. 116.
11. Ibid., p. 121.
12. Ibid., pp. 132–33.
13. Ibid., p. 98.
14. G. W. F. Hegel, *Phänomenologie des Geistes,* ed. Johannes Hoffmeister (Hamburg, 1952), pp. 415–21. For Hegel's description of the widespread sense of millennial expectation evoked by the early period of the Revolution, see his *Vorlesungen über die Philosophie der Weltgeschichte,* ed. Georg Lasson (Leipzig, 1919), II, 926.
15. *The Prelude* (1805 text), XI, 6–7, 47–48; XII, 21.
16. *Confessions,* VIII, xi; cf. VIII, viii.
17. *Biographia Literaria,* I, 137.
18. *The Friend,* ed. Barbara E. Rooke (London, 1969), I, 203 n.; *Collected Letters,* IV, 956.
19. Ibid., pp. 758–59. See *The Friend,* ed. Rooke, I, 446–47, on the pervasive effects of the "Mechanical Philosophy," which include its being "hailed as a kindred revolution in philosophy, and espoused, as a common cause, by the partizans of the revolution in the state"; and see also *The Statesman's Manual,* in *Lay Sermons,* ed. R. J. White (London, 1972), pp. 11–17.
20. Richard Kroner, *Von Kant bis Hegel* (Tübingen, 1921–24), I, 1–3.
21. *Kants gesammelte Schriften* (Berlin, 1902–   ), VIII, 27, and VI, 34, 134–36.
22. C. L. Reinhold, *Briefe über die Kantische Philosophie* (Leipzig, 1790), I, 9–16.
23. To Baggesen, April 1795, in J. G. Fichte, *Briefwechsel,* ed. Hans Schulz (Leipzig, 1925), I, 449–50.
24. Friedrich Schelling, *Sämmtliche Werke,* ed. K. F. A. Schelling (Stuttgart and Augsburg, 1856–61), Pt. I, Vol. I, pp. 156–59. Cf. Schelling's statement that his system "entirely alters, even inverts the ruling views not only in ordinary life, but in the greater part of systematic philosophy" (Vol. III, p. 329). On the "true revolution" in philosophy that will bring on a nonpolitical "golden age," see Vol. VI, pp. 562–64.
25. *Phänomenologie des Geistes,* pp. 563–64.
26. Preface to the *Phenomenology of Spirit,* trans. Walter Kaufmann in his *Hegel* (New York, 1965), p. 380.
27. *Notebooks,* II, entry 2541; *Collected Letters,* III, 314. In *The Friend,* ed. Rooke, I, 368, Coleridge alludes to Wordsworth's *Prelude,* with its double aspect of mental growth and mental crisis-and-conversion, as Wordsworth's "Poem on the Growth and Revolutions of an Individual Mind."
28. *Biographia Literaria,* I, 137.
29. 30 March 1820, *Collected Letters,* V, 28; *Biographia Literaria,* I, 166–67, and see also p. 199. In *The Statesman's Manual,* in *Lay Sermons,* pp. 14–15, Coleridge asserts that "all the *epoch-forming* Revolutions of the Christian World," in all areas of life and thought, "have coincided with the rise and fall of metaphysical systems."

30. *Biographia Literaria*, I, 59–60; the passage, with some differences, occurs also in *The Friend*, ed. Rooke, II, 73–74. In *The Prelude*, Wordsworth described his crisis as marked by a "tyranny" of the eye, a slavery to customary ways of seeing which yielded the perception of "a universe of death," and described his recovery from this crisis as the breakthrough to an alternative vision of the world—a world "which moves with light and life informed, / Actual, divine, and true" (1850 text, XI, 127–39; XIV, 157–62).

31. *The Friend*, ed. Rooke, I, 519–21. Coleridge remarked, with respect to demonstrating "the absurdity of the corpuscularian or mechanic system": "But we cannot force any man into an insight or intuitive possession of the true philosophy, because we cannot give him abstraction, intellectual intuition, or constructive imagination" (*Hints Towards the Formation of a More Comprehensive Theory of Life*, ed. Seth B. Watson, London, 1848, pp. 57–58). For Schelling on the founding intuition of a philosophy, see *Sämmtliche Werke*, Pt. I, Vol. II, pp. 12, 46, 343; Vol. IV, p. 77; Vol. V, p. 275.

32. "My Mental Development," in *The Philosophy of Bertrand Russell*, ed. P. A. Schilpp (New York, 1963), pp. 10–12.

33. Ludwig Wittgenstein, *Philosophical Investigations*, trans. G. E. M. Anscombe (Oxford, 1953), Foreword, p. x, Sections 124, 400–401; see also Section 122. Commentators on the *Philosophical Investigations* have noted its likeness in procedure to Augustine's *Confessions*, in that the radically altered Wittgenstein harshly criticizes his former self, conducts a dialogue in which he combats the persistent temptations to fall back into former errors, and attempts to help his readers to achieve a similar philosophical conversion. See Stanley Cavell, "The Availability of Wittgenstein's Later Philosophy" (1962), reprinted in his *Must We Mean What We Say?* (New York, 1969), pp. 70–72; K. T. Fann, *Wittgenstein's Conception of Philosophy* (Berkeley, 1971), pp. 106–108.

34. *Biographia Literaria*, I, 99. On the same page Coleridge speaks of his "fifteen years' familiarity" with Kant's major works. On the dating of Coleridge's reading of Kant see G. N. G. Orsini, *Coleridge and German Idealism* (Carbondale, Ill., 1969), pp. 47 ff.

35. *Collected Letters*, II, 669, 671, 706–707. In the last letter, of 16 March 1801, Coleridge goes on to say that he is planning a book on "Locke, Hobbes, & Hume" which will manifest his "attentive Perusal" of his philosophical predecessors "from Aristotle to Kant" (p. 707).

36. Ibid., III, 490.

37. 22 June 1806, *Notebooks*, II, entry 2866.

38. *Collected Letters*, III, 477.

39. *Biographia Literaria*, I, 102. In an annotation to a work by Schelling, Coleridge describes it as "a book I value, I reason and quarrel with *as* with myself when I am reasoning" (quoted by Orsini, p. 50).

40. *Biographia Literaria*, I, 103–104. In referring to Kant as putting forward the "germs" of the "Dynamic System" which was developed by Schelling (pp. 103–104 and n.), Coleridge has in mind especially Kant's essay "Metaphysische Anfangsgründe der Naturwissenschaft" (1796), which proposed a "metaphysical" analysis of "matter" as a product of the elemental "powers" of attraction and repulsion. On p. 99 Coleridge

lists this essay as one of the four works of Kant that "took possession of me as with a giant's hand."

41. This section parallels the account of Coleridge's metascience in section I of the preceding essay, which, like the present essay, was originally delivered as a lecture. For the convenience of those who read either essay independently of the other, the exposition has been retained in both places.

42. Joseph Warren Beach, "Coleridge's Borrowings from the German," *ELH*, 9 (1942), 38 n., 50; Norman Fruman, *Coleridge, the Damaged Archangel* (New York, 1971), p. 126.

43. *Mill on Bentham and Coleridge*, ed. F. R. Leavis (London, 1950), pp. 99–100.

44. *Collected Letters*, IV, 750; *The Statesman's Manual*, in *Lay Sermons*, p. 85. As early as 23 March 1801, when he began to study the *Opticks*, Coleridge discriminated between the experimental and theoretical elements in Newton's work. He was, Coleridge said, "exceedingly delighted" with Newton's "experiments, & with the accuracy of his *immediate* Deductions from them"; but the opinions which Newton "founded on these Deductions, and indeed his whole Theory" are so superficial as "to be deemed false" (*Collected Letters*, II, 709). For Coleridge's lifelong interest in experimental science, and his varied judgments on Newton, see *Coleridge on the Seventeenth Century*, ed. Roberta F. Brinkley (Durham, N.C., 1955), pp. 393–408.

45. Newton, *Opticks* (4th ed.), ed. I. Bernard Cohen et al. (New York, 1952), Query 31, p. 400, and Queries 17–23, pp. 347–53.

46. Ibid., Query 31, p. 403, and Query 28, p. 370.

47. "Conclusion," in *Aids to Reflection* (London, 1913), pp. 268–69.

48. *The Statesman's Manual*, in *Lay Sermons*, p. 96; *Collected Letters*, IV, 760–61.

49. *The Statesman's Manual*, in *Lay Sermons*, p. 89; see also *Biographia Literaria*, I, 197–98. In 1815 Coleridge described the "substitution of Life, and Intelligence" for "the philosophy of mechanism which . . . strikes *Death*" as "a general revolution" in the discipline of the mind (*Collected Letters*, IV, 575).

50. *The Friend*, ed. Rooke, I, 94 and n.

51. *Hints Towards the . . . Theory of Life*, p. 69; *Collected Letters*, IV, 760, 771, 775; and the MS quoted by Owen Barfield, *What Coleridge Thought* (Middletown, Conn., 1971), p. 141. The pioneering study of Coleridge's nature-philosophy is Craig W. Miller, "Coleridge's Concept of Nature," *Journal of the History of Ideas*, 25 (1964), 77–96; the fullest account of the role of such concepts in various areas of Coleridge's concern is Barfield's.

52. *Biographia Literaria*, I, 188–89, 196–98.

53. *Hints Towards the . . . Theory of Life*, pp. 38, 40–42, 51–52, 70.

54. Ibid., pp. 85–86; *Philosophical Lectures*, ed. Kathleen Coburn (New York, 1949), p. 179.

55. *The Friend*, ed. Rooke, I, 520.

56. *The Complete Works of Samuel Taylor Coleridge*, ed. W. G. T. Shedd (New York, 1853), III, 709. See Thomas McFarland's thorough study, *Coleridge and the Pantheist Tradition* (Oxford, 1969), esp. chap. 3.

57. *The Friend*, ed. Rooke, I, 519.
58. 20 January 1820, *Collected Letters*, V, 18.
59. *The Statesman's Manual*, in *Lay Sermons*, pp. 28–31.
60. *Collected Letters*, IV, 771.
61. E.g., Hegel, *Phänomenologie des Geistes*, pp. xxxviii, 536–44, 549; Hegel, *Lectures on the Philosophy of Religion*, trans. E. B. Speirs and J. B. Sanderson (New York, 1962), I, 20.
62. *Collected Letters*, II, 961; *Biographia Literaria*, I, 98, 137.
63. *The Statesman's Manual*, in *Lay Sermons*, pp. 69–70.
64. Ibid., pp. 49–50.
65. *Collected Letters*, V, 19.
66. *The Statesman's Manual*, Appendix C (Appendix B in 1839 ed.), in *Lay Sermons*, pp. 72–73.
67. *Coleridge the Talker*, ed. R. W. Armour and R. F. Howes (Ithaca, 1940), p. 291.
68. Ibid., p. 182.
69. *Notebooks*, II, entry 2372.
70. Jan Ingenhousz, *Experiments upon Vegetables*, in *Jan Ingenhousz, Plant Physiologist*, by Howard S. Reed, *Chronica Botanica*, Vol. XI, No. 5/6 (1949), esp. pp. 316, 329; Ingenhousz, *An Essay on the Food of Plants*, reprinted by J. Christian Bay (1933), pp. 3–6, 10. See also Julius Wiesner, *Jan Ingen-Housz: Sein Leben und Sein Wirken* (Vienna, 1905). Erasmus Darwin in *The Botanic Garden* refers to Hales, Priestley, and Ingenhousz in discussing plant transpiration and interchanges with the atmosphere. This work was known to Coleridge, but his description of plant processes is much more precise and accurate than Darwin's. See *The Botanic Garden*, 2nd ed. (London, 1794–95), notes to Pt. I, Canto I, line 462, and Canto IV, line 34, and Additional Notes XXXIV and XXXVII.
71. *Inquiring Spirit*, ed. Kathleen Coburn (London, 1951), pp. 223–24.
72. *On the Constitution of the Church and State*, 2nd ed. (London, 1830), p. 233; see also *Philosophical Lectures*, p. 358.
73. *The Statesman's Manual*, in *Lay Sermons*, pp. 30–31; see also p. 79, and *Aids to Reflection*, pp. 250–55 nn.
74. *Hints Towards the . . . Theory of Life*, p. 85; *Collected Letters*, IV, 769.
75. *Biographia Literaria*, II, 131. For the original letter in which Coleridge described this episode, see *Collected Letters*, I, 420 ff. Coleridge first revised the letter for inclusion in *The Friend* (1809) and then reprinted it, with slight changes, in *Biographia Literaria*, II, 132 ff.
76. Wallace Stevens, *The Necessary Angel* (New York, 1960), pp. 40–41.

N I N E / *Apocalypse: Theme and Romantic Variations*

From *The Apocalypse in English Renaissance Literature*, ed. C. A. Patrides and Joseph Anthony Wittreich, Jr. (Ithaca: Cornell University Press; Manchester: Manchester University Press, 1983), the concluding essay. Reprinted by permission of the publishers.

1. D. H. Lawrence, *Apocalypse* (1931) (London, 1972), pp. 3, 5–6.
2. See Frank E. Manuel, *The Religion of Isaac Newton* (Oxford, 1974); and, on Priestley's writings on Revelation, Clarke Garrett, *Respectable Folly: Millenarians and the French Revolution in France and England* (Baltimore, 1975), chap. 6.
3. P. J. Proudhon, *System of Economical Contradictions* (1846), trans. Benjamin R. Tucker (Boston, 1888), I, 27, 30–31.
4. On biblical patterns in Western fiction see Frank Kermode, *The Sense of an Ending: Studies in the Theory of Fiction* (New York, 1967).
5. Milton, *The Christian Doctrine*, I, xxxiii. See also *Paradise Lost*, XII, 463–64: "Whether in Heav'n or Earth, for then the Earth / Shall all be Paradise. . . ."
6. H. C. Robinson, *Blake, Coleridge, Wordsworth, Lamb, etc.*, ed. Edith J. Morley (Manchester, 1922), p. 12; Blake, *Jerusalem* 17.33–35, and *The Marriage of Heaven and Hell*, Plate 3.
7. Karl Löwith, *Meaning in History* (Chicago, 1949), p. 183.
8. Friedrich Schelling, *Denkmal der Schrift . . . des Herrn F. H. Jacobi*, in *Sämmtliche Werke*, ed. K. F. A. Schelling (Stuttgart and Augsburg, 1856–61), Pt. I, Vol. VIII, p. 81.
9. Schelling, *Vorlesungen über die Methode des akademischen Studiums*, in *Sämmtliche Werke*, Pt. I, Vol. V, p. 275.
10. *The Logic of Hegel*, trans. William Wallace, 2d ed. (Oxford, 1892), p. 379.
11. G. W. F. Hegel, *Phenomenology of Spirit*, trans. A. V. Miller (Oxford, 1977), pp. 10–11.
12. Rufus M. Jones, *The Eternal Gospel* (New York, 1938), p. 5.
13. Francis Bacon, *The New Organon and Related Writings*, ed. Fulton H. Anderson (New York, 1960), pp. 90–92. As Lord Acton, late in the nineteenth century, put the relation between Providence and what Bacon called "fate" in history: "Progress was Providence: unless there was progress there could be no God in history" (quoted by Herbert Butterfield, *Man on His Past*, Cambridge, 1955, p. 130).
14. *The New Organon and Related Writings*, pp. 3, 14, 15, 66, 22–23.
15. Coleridge's interpolation in his translation of Schiller's drama *The Piccolomini*, II.iv.123 ff.
16. J. F. C. Harrison, *Robert Owen and the Owenites in Britain and America* (London, 1969), pp. 106, 126, 134.
17. Marx, especially in his earlier writings, incorporated the theory of absolute revolution into the Romantic pattern of history as a spiral movement. The ultimate state of mankind will be a return to the primitive state of communal unity, but on a higher level because, as Marx puts it, it will be "a return which assimilates all the wealth of previous development." See M. H. Abrams, *Natural Supernaturalism* (New York, 1971), pp. 313–16.
18. The rationale and practice of absolute revolution in non-European civilizations has been either taken over from Western theorists or else exported to underdeveloped countries by the indefatigable Christian missionaries who, preaching the religion of peace, unwittingly brought a sword—the apocalyptic faith in a divine, or divinely appointed, champion who would reverse the local status of oppressor and oppressed, to inaugurate a world of universal abundance and happiness. See Vit-

torio Lanternari, *The Religions of the Oppressed: A Study of Modern Messianic Cults*, trans. Lisa Sergio (New York, 1963).

19. *The New Law of Righteousnes* (1649), in *The Works of Gerrard Winstanley*, ed. George H. Sabine (Ithaca, 1941), pp. 214–15, 170–74.

20. *The Marriage of Heaven and Hell*, plates 11, 14; *Jerusalem*, plate 77; *The Mental Traveller*, line 62.

21. This vatic passage, originally used at the end of *Home at Grasmere* to announce the "theme" of the new poetry Wordsworth felt that it was his special mission to sing, was printed as "a kind of *Prospectus*" to his projected masterpiece, *The Recluse*, in his Preface to *The Excursion* (1814).

22. Edward Johnson, *Wonder-Working Providence*, ed. J. Franklin Jameson (New York, 1910), p. 25; Jonathan Edwards, *Thoughts on the Revival of Religion in New England*, in *Works of Jonathan Edwards* (New York, 1881), III, 314.

23. Quoted by Henry Nash Smith, *Virgin Land* (New York, 1957), p. 40.

24. Melville, *White Jacket* (1850), chap. 36, quoted by Ernest Lee Tuveson, *Redeemer Nation* (Chicago, 1968), pp. 156–57; *Clarel* (1876), in *The Works of Herman Melville* (New York, 1958), XV, 250.

25. For a detailed discussion of the pervasive apocalyptic design and imagery in Romantic thought and literature see M. H. Abrams, *Natural Supernaturalism*, esp. chaps. 3–7; see also "English Romanticism: The Spirit of the Age," pp. 44–75 in the present volume.

26. *The Correspondence of Robert Southey with Caroline Bowles*, ed. Edward Dowden (Dublin, 1881), p. 52.

27. G. W. F. Hegel, *Vorlesungen über die Philosophie der Weltgeschichte*, ed. Georg Lasson (Leipzig, 1919), II, 926.

28. Joseph Priestley, quoted by Garrett, *Respectable Folly*, pp. 142–43.

29. *Collected Letters of Samuel Taylor Coleridge*, ed. E. L. Griggs (Oxford, 1956–71), I, 527.

30. To Byron, *The Letters of Percy Bysshe Shelley*, ed. F. L. Jones (Oxford, 1964), I, 361; *Shelley's Prose*, ed. D. L. Clark (Albuquerque, 1954), pp. 239–40, 296–97.

31. T. N. Talfourd, "An Attempt to Estimate the Poetical Talent of the Present Age," *Pamphleteer*, 5 (1815), 432–33.

32. Mary Shelley, notes in *The Complete Poetical Works of Shelley*, ed. Thomas Hutchinson (London, 1934), pp. 156, 551; Thomas Medwin, *Life of Shelley*, ed. H. B. Forman (Oxford, 1913), p. 255.

33. *Kants gesammelte Schriften* (Berlin, 1902–   ), VIII, 109–10, 27; see also VI, 34, 134–36.

34. On the role of the French Revolution in man's progress toward a secular millennium, see Kant, "The Victory of the Good Principle over the Evil One and the Establishment of the Kingdom of God on Earth" (1792), and "Whether the Human Race Is Continually Advancing Toward the Better" (1792).

35. Novalis, *Briefe und Werke* (Berlin, 1943), III, 702.

36. *The Logic of Hegel*, p. 54.

37. Hegel, *Phenomenology of Spirit*, p. 479. For Hegel's systematic translation of the Christian history and creed into his philosophical equivalents, see esp. the section "The Revealed Religion," pp. 453–78.

38. Carlyle, *Sartor Resartus*, ed. C. F. Harrold (New York, 1937), p. 194.

39. *Phenomenology of Spirit*, p. 492. In his Preface, Hegel represents the

imminence, and abruptness, of the coming of the apocalyptic new world, spiritually interpreted, in his own post-Revolutionary age: "It is not difficult to see that ours is . . . a period of transition to a new era. Spirit has broken with the world it has hitherto inhabited and imagined. . . . The Spirit . . . [is] dissolving bit by bit the structure of its previous world. . . . The gradual crumbling . . . is cut short by a sunburst which, in one flash, illuminates the features of the new world" (ibid., pp. 6–7).

40. Schiller, *On the Aesthetic Education of Man*, trans. and ed. Elizabeth M. Wilkinson and L. A. Willoughby (Oxford, 1967), pp. 25, 205, 215–19.

41. *The Way Towards the Blessed Life*, in *The Popular Works of Johann Gottlieb Fichte*, trans. William Smith, 4th ed. (London, 1889), II, 306–309. In 1795 Fichte had said that the French Revolution inspired his first major work, the *Wissenschaftslehre*, and that this work is the equivalent in philosophy of the political revolution in history (to Baggesen, April 1795, in J. G. Fichte, *Briefwechsel*, ed. Hans Schulz, Leipzig, 1925, I, 449–50).

42. Schelling, *System der gesammten Philosophie* (1804), in *Sämmtliche Werke*, Pt. I, Vol. VI, pp. 562–64. For Schelling's description, in 1795, of his philosophy as a "revolution of knowledge" which will reestablish the original conditions of intellectual life, see *Sämmtliche Werke*, Pt. I, Vol. I, pp. 156–59.

43. Novalis, *Schriften*, ed. Paul Kluckhohn et al. (Stuttgart, 1960), I, 347, 110–11.

44. *Sartor Resartus*, pp. 220, 186, 264, 222.

45. *Of Reformation*, in *Complete Prose Works of John Milton* (New Haven, 1953), I, 615–16. Bacon, it will be recalled, had also represented himself as intoning "the bridal song" of the millennial state to be achieved by natural science.

46. Schelling, *The Ages of the World*, ed. and trans. Frederick de Wolfe Bolman, Jr. (New York, 1942), pp. 90–91. On Schelling's uncompleted epic poem, see Fritz Strich, *Die Mythologie in der deutschen Literatur* (Halle, 1910), II, 31–39. As early as 1795 the young Schelling had proclaimed himself a prophetic herald of a messianic philosopher who would bring about the liberation and reintegration of the enslaved and divided human intellect—"a deed reserved . . . perhaps only for one man—but may it nonetheless be granted to the individual who has a presentiment of the coming day to rejoice in it by anticipation" (*Von Ich als Princip der Philosophie*, in *Sämmtliche Werke*, Pt. I, Vol. I, pp. 156–59).

47. See John Holloway, *The Victorian Sage* (London, 1953).

48. Wordsworth, MS D, lines 686 ff., in *Home at Grasmere*, ed. Beth Darlington (Ithaca, 1977). In the passage excerpted from this poem that he later called his "Prospectus," Wordsworth indicates that he is emulating Milton, whom he denominates "the Bard, / Holiest of Men." In the great ode *To William Wordsworth* that Coleridge wrote in 1807, after hearing the author read *The Prelude* aloud, he repeatedly hailed Wordsworth as a "Bard," singer of that "more than historic, that prophetic Lay."

49. Friedrich Hölderlin, *Hymne an die Menschheit*.

Index

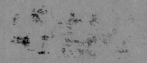